Development and Distribution

Development and Distribution

Structural Change in South East Asia

Andy Sumner

OXFORD
UNIVERSITY PRESS

OXFORD
UNIVERSITY PRESS

Great Clarendon Street, Oxford, OX2 6DP,
United Kingdom

Oxford University Press is a department of the University of Oxford. It furthers the University's objective of excellence in research, scholarship, and education by publishing worldwide. Oxford is a registered trade mark of Oxford University Press in the UK and in certain other countries

First Edition published in 2018
Impression: 1

Published in the United States of America by Oxford University Press
198 Madison Avenue, New York, NY 10016, United States of America

British Library Cataloguing in Publication Data
Data available

Library of Congress Control Number: 2017958473

ISBN 978–0–19–879236–9

Printed and bound by
CPI Group (UK) Ltd, Croydon, CR0 4YY

Acknowledgements

I am grateful to those who have influenced my work through discussion and collaboration. With apologies for any omissions, I would like to particularly thank the following people (in alphabetical order): Tony Addison, Peter Edward, Andrew Fischer, and Arief Anshory Yusuf. I would also like to thank participants at seminars at Padjadjaran University, Indonesia, at the National University of Malaysia; at the Institute of Strategic and International Studies, Kuala Lumpur; at Chulalongkorn University, Bangkok, and the Thailand Development Research Institute, Bangkok. Further, for assistance and comments, I would like to thank the following: Shamsulbahriah Ku Ahmad, Artur Borkowski, Kyunghoon Kim, Arriya Mungsunti, Anisa Muzaffar, Eva Renon, Diding Sakri, Lukas Schlögl, and Dharendra Wardhana. I would like to add to the list of thanks, Adam Swallow at OUP and Dee Scholey. Finally, thanks are very much due to my family for their support. Any errors and omissions are the responsibility of the author.

Contents

List of Figures

One day in August, 1952, walking down the road in Bangkok, it came to me suddenly [. . .] a dual (national or world) economy.

W. Arthur Lewis (cited in Lindbeck 1992, p. 397)

1

Introduction

1.1 Overview

Since the Second World War, surprisingly few developing countries have experienced a truly sustained episode of economic and social convergence towards the structural characteristics of the advanced nations.[1] The region of the world that has gone the furthest in that convergence is East Asia. Much has been written on comparative industrialization and development in North East Asia but relatively less on South East Asia. This book focuses on the latter and, more specifically on Malaysia, Indonesia, and Thailand (henceforth, MIT). These three nations have all undergone a major transformation—in a way never anticipated—from being poor, agrarian countries to middle-income countries who have developed an industrial and manufacturing base.[2] Malaysia and Thailand have virtually eradicated absolute poverty and Indonesia has the potential to do so too in the next decade. Furthermore, MIT achieved all of the above without a dramatic rise in income inequality.

The 'puzzle' that flows from that achievement and which led to the writing of this book is as follows: how did MIT achieve such a transformation, and how did they achieve the transformation with a form of economic growth that was driven by structural transformation, but that was 'inclusive'? (Given that, historically, it has been thought that structural transformation tends to push up inequality, whilst inclusive growth necessitates static or even falling inequality, this last point is particularly salient to developing countries). Understanding how the transformation was possible in a relatively small

[1] World Bank (2008) listed just thirteen countries since 1950 that had sustained high growth rates for 25 years or longer, and two further countries that might join this group. Northeast East and South East Asia account for all but five of this set of fifteen countries.

[2] To paraphrase Rock (2017, p. 13): In the 1960s Indonesia was one of the poorest countries in the developing world; Thailand had experienced a long period of no growth in income per capita from 1900–1950; and incomes fell in Indonesia and Malaysia from 1930–1950; it was anticipated that an ethnic conflict would engulf Malaysia following independence.

space of time, the extent to which it was inclusive, and the caveats and prospects for South East Asia is thus an area of enquiry significant to all developing countries as they seek economic and social transformation.

In order to 'solve' the puzzle, the discussion of the transformation of South East Asia in this book focuses on a set of three core questions. These questions are: How deep, and of what nature was the structural transformation and inclusive growth in MIT? How did MIT deal with the distributional tensions that rapid transformation often entails? And how did Malaysia, Indonesia, and Thailand achieve such rapid economic and social transformation in a relatively short space of time? In other words, what does the experience of those countries imply for theories of economic and social transformation.

The two key arguments of the book are as follows: first, that *old and new varieties of orchestrated developmentalism* are the underlying basis of this transformation, but that each of these developmentalist models entails a variety of dependency, subordination, or peripherality with reference to the global economy that provides the seeds of an eventual crisis. The crisis leads to a reincarnation of—a new variety of—developmentalism every so often, to allow capital accumulation to recommence driven by changes in the global economy. The experience of South East Asia thus validates a key postulate of heterodox theories of structural transformation in the sense that structural transformation-led capital accumulation in the developing world has to be state-directed to a greater or lesser extent, but the parameters and timing are framed by global incorporation and global accumulation in that period of history.

Second, that whilst capital accumulation and structural transformation tend to generate distribution tensions, those tensions are diffused by expanding public policy interventions to address the three forces of internal divergence unleashed by structural change between and within 'sectors': specifically, urban–rural sectors, skilled–unskilled workers, and capital–labour (and their capture of productivity gains). Thus, structural transformation-led capital accumulation that is broad-based requires, counter-intuitively, highly activist rural and agricultural policy, and public investments to constrain the urban–rural divergence; redistribution of the near future by large investments in public education to constrain the skilled–unskilled worker wage divergence; and state–capital–labour pacts—formally or informally—to ensure employment growth rather than large real-wage rises are the consequence of productivity growth as one pioneer of development economics, W. Arthur Lewis originally outlined in the 1950s.

1.2 The Developer's Dilemma

The transformation of South East Asia illustrates the distributional friction inherent in late economic development. Contemporary developing countries are seeking to achieve two goals: structural transformation and inclusive growth. We have introduced the former. The latter we take to mean spreading the benefits of growth broadly. The first, structural transformation or a shift towards higher productivity activities, is essential to economic development in developing countries. This is because economic growth led by structural transformation is likely to be sustained in the medium term in a way that commodity boom-led growth is not.

The second, inclusive growth, which has a genealogy in pro-poor growth, growth with equity, and other predecessors, is essential for the social stability which underpins waves of capital accumulation, in that it raises incomes/consumption across the population, particularly at the lower end. That said, inclusive growth can take various manifestations in terms of who is 'included', how much, and in what way (and who decides who is included and the terms of inclusion). Historically, it has been thought that structural transformation tends to entail a rise in income inequality during growth, as originally posited by Arthur Lewis and Simon Kuznets (although neither necessarily saw it as inevitable), and that inclusive growth is ideally achieved with steady or even falling inequality (and certainly not with rising inequality) during transformation so that the incomes/consumption of the poorest rise substantially to reduce poverty rates.[3] How are countries to manage this tension and what are the experiences of countries that have managed the tension?

The countries of South East Asia are examples of countries which, at some level at least, have managed to achieve both structural transformation in terms of large increases in productivity as well as inclusive growth in terms of reducing poverty and curtailing the tendency for inequality to rise during transformation. This book therefore takes the experience of South East Asia to have a wider significance for theorizing about the processes of late economic development.

1.3 Theories of Structural Transformation and Inclusive Growth

Revisiting the historical theoretical and empirical literature on structural transformation and inclusive growth is useful in understanding the tension between them. In particular, the works of Arthur Lewis and Simon Kuznets as noted are of relevance. The Lewis dual economy model is a useful heuristic device to compare reality to and although Simon Kuznets' hypothesis of rising inequality in the early stages of that transition is discredited as a universal law,

[3] Indeed the title of this book is based on the Lewis (1976) account of these issues, and Fields (2001) inverting of the same title.

it has been the experience of many fast-growing developing countries under contemporary globalization.[4]

There have been various scholars writing in the tradition of Lewis and Kuznets, or in reaction to their work, demonstrating the issues of late industrialization and the transformation or transition of a society from an agrarian one to a modern, urban one is of enduring importance. The literature includes those writings in a heterodox tradition such as those in the structuralist lineage and others that seek to explain the enablers or impediments to the Lewis transition. Orthodoxy theory, however, tends to underplay the role of structural transformation by abstracting to one sector growth model, and making little reference to distribution (as noted by Herrendorf et al. 2013; McMillan and Rodrik 2011). Heterodox theories have much to say on the issues of structural transformation and distribution, though their arguments are weakened by an overemphasis on one capitalism (global or national) rather than heterogeneous late capitalisms.

Contemporary discussion has coalesced around what can be called varieties or regimes of late capitalism, which adds the heterogeneity of capitalism into the discussion. There are two notable strands in this literature. The first is the 'varieties of capitalism' literature, and the institutional configurations that promote different capitalisms and its iterations, emerging in business studies, since the original statement of Hall and Soskice (2001). The second is the 'welfare regimes' literature from sociology and social policy and its iterations, since the exposition of Esping-Andersen (1990). Both these literatures have begun to evolve to consider varieties of capitalism and their welfare regimes in developing countries.

The heterogeneity of experience in the developing world is immediately evident. The United Nations Research Institute for Social Development (UNRISD) (2010), for example, characterizes several pathways thus: first, a 'classic manufacturing growth path' followed by many countries in East Asia. This was led by a strong state, and predicated, in some instances, on substantial land reform or agricultural modernization, and public investment in rural areas. Import-substitution industrialization was synthesized with export-led growth based on industrial policy and directed credit. Foreign investment was managed through joint ventures and performance requirements to extract benefits for the host economy.

The second pathway was followed by natural resource-abundant developing countries, such as those in sub-Saharan Africa. This pathway is characterized

[4] That is, in rapidly growing countries with structural change and a shift away from agriculture, there is a compression of the shares of national income to the poorest four deciles of the population, and an expansion of the share of the richest decile (see discussion of Sumner 2016a, 2016b). For further empirical support for an association between rising income inequality and a shift of employment shares away from agriculture, see Baymul and Sen (2017).

by a shift from agriculture to mining, including or excluding oil. In short, an intra-sectoral structural change confined to the primary sector, and higher productivity within the primary sector. This provides export earnings but few jobs, given that mining is typically capital intensive. Governments can then redistribute mineral rents to more productive sectors or social spending. However, exchange rate appreciation may impact the tradable sector, and growth may be rather exclusive due to enclave economies.

Third, there is a pathway of service sector-led growth, such as that followed in India, ideally in higher value-added and internationally traded services. This approach tends to disconnect labour market participation and welfare regimes because much of employment is in the informal sector and not covered by social protection programmes.

Finally, there is a pathway of industrialization which may be labelled stalled structural change that is evident in upper middle-income countries in Latin America which followed import-substitution industrialization (ISI) but retained dualism to some extent. These countries have the economic structures of both capital-intensive farming and a low-productivity, self-employed, urban informal service sector. In these countries, growth reduced poverty to some extent, but structural change is stagnant because the transformation was partial, welfare regimes and labour markets remain segmented, and high levels of income inequality and unemployment or underemployment persist.

1.4 Methodology and Analytical Approach Taken

This book sets out to explore the issues outlined and to investigate how South East Asia has approached the developer's dilemma. The methodology of this book is one of a detailed empirical comparative case study. It is inductive and empirical in terms of methodology in the tradition of the pioneers of development economics such as Lewis and Kuznets and structuralists, and the methods used are quantitative statistics on historical trends and regularities, and analysis of structures and systems. The approach is also one of 'thick description', meaning a detailed account of the social and economic relations within the context they exist in, so that not only the action of social groups can be explained, but also the broad context for the action in the tradition of Geertz (1973). Finally, the approach is substantivist in the Polanyi (1944, 1957) sense: there is no assumption about scarcity or rationality; instead reference is made to how human beings live within interacting social and natural environments which may or may not be optimizing.[5]

[5] Polanyi (1944) argued that 'economics' had two meanings, one formal, as used in neoclassical economics (an assumption of scarcity leads to the study of decision-making and rational

The analytical approach of the book is one of a broad and eclectic school of thought called the 'Social Structure of (Capital) Accumulation' (the addition of 'capital' is that of the author here).[6]

This book seeks to explain the set of distinct 'waves' of capital accumulation in South East Asia since the 1960s, that have taken Malaysia, Indonesia, and Thailand from low-income, high-poverty countries towards higher-income, low-poverty countries. The focus is the social structure—that is, the institutional arrangements and their integrity—that sustains the upswings of each wave of capital accumulation by favouring investment, with emphasis on the recuperative and regenerative power of capitalism to revive and reinvent following intermittent crises.

In short, the book is a comparative, interdisciplinary study of poverty, inequality, and structural transformation in South East Asia from the late 1960s to the present day. The book thus extends the global discussion of poverty, inequality, inclusive growth, and structural transformation in Sumner (2016a, 2016b) and revisits the author's own Ph.D. (see Sumner 2002) in a set of comparative country case studies.

1.5 The Intended Contribution of this Book

The intended intellectual contribution of the book is threefold: first, to provide a comparative, historical analysis of the processes of structural transformation and to do so with reference to their relationship to distributional tensions.

Often, poverty (and to some extent even individual inequality) has come to be viewed in a vacuum, separate from the processes of economic development. In short, poverty is often analyzed by its effects or proximate factors, such as a lack of assets, rather than the processes of economic development and social relations.[7] The inclusive growth literature tends to focus on how much income or assets people have in their possession rather than how people

optimizing choices), and the other substantive, which makes no assumption about scarcity or rationality and instead refers to how human beings live within an interaction of social and natural environments which may or may not be optimizing.

[6] See for discussion, Gordon (1978, 1980), Gordon et al. (1982, 1994, 1996), Houston (1992), Kotz (1994, 2015, 2016), McDonough (1994, 2008), Reich (1994), Wolfson (1994), and Wolfson and Kotz (2009).

[7] Harriss (2007, p. 5) puts it eloquently thus: 'the way in which poverty is conceptualised separates it from the social processes of the capital accumulation and distribution of wealth, which depoliticises it'. Green and Hulme (2005, pp. 869, 872) concur noting that

> [p]overty comes to be seen as a lack of resources rather than an absence of entitlements, as an 'economic' rather than a political problem... [t]he question becomes not why are some people poor in society, but why some societies tolerate poverty as an outcome and for whom, and how this toleration becomes embedded within institutional norms and systems.

earn that money. On the other hand, the structural transformation literature has largely focused on production and employment composition and hence productivity of various economic sectors rather than the effects of structural change on people. As a result, its policy recommendations have focused on industrial policies, business environment and capital, skills and capital accumulation.

There has been a resurgence in interest in developing countries' structural transformation with the fall of commodity-dependent emerging nations, a possible seismic shift within the 'Factory Asia', an acceleration of automation in manufacturing, and the talk of reshoring of advanced country companies. Some recent analyses on structural transformation, such as UNCTAD (2017), UNIDO (2016), and World Bank (2017) touch upon the issues of inclusive and sustainable growth; however, they have not gone far enough in integrating the analysis of growth, poverty and inequality within the process of structural change. This integration of poverty and inequality in the analysis of processes of structural transformation is at the core of the book, as it situates poverty and inequality as integral dynamics of economic development rather than 'residuals'.

Second, in light of the experience of South East Asia, the book reconsiders the contemporary relevance of theories of structural transformation. Orthodox theories such as comparative advantage remain dominant whilst heterodox theories of peripherality such as structuralism have become peripheral intellectually despite being the intellectual underpinning for many policies that were pursued in the region under what might be called 'classical developmentalism', meaning the ISI of the 1960s. The book shows that such policies are experiencing a renaissance in the contemporary period and discusses why.

Third, the nature of structural transformation and industrialization has radically shifted from infant domestic industry-building to integration into global value chains via foreign direct investment or supplying global value chains.[8] This has provided new constraints as well as opportunities for structural transformation, and new questions which this book explores.

1.6 The Existing Literature

Numerous books have been written on the issues of structural transformation in the broad region of East Asia. Many of those contain some emphasis on the inclusive nature of growth. However, much of the writing has focused on

[8] Further, transnational companies (TNCs) have moved away from direct production in the form of foreign direct investment to indirect forms and outsourcing which has generated 'buyer chains' controlled by TNCs rather than solely direct production by TNCs.

North East Asia (for example, Amsden 1989, 2001; Wade 1990; and more recently, Boyer et al. 2012; Walter and Zhang 2014).

Although industrialization and development in South East Asia has been similar in some ways, it has also been different in other ways (see Amsden 1995; Booth 1999; Doner et al. 2005; Vu, 2010).

South East Asia has received less attention relative to North East Asia. Many of the books covering the region date from a decade ago or longer, and the period shortly after the Asian financial crisis (for example, on Malaysia, see Alavi 2002; on Indonesia, see Dick 2002; Hill 2002; on Thailand, see Dixon 1999). There are some more recent exceptions (see for Malaysia, Hill 2012; Jomo and Wee 2014; for Thailand, see Doner 2009; Raquiza 2012; for Indonesia, see Booth 2016; Hadiz 2010; Thee 2012; van Zanden and Marks 2014) though these tend to focus on single countries rather than comparative industrialization and development across South East Asia. And whilst the study of politics across South East Asia has received attention (for example, Robison 2012), the comparative study of economic and social development in South East Asia has received relatively less attention, at least in terms of a dedicated monograph (not withstanding there are numerous articles and papers). One key recent contribution is Rock (2017), which has a particularly strong emphasis on a political understanding of growth though it does not focus directly on the distributional tension considered in this book. That said, the discussion of this book does resonate clearly with Rock and also with Jomo and Wee (2014, p. 58) who, although discussing only Malaysia, outline their thesis with eloquence and a thesis that equally applies to Indonesia and Thailand and indeed, any country:

> [Malaysia's] economic development policy has been primarily shaped by the nature of the regimes, the dominant interests represented, and their respective views of what would be desirable to advance their own interests and to secure legitimacy in order to remain in power.

In short, as Arthur Lewis put it, '[i]n the end, economics is not enough' (Lewis 1985, p. 121). Other recent books that seek to cover the entire region of South East Asia tend to take a very long-term historical sweep (for example, Ricklefs et al. 2010; Rigg 2012), but they tend to say relatively little on the post-Asian financial crisis period. Nor do they address the distributional tension that is central to this book.

1.7 The Structure of the Book

The structure of the book is as follows: this introduction outlines the background, rationale, scope, and content to the reader. Chapter 2 then sets the scene in terms of the points of departure and the concepts of structural transformation and inclusive growth. The chapter discusses their meanings, the 'basic' model of economic development, meaning the dual model as developed by Arthur Lewis (emphasizing the use of the model as an 'ideal type' or a heuristic device) within which the capture of productivity gains is central to capitalists and capital accumulation. The chapter builds on this with a discussion of Simon Kuznets' theories on economic transition and distribution.

Chapter 3 revisits the stock of theoretical literature on structural transformation, industrialization, and distributional questions covering both orthodox and heterodox theories. Much of this literature, building on or reacting to the transition outlined in the Lewis model, asks why developing countries do not experience the transition that the Lewis model optimistically envisaged. Discussion centres on the nature of incorporation, adverse or otherwise, of developing countries into the global economy. The contemporary literature on the heterogeneity of regimes of late capitalism is also discussed. This sets the scene for the rationale and exposition of the analytical framework for the book in the social structure of capital accumulation.

Chapters 4, 5, and 6 focus on South East Asia's experience since the 1960s. Chapter 4 begins with the period of 'classical developmentalism' from the late 1960s to the mid 1980s. The thesis of Chapter 4 is that classical developmentalism achieved radical structural transformation with inclusive growth. That said, by the early 1980s, this variety of developmentalism was exhausted due to changes in the global economy leading to economic crises. Until the 1980s, structural transformation was largely based on ISI and was distributionally neutral. This modality of structural transformation, however, left Malaysia, Indonesia, and Thailand dependent on global accumulation. This was positive whilst the good times lasted, especially so for Indonesia and Malaysia, given the oil boom. However, rising oil prices forced Thailand into an early adjustment, whilst in Indonesia and Malaysia, 'voluntary' adjustment followed the drop in oil prices of the early 1980s.

Chapter 5 picks up the narrative from the mid 1980s and the reincarnation of developmentalism into a 'two-tier developmentalism' as its starting point.[9] As a result of changes in the relative values of national exchange rates vis-à-vis the US dollar, the Japanese yen, and the currencies of Northeast Asia, the

[9] The terms 'classical developmentalism' and 'two-tier developmentalism' complement or compare with other terms such as 'crony capitalism', 'oligarchic capitalism', and 'predatory capitalism' that have often been used to describe MIT's development during the high-growth period in the sense that 'classical developmentalism' and 'two-tier developmentalism' aim to describe the intertwined outcome of overall macroeconomic and social development whilst other terms (e.g. crony, oligarchy, predatory) are from an account of the dominant economic force during economic development and its surrounding institutions during the period.

countries of Southeast Asia—Malaysia, Indonesia, and Thailand—at a stroke became ultra-competitive and thus MIT became very attractive to foreign investors. The period from the mid 1980s to the mid 1990s was an episode of rip-roaring capital accumulation and global incorporation at staggering speed. This was largely driven by these exchange rate movements and the resulting large inflows of foreign direct investment. It also involved increasingly deregulated foreign borrowing by the domestic private sector and portfolio investment inflows into new stock markets.

This wave of capital accumulation ended in crisis which, as before, was related to the mode of global incorporation. When national exchange rates appreciated, South East Asia became less competitive, and the unregulated borrowing and speculative inflows that had fuelled the boom became unsustainable.

Chapter 6 picks up the story in the mid 1990s immediately prior to the Asian financial crisis of the late 1990s. It argues that in the same way the global economy made South East Asia a highly competitive region for relocating foreign direct investment via exchange rate movements, movements in exchange rates in the opposite direction removed that attractiveness. The mass capital outflows, although made possible by policies of capital account and financial liberalization, were a symptom of the crisis rather than a structural cause. The appreciation of national exchange rates, coupled with new competition from China and elsewhere in similar manufactures, led to weakening export growth, and this was the ultimate cause of the crisis. The chapter considers the emergence since the crisis of 'premature deindustrialization' (see for discussion, Palma 2005; Rodrik 2015) in South East Asia from around 2000 onwards. Although growth resumed after the crash of the late 1990s for Malaysia, Indonesia, and Thailand, growth has been substantially slower in each of these countries since then, and each country has experienced at least a plateauing of structural transformation. Additionally, the political consensus that was conducive to rapid industrialization has broken down to some extent, in different ways, in the three countries due to the rise of populist and democratic political forces that the Asian financial crisis unleashed.

It is argued that the end of the commodity boom, which had hidden underlying weaknesses until the late 2000s, triggered the next reincarnation or a 'new developmentalism' legitimatized by state-directed capitalism in China, and the US government bailout of its own companies in response to the global crash in 2007/8. However, this reinvention is constrained by the boundaries of global rules and thus favours non-traditional protectionism such as non-tariff barriers rather than traditional measures such as tariff barriers. The thesis of Chapter 6 is that, as before, new varieties of developmentalism evolve in response to a crisis and bring within them new dependencies or subordination related to global incorporation. Due to the foreign ownership or ties of much manufacturing capacity, few domestic firms are able to access higher entry points in global value chains and this has limited the potential for domestic company upgrading. At the same time, current entry points to global value chains face competition with China and other newly emerging countries.

Chapter 7 concludes the book, drawing together the key arguments in terms of the varieties of developmentalism in South East Asia and how they have sought to address the developer's dilemma. It is argued that structural transformation and industrialization are made possible by international trade and foreign investment, contradicting the more pessimistic historical predictions of heterodox theorists, but only to a point, after which new forms of dependency, subordination, and peripherality have emerged. In sum, South East Asia demonstrates the possibilities as well as the limitations for economic development in developing countries today.

1.8 Conclusion

This book discusses the economic history and the developmental experience of structural transformation and inclusive growth in Malaysia, Indonesia, and Thailand from the 1960s onwards. The book utilizes a methodological approach of a detailed comparative case study that is inductive and empirical. The book employs methods that draw on quantitative statistics on historical trends and regularities, and analyses of global and national structures. Transformation is attributed to orchestrated developmentalism of various types: classical developmentalism (1960s to 1980s), meaning an ISI-led model; two-tier developmentalism (1980s to 1990s), meaning protection of domestic capital with selective openness to international capital and opportunism built on changes in global capital accumulation (and in relative exchange rates and interest rates); and a new, or revivalist developmentalism (2000s to the present day), meaning the resurgence of the importance of, and financing for, state-owned enterprises (SOEs) and state agencies of economic development.

It is argued throughout this book that transformation in MIT was strongly shaped by the global dynamics of the time: the oil boom (1960s to 1970s), exchange rate and interest rate differentials (1980s to 1990s), and China's awakening (2000s to present). It is also argued that structural transformation unleashes the forces of divergence between and within 'sectors' of urban and rural, skilled and unskilled workers, and between capital and labour. However, these Lewis–Kuznets types of tensions were counterbalanced, and even neutralized by—counter-intuitively—a strong focus on rural and agricultural development; a focus on redistributing in the near future via a continual education expansion until exhausted, and a focus on employment growth as opposed to the translation of productivity gains into more substantial real-wage growth. In short, structural transformation with inclusive growth requires a counterbalancing of the inequality pressures unleashed by structural transformation, and a focus not solely on urban/manufacturing, but also on the rural/agricultural sector; a focus not solely on current income redistributive measures, but also on future income inequality (tomorrow's inequality of outcome); and a focus not solely on real-wage growth, but on employment growth. This is how the countries of South East Asia have managed the developer's dilemma. In doing so, elites—of course—got rich in absolute terms even if relative income inequality did not rise dramatically in the process and in all likelihood only a small proportion of the rents from natural resources were channelled directly into development. Still that was sufficient, coupled with domestic regimes and patterns of global accumulation, to transform a set of low-income, high-poverty, agrarian economies into middle-income countries with industrial bases.

2

Structural Transformation and Inclusive Growth

Conceptual Points of Departure

2.1 Introduction

Chapter 1 outlined the 'developer's dilemma'. To recap, developing countries are seeking economic development, which requires structural transformation and productivity growth via intra- and inter-sectoral reallocation of economic activity. At the same time, developing countries are also seeking some form of broad-based or 'inclusive growth' which can be defined in various ways, typically in terms of who benefits from growth and by how much. The dilemma is the trade-off between structural transformation and inclusive growth. There is a 'developer's dilemma', in that structural transformation has historically been thought to have a tendency to push up inequality, as Arthur Lewis and Simon Kuznets originally posited, though they differed to some extent on whether this is inevitable and what the countervailing forces are. On the other hand, inclusive growth implies a need for steady or even falling inequality to spread the benefits of growth as broadly as possible. In short, the 'developer's dilemma' is a distribution dilemma or tension at the heart of economic development. Empirical support for this potential trade-off or developer's dilemma—that structural change is associated with rising inequality—was originally offered in Sumner (2016a, 2016b), and then offered in greater detail by Baymul and Sen (2017).[1] Given the empirical support for

[1] Baymul and Sen (2017) make use of the Timmer et al. (2015) dataset and the United Nations University World Institute for Development Economics Research (UNU-WIDER) World Income Inequality Database (WIID) (UNU-WIDER forthcoming). They find that a movement of workers away from agriculture is unambiguously associated with rising income inequality. However, in most cases, the shift of employment is from agriculture to services, not agriculture to manufacturing.

the developer's dilemma, how are countries to manage the tension and what are the experiences of countries who have managed the tension?

The purpose of this chapter is three-fold. First, to outline the components of the developer's dilemma in terms of the conceptual points of departure for the book in terms of structural transformation (ST) and inclusive growth (IG). Second, to situate those concepts of ST and IG in a model of economic development appropriate for the study of the developer's dilemma. Third, to contextualize Lewis and Kuznets to contemporary times to take account of multiple forms and dimensions of structural change.

The following chapter (Chapter 3), then focuses on the stock of theory relating to the facilitators and impediments to structural transformation and industrialization, and the distributional questions arising. Much of this theory is focused on the nature of the adverse incorporation of developing countries into the global economy and extends the discussion of the Lewis model of economic development. This is followed by a discussion of the contemporary literature on the heterogeneity or differentiated regimes of late capitalism and culminates in the rationale for, and outline of, the 'Social Structure of Capital Accumulation' approach as the analytical approach of the book. Chapters 4, 5, and 6 then consider how the developer's dilemma played out in South East Asia in three distinct 'waves', each culminating in crisis, and all of which, were, it is argued, triggered by changes in the global economy and by the nature of countries' incorporation into the global economy.

The core arguments of this chapter are as follows: first, that both ST and IG have tended to be defined in a reductionist sense, in a way that disconnects the two concepts (in fact those who study one would, most likely, not study the other). It is posited that, by defining ST solely by shares of gross domestic product (GDP) or employment, more important aspects of ST are neglected. In a similar vein, by defining IG as the reduction of absolute poverty (or the consumption or income of the poorest only) and—sometimes—by changes in individual income inequality, some other aspects of IG, notably capabilities, inequality of opportunity and importantly, employment, have been neglected. It is argued that this matters because the relationship between ST and IG is embedded in—rather than separated from—the modality of late capitalism pursued.

The second part of the thesis is that both the work of pioneering development economist, W. Arthur Lewis, and the Lewis dual economy model, provide a useful heuristic device for thinking about the developer's dilemma and the relationship between ST and IG. Further, although Lewis did not ignore inequality, the seminal work of Simon Kuznets, who used a dual economy model, and those writing in the Kuznetsian tradition, are useful to revisit in order to understand the inequality dynamics of the transition from a traditional to a modern economy though Kuznets and Lewis need to be contextualized because of multiple forms of contemporary structural change, not least 'premature deindustrialization' and circular (back-and-forth) or 'commuting' labour movements; non-farm rural income; the growth of intersectoral resource flows and the multiple dimensions of inclusive growth.

Contributions since Lewis and Kuznets seminal work have placed emphasis on the modality of incorporation into the global economy.[2] For instance, much of the theory discussed in the following chapter takes the view that the modality of incorporation into the global economy and the intermittent tectonic plate-type changes in the global economy, such as changes in global oil prices, are important for understanding national economic development. At the same time, others have focused on domestic factors and/or the interplay of both.

The current chapter is structured as follows: Sections 2.2 and 2.3 discuss the conceptual components of the developer's dilemma—the concepts of structural transformation and inclusive growth, and their meaning. The argument of this section is that important aspects have been neglected in the reductionist definitions of ST and IG. Further, that ST and IG have been considered separately, rather than as interconnected phenomena. Section 2.4 situates the concepts within the transition as outlined by Arthur Lewis, and the application by Simon Kuznets of income inequality dynamics within the transition. The Lewis model postulates that the transfer of labour, from low productivity to higher productivity activities and sectors, is the key driver of economic development.[3] The Kuznets hypothesis on rising inequality during structural transformation implies a pattern of growth that constrains income/consumption gains at the poorest end of the distribution. Empirically, the Kuznets hypothesis has been generally rejected in cross-sectional data, though it has seen an empirical resurgence in recent time-series data for fast-growing developing countries where growth is accompanied by structural transformation (see Sumner 2016a, 2016b). Various contemporary authors, writing in the Lewis/Kuznets tradition (for example, Acemoglu and Robinson 2002; Aghion and Bolton 1997; Gallup 2012; Lindert 1986; Lindert and Williamson 2001; Oyvat 2016; Roine and Waldenström 2014; Williamson 1985) are discussed. Finally, Section 2.5 concludes and sets the scene for the next chapter.

[2] Though there is only one section explicitly on the open economy in the original exposition of the Lewis (1954) model, more is evident implicitly and Lewis, himself, elucidated more in later works. Specifically, an open economy would delay the Lewis turning point where surplus labour was exhausted and wages would rise. Lewis (1954) argued, using an open economy and factoral terms of trade, that the benefits of productivity growth accrue to Northern importers of exports of developing countries by way of lower prices because wages are set in the subsistence sector where there is an unlimited supply of labour.

[3] It is not given that structural change *will* always be growth-enhancing as Diao et al. (2016) note, and Baymul and Sen (2017) concur.

2.2 Structural Transformation: Conceptual Points of Departure

2.2.1 *Overview*

The purpose of this section is to discuss, first, what might be called the dominant definitions of both core concepts, ST and IG. This section argues that such definitions neglect deeper aspects of ST and IG, and that, in doing so, they disconnect the concepts of ST and IG, thus delinking poverty, inequality, and capital accumulation. This section is structured as follows: this overview is followed by a discussion of the meanings of ST and IG. This is succeeded by a proposal for alternative definitions of ST and IG that link the two conceptually. In short, the argument of this section is that the two conceptual aspects of the 'developer's dilemma' have been historically approached in a more reductionist sense and treated as analytically separate. Consequentially, the relationship between ST and IG has not been teased out in greater depth.

2.2.2 *Structural Transformation: Definitions*

The purpose of this section is to critically discuss different definitions of ST. In considering the conceptualization of ST, one is pushed to consider ST *from what, between what,* and *in what direction,* and the possibility of multiple and co-existing/co-evolving transitions beyond that of a shift from the 'traditional' or agriculture or rural or informal sector to the 'modern', manufacturing, urban, or formal sector. This section argues that dominant approaches to defining ST have generated understandings based largely on sectoral shares of GDP and employment. Yet, the broader set of structures related to the factoral composition of growth, labour productivity, and international trade are just as important in garnering a deeper understanding of ST. One could potentially cast the net even wider to include political and social institutional change.

First, we consider the neglect of ST in developing countries (relative to the attention to IG). It is reasonable to say that structural transformation—in the first instance meaning the reallocation of economic activity not only between, but also within, sectors towards higher productivity—has been neglected at least relative to the attention to IG with reference to developing countries.[4] Although the importance of the shift to higher productivity is not disputed in neoclassical economics, a one-sector model of economic growth has become

[4] See Herrendorf et al. (2013), and earlier reviews of structural transformation, notably Matsuyama (2008), Ray (2010), and Greenwood and Seshadri (2005). One can also note the works of Clark (1957), Chenery (1960), Kuznets (1966), and Syrquin (1986).

standard in macroeconomics. In this one-sector model of economic growth there is no account of the process of inter-sectoral reallocation of economic activity or structural transformation. This is because, in the neoclassical growth model (of Solow 1956), growth is driven by incentives to save, accumulate physical and human capital, and innovate. In contrast, for most heterodox economists, growth is due to reallocation of economic activity to more productive sectors or more productive sub-sectors.

In some ways, this debate is embedded in historic discussion on the need, or not, for 'balanced growth' across sectors.[5] Regardless of whether growth should be balanced or not, ST in itself is an important driver of growth because of (often dramatically) differing productivity levels between, and even within, sectors. Although whether productivity can be accurately measured is contested by Fischer (2011) who refers to a 'fallacy of productivity reductionism', which is the assumption that productivity can be measured in a complex economy. Measuring productivity relies on value-added account data, but such data is a combination of output and prices/wages. So, most measurements for productivity show *price or wage differentials* not actual effort, output, or skill. This is an even bigger problem in the service sector as the comparability of services is more problematic because they are not physical goods that can be compared. Fischer (2014) also notes another problem that, because transnational companies (TNCs)—who dominate production and its coordination in global value chains—conduct practices such as transfer pricing and the transferring of profits from Southern subsidiaries to Northern HQs (for example, low-interest loans from subsidiary to parent company), such actions could make the subsidiary look less productive. These are clearly important issues that, although not easily resolved, should not be forgotten.

If one assumes, for the sake of continuing further, that productivity can be measured albeit imperfectly, McMillan and Rodrik (2011, p. 1), in taking sectoral and aggregate labour 'productivity' data empirically, show that the

[5] On balanced growth, the key seminal (and first) promoter of this idea was Rosenstein-Rodan. Scholars are/were divided on the need to which growth should be balanced. For example, Singer and Hirschman, for example, both argued that growth need not take place in an inter-sectorally balanced way. In contrast, Kalecki (1954, 1955, 1967) argued that 'balanced development' in the agriculture and industrial sectors is required. Kalecki argued that the inter-sectoral terms of the trade between the agriculture and industrial sectors need managing so that the terms of trade do not undermine the agriculture that provides food, and that failure to do so would slow down industrialization as it would depress real wages in industry and profits. Lewis also noted,

> In unenlightened circles agriculture and industry are often considered as alternatives to each other. The truth is that industrialization for a home market can make little progress unless agriculture is progressing vigorously at the same time, to provide both the market for industry, and industry's labour supply. If agriculture is stagnant, industry cannot grow. (Lewis 1953, cited in Kanbur 2016, p. 6)

transfer of labour and other inputs to higher productive activity is a driver of economic development, as Lewis hypothesized.[6] They note:

> One of the earliest and most central insights of the literature on economic development is that development entails structural change. The countries that manage to pull out of poverty and get richer are those that are able to diversify away from agriculture and other traditional products. As labour and other resources move from agriculture into modern economic activities, overall productivity rises and incomes expand. The speed with which this structural transformation takes place is the key factor that differentiates successful countries from unsuccessful ones.

They go on to note that ST can in fact be growth-enhancing or growth-reducing depending on the reallocation of labour.[7] This is an important point and relates to the multiple modes of ST and direction between sectors, which may be regressive as well as progressive in the sense of productivity gains or losses. They show how ST had been growth-enhancing in Asia because labour has transferred from low to higher productivity sectors. However, the converse is the case for sub-Saharan Africa and Latin America because labour has been transferred from higher to lower productivity sectors and this has reduced growth rates.[8]

Is manufacturing 'special'? Rodrik (2013) shows that unconditional convergence is evident in manufacturing, meaning faster productivity growth the further away from the labour productivity frontier. Furthermore, returns to scale imply that as costs fall, demand rises for manufacturing foods (high-income elasticities of demand), triggering more manufacturing and higher incomes, more demand, and cost reductions. Many such as Rodrik (2015) argue that most services are (i) non-tradable, and (ii) not technologically

[6] For a contrarian view see Roy (1951). Specifically, the causality could run from growth to ST, meaning ST is an outcome of growth not a cause of growth; what appear to be sectoral differences in productivity are not necessarily due to sectors but could be skills, for example; further that inter-sectoral relocations may occur without changes in productivity gaps between sectors. One needs to show not that incomes are higher in urban than in rural areas (or different sectors) but that the income of the same individual would be higher in an urban area than in a rural area if they migrated. Importantly, if Roy (1951) is correct then the transition of labour from low productivity to higher productivity sectors will not reduce inequality; rather, it will increase it, because the same person would earn less in the high productivity sector.

[7] McMillan and Rodrik (2011) find that countries with a large share of exports in natural resources tend to experience growth-reducing structural transformation and, even if they have higher productivity, cannot absorb surplus labour from agriculture. In a similar vein, Gollin et al. (2016), too, argued that natural resource exports drive urbanization without structural transformation because natural resources generate considerable surplus which is spent on urban goods and services, and urban employment tends to be in non-traded services. McMillan and Rodrik (2011) also find that an undervalued (competitive) exchange rate, which operates effectively as a subsidy on industry and labour market characteristics (so labour can move across sectors and firms easily), leads to growth-enhancing structural transformation.

[8] In a similar vein, Diao et al. (2017) argue that the most recent growth accelerations in the developing world, unlike East Asia's historical experience, have not been driven by industrialization but by within-sector productivity growth (in Latin America) and growth-increasing structural transformation, but this has been accompanied by negative labour productivity growth within non-agricultural sectors (in Ethiopia, Malawi, Senegal, and Tanzania).

dynamic, and that (iii) some sectors are tradable and dynamic, but they do not have the capacity to absorb labour. Similar shortcomings can be observed about the manufacturing sector. A significant share of manufacturing is (i) non-traded (even though it is tradable) and (ii) much of manufacturing in developing countries is not technologically advanced (at least in relative terms to other modern sectors), and (iii) where some manufacturing sectors are technologically dynamic, they may not create much employment, as some service sectors do. This is especially true now that it is robots and machines that perform more factory work in the electronics sector. Developing the manufacturing industry is important, but one should be careful of 'industrial fundamentalism'. To achieve the goal of upgrading the economy and creating jobs, one should not overlook opportunities in other sectors. In short, there is a need to go beyond blue-collar jobs and manufacturing investment, and a need for policies that boost the service sector (see discussion of Kim et al., 2017).

Others, such as Herrendorf et al. (2013), concur empirically with the argument that the sectoral composition of economic activity is key to understanding not only economic development but also regional income convergence, productivity trends, business cycles, and inequality in wages. This echoes Kuznets (1971, p. 1), who, writing almost fifty years ago, listed a high rate of structural transformation as one of the six main features of 'modern economic growth' about which he said,

> [t]he rate of structural transformation of the economy is high . . . [and] [m]ajor aspects of structural change include the shift away from agriculture to non-agricultural pursuits and, recently, away from industry to services; [also included is] a change in the scale of productive units, and a related shift from personal enterprise to impersonal organisation of economic firms, with a corresponding change in the occupational status of labor.

Many of the other features of 'modern economic growth' outlined by Kuznets relate to a broader conceptualization of ST beyond GDP and employment shares alone. Changes in societal structures, many of which are related to ST, such as urbanization and technological progress, were also included in Kuznets' conceptualization. This raises the question of definitional scope noted at the outset of this section, and the structural change *of what*, *between what*, and *in what direction*, to which we next turn.

Kuznets (1971, p. 348) made a case that ST was a much broader societal process as it was embedded in societal change beyond economic structure alone. ST could be extended to population, legal, political, and social institutions, social ideology, and beliefs, and such shifts were prerequisites for the 'modern economic growth' he outlined. This argument also resonates with the 'special case' outlined by Dudley Seers (1963) when he referred to the 'highly special case' of advanced countries. One could call such countries the 'arrived' cases of ST (with caveats for the socio-economic problems in advanced countries). Seers went beyond a definition of ST based solely on shares of GDP and employment, and the characteristics set out by Seers of the 'special case' remain an enduring set of features that define an advanced economy or an 'arrived' case in terms of ST (and indeed, IG, given the aspects of poverty and inequality noted).

In terms of the structural transformation of the economy, foreign trade, and other matters, Seers (1963, pp. 81–3) identified the following list (summarized here) to demonstrate how one might differentiate developed nations from developing nations: by factors of production (a literate and mobile labour force who are mostly in employment; substantial quantities of skilled labour; most available land cultivated; all sectors heavily capitalized, with spare capacity; comprehensive transport and power systems; a favourable climate for enterprise; firm legal basis for companies); by sectors of the economy (for example, agriculture wholly commercial; mining of limited size; manufacturing diversified and much larger than either agriculture or mining); by public finance (for example, reliance on direct taxes; tax laws enforceable; big outlays on social security and agricultural subsidies); by foreign trade (exports that have a large internal market and are sold to many countries with high price and income elasticities; imports largely of primary products and income elasticity of demand not high); by household consumption (for example, very few people below subsistence level and a moderately equal distribution of income post-tax; food not the overwhelming majority of household expenditure); by savings and investment (for example, well-developed financial intermediaries; significant personal savings and high investment); and by 'dynamic influences' (no chronic tendency to deficits; slow population growth and high urbanization). In short, this resonates with Kuznets (and Polanyi) and an embedding of ST in broader societal social, political, and economic change. Seers, however, argued that the ST or development of the advanced countries was a special case and not a general one that could simply be reproduced.[9]

More recently, echoing somewhat Kuznets' and Seers' thinking on ST, Pritchett et al. (2010, pp. 3–4) conceptualized 'development' in a broader way, as follows:

> When people speak of the 'development' of societies most people refer, implicitly or explicitly, to a cumulative historical process whereby economies grow through enhanced productivity, prevailing political systems represent the aggregate

[9] Seers (1963, pp. 79–80) noted the 'special case' of 'First World' or developed industrial economies as, 'by no means typical' and developing countries as having a 'largely unindustrialised economy, the foreign trade of which consists essentially in selling primary products for manufactures'. He argued that orthodox economics pays too little attention to the role of the export sector and that developing countries cannot be understood without reference to the global economy, and how the public sector automatically compensates for fluctuations in the private economy in industrial economies, which is much harder or impossible for developing countries.

> preferences of citizens, rights and opportunities are extended to all social groups, and organisations function according to meritocratic standards and professional norms (thereby becoming capable of administering larger numbers of more complex tasks). A given society undergoes a four-fold transformation in its functional capacity to manage its economy, polity, society and public administration, becoming, in time, developed.

Of course, one cannot deny that ST is a much broader process and economic ST is interwoven into socio-political institutions. However, there is the usual trade-off of excessively broad definitions (everything is ST) versus narrower definitions (ST is economic in nature), which are manageable for analysis.

Even if one decides to focus on economic ST alone, a set of methodological questions arises. Syrquin (2007) briefly identifies such questions and they include defining what is meant by 'sectors' and thus what ST means (inter- or intra- depends on the breadth of definitions of sectors) and the blurring between 'services' and 'manufacturing' due to technological advances and outsourcing (see later discussion on 'premature deindustrialization'). Furthermore, it is necessary to discuss the related changing nature of industrialization itself in developing countries and globally. Industrialization used to mean vertically integrated national economic development to be realized in domestic industry building, but over time industrialization has come to mean horizontal integration into global value chains via foreign direct investment or as domestic suppliers. Thus, the meaning of what is to be achieved in industrialization has changed, which is not inconsequential. The changing nature of industrialization is of relevance as assessments of ST tend to overemphasize shares of GDP and employment and pay limited attention to the questions of ownership and the national capture of economic value added.

In sum, one could say that a conceptualization of ST has three discernible dimensions framed around a shift towards higher productivity activities. These are sectoral, factoral, and integrative. The first dimension—the sectoral aspects of ST—is about the inter- and intra-reallocation of sectoral activity towards higher productivity. This includes the common measures of ST, notably shares of GDP and employment. However, ST may not only be agriculture to industry or manufacturing, but agriculture to services or other sectors (see later on the modes of sectoral ST). The second dimension is the factoral aspects of ST and is about the composition or drivers of economic growth in terms of a shift of factors of production towards higher productivity activities. Underlying this are questions of demography too with reference to labour. Third are the integrative aspects of ST. This is the extent of integration in terms of the global economy and a shift from forms of incorporation—trade deficits and capital inflows that come with liabilities (for example, profit repatriation or debt repayment)—towards trade surpluses and outward FDI. Here the changing nature of global capital accumulation is important.[10]

2.3 Inclusive Growth: Conceptual Points of Departure

The purpose of this section is to critically assess different meanings of IG. The argument of this section is that common approaches to defining IG have generated limited understandings based largely on absolute poverty lines and—sometimes—on reductions in inequality of outcomes. Instead, it is argued that a broader set of measures is important in garnering a deeper understanding of IG and conceptually linking IG to ST. In this section we discuss first the emphasis given to IG: we discuss first the relative overemphasis given to IG in developing countries (relative to the neglect of ST), albeit defined in a narrow way. Research has tended to show almost all growth to be, at least minimally, inclusive, although there are emerging signs that some are empirically questioning this once again (for example, Shaffer 2017; Sen 2014). Second, we discuss the basic dimensions for conceptualizing IG in terms of who to include, how much, and in what way (though this latter dimension is implicitly material- or consumption-based now or at some point in the future). There is the further question of who decides who to 'include' and on what terms, which relates to the social structure supporting and sustaining capital accumulation (see Chapter 3).

The substantial attention to IG in developing countries (certainly relative to ST) demonstrated by the sheer volume of literature, has tended to show growth in general *is* inclusive at least in a minimal way. In contrast to ST, IG has received a considerable amount of attention in academic (and policy) literature, albeit among a different scholarly community (one who works on poverty and inequality issues rather than on economic development, ST, productivity, and growth per se). IG, like ST has a lengthy genealogy with an evolutionary path into the contemporary concept of IG. IG is a term

[10] Singh (1977), for one, argued that one should look beyond the share of manufacturing in GDP or employment and towards shares of external trade. Singh (1977) notes,

> given the normal levels of the other components of the balance of payments, we may define an efficient manufacturing sector as one which . . . not only satisfies the demands of consumers at home, but is also able to sell enough of its products abroad to pay for the nation's import requirements. This is, however, subject to the important restriction that an 'efficient' manufacturing sector must be able to achieve these objectives at socially acceptable levels of output, employment, and the exchange rate . . . In operational terms, a structural problem can arise in this sense, if the manufacturing sector, without losing price or cost competitiveness, is unable to export enough to pay for the full-employment level of imports.

which some associate with the World Bank, though the use of the term need not be, as we shall come to see shortly.

There has, without a doubt, been a substantial amount of attention given to IG in developing countries. Historically, the interest in the broad area—defined as who benefits from growth and by how much—grew from debates in the early 1970s that were critical of the then distribution of the benefits of growth (for example, Adelman and Morris 1973; Chenery et al. 1974). Such issues received a lot of attention in the late 1990s through to the mid 2000s under different but related terms. For example, 'growth with equity', drew on critical debates on East Asian development (see for example, Fei et al. 1979; Jomo 2006; World Bank 1993). Then 'growth with equity' was supplanted by the label of 'pro-poor' growth (see for example, Besley and Cord 2006; Grimm et al. 2007; Shorrocks and van der Hoeven 2004) that in turn was supplanted by the term 'inclusive growth' (see Ali and Zhang 2007; Klasen 2010; McKinley 2010; Rauniyar and Kanbur 2010) which became the umbrella term for considering who benefited from growth.[11]

This range of labels entails some differences. For example, 'growth with equity' was typically defined as growth where inequality does not rise or may even fall (and is a term associated with World Bank 1993). In contrast, 'pro-poor growth' was taken to be absolute pro-poor growth if growth was accompanied by a falling poverty headcount (or rising incomes of the poor by a poverty line or fractile line), or relative pro-poor growth if that fall in poverty headcount was accompanied by falling inequality of outcome (see discussions in Bourguignon 2003; Kakwani and Pernia 2000; Ravallion 2004).

In contrast, 'inclusive growth' was framed as poverty reduction both in monetary and non-monetary terms. This entailed the participation of the poor or a broader group beyond just the poor in growth processes, via employment and the expansion of capabilities (in terms of public good access), which reduced poverty and potentially reduced the inequality of opportunity and/or inequality of outcomes.

The body of literature discussed above provides the empirical basis for a generally accepted notion that economic growth *is* inclusive in a general sense: on average, the poverty headcount falls and the incomes of the poorest rise in line with average income growth (see Dollar and Kraay 2002; Kraay 2006; Dollar et al. 2013). However, two recent contributions have reopened this debate. First, Shaffer (2017) notes that in 15–35 per cent of episodes of growth, absolute poverty actually rises with per capita growth and he connects this with historical debates on 'immiserizing growth', a term which has been

[11] The term 'shared prosperity' is one more label sitting under the umbrella of 'inclusive growth'. It is a term that is again associated with the World Bank (for example, World Bank 2016) though it need not necessarily be.

used (see Bhagwati 1958) to demonstrate that export-led growth could lead to a country being worse off due to changes in the terms of trade. However, for Shaffer it refers to growth accompanied by no change in, or even increasing poverty.

Second, Sen (2014) concurs with this, finding that there is a surprising number of growth episodes that are not inclusive based on 'traditional' interpretations of IG (that of falling poverty with or without non-rising inequality). Sen separates types of growth episodes between 'growth acceleration' and 'growth maintenance' and finds that the former is much less likely to benefit the poor than the latter. Sen argues that this is because the institutional factors that lead to growth accelerations are different from those that lead to growth maintenance.[12] This suggests that during periods of growth, potentially when ST is most rapid—a growth acceleration episode—IG may suffer and only recover when or if that growth acceleration becomes a growth maintenance episode and institutional arrangements change. This points towards a well-noted argument, even in the traditional IG studies, that the average inclusivity of growth can be misleading as it is subject to enormous variation across countries and highly sensitive to where the poverty line is set (see also the discussion of Edward and Sumner 2015; Sumner 2016a, 2016b). Much of the debate turns on whether inequality is high or rising, as high and rising inequality can hamper not only poverty reduction but also future growth prospects, which can impact future poverty reduction.[13] This brings us to our second question and a taxonomy of IG.

If we turn next to the basic dimensions for conceptualizing IG in terms of who to include, how much they are 'included' relative to others, and in what way they are 'included' (implicitly current or future consumption), it is immediately evident that the debate about the distributional pattern of growth raises a number of normative issues: should the poor (by whatever poverty line) see their standards of monetary and non-monetary living improve more than the non-poor? If so, where does one draw the poverty line? Or should the line be at median consumption or even, for example, at say $10 per day, which is a line associated with permanent escape from the risk of falling back into poverty (see López-Calva and Ortiz-Juarez 2014)? That level of daily consumption would capture most of the population of many developing countries. Then, once the line is taken and a normative decision is made to favour those

[12] In fact, the average relationship during a growth acceleration episode was negative for the poorest quintile (and, on average, the Gini coefficient rises) and the poorest 20 per cent were worse off in a range of countries including Bangladesh, China, and Nigeria, each home to large populations of the world's poorest. In contrast, during a growth maintenance episode, the income of the poorest quintile, on average, rises and the Gini falls.

[13] The debate in the literature on the relationship between inequality and growth received a detailed review in Cunha Neves and Tavares Silva (2014). Although numerous methodological issues remain, inequality may support growth at low levels of average income, but rising or high inequality can hamper growth at middle-income levels.

below the line more so than those above the line, what are the intra-poor weightings? Again, this is a normative question. If the poor are 90 per cent of the population, their incomes could rise at a faster rate than the top 10 per cent across the 90 per cent, but within the 90 per cent should there be progressive weighting with the strongest weighting on the poorest? These questions point towards the complexity of defining precisely what an 'inclusive growth' episode should look like. Further complicating matters is the relative simplicity of the relationship of growth to expenditure or monetary poverty versus the more complex relationship of growth to multi-dimensional poverty.[14]

One could say the contemporary concept of IG has several discernible dimensions. All of these IG types have something to say on who is 'included' and how much they are included. To recap, the assumption is that the 'in what way included' dimension is answered as consumption broadly defined now and/or in the near future. The first dimension or type of IG entails a focus on the benefits of growth to those under a poverty or population fractile line and their absolute or relative income or consumption. There are also sub-types. This definition includes IG as poverty reduction or absolute pro-poor growth. This refers to growth whereby those under a specific poverty line or fractile of consumption (e.g. the poorest 40 per cent) benefit in absolute terms and the proportion of population under that line diminishes. The definition also includes poverty reduction with falling inequality of outcome or relative pro-poor growth. This refers to growth whereby those under a specific poverty line or fractile of consumption (that is, the poorest 40 per cent) benefit more than those above that line (meaning inequality falls).

In contrast, a further dimension or type of IG entails a focus on the benefits of growth to the entire population, or at least a much broader group than those under a specific poverty or population fractile line, and their *capabilities* in terms of the expansion of education levels or employment prospects. A type II IG is growth that focuses on 'equalizing opportunities' *ex ante* or redistributing opportunity in the future. This is more in keeping with the recent evolution of the field of enquiry. This refers to growth whereby the education attainment expansion is prioritized (and one could add health access policies

[14] In this book, focus is on consumption/income/monetary poverty (though not exclusively). This is not to say poverty is not multidimensional. Clearly it is. The link, however, between monetary poverty and ST is clearer than that between multidimensional poverty and ST. The relationship between multidimensional poverty and growth is more complex than the mathematical identity for monetary poverty. Santos et al. (2016) find the relationship between multidimensional poverty and growth much weaker than monetary poverty and growth. Rising incomes among the monetary or multidimensional poor can lead to improved nutrition intake and outcomes, or improved access to education and health and outcomes, but public spending may be important in terms of the provision of free or subsidized public education and health. Social policy, such as redistributive transfers, can further support the reduction of both monetary and multidimensional poverty (see, for a discussion of countries with multidimensional poverty data over time, Alkire et al. 2015).

and social protection access) and is configured to ensure an equalizing of opportunity across the whole population. In short, the divergence between skilled and unskilled workers is constrained by expanding the education levels of the lesser skilled. During growth, it is likely that skilled workers will benefit first if growth opportunities are focused in higher skilled employment or sectors. The expansion of education attainment thus provides for a means to constrain the divergence of the skilled–unskilled worker pay differentials by expanding the supply of skilled labour and reducing the supply of unskilled labour. A third dimension or type III IG is full or fuller employment or employment-generating or labour-intensive growth or productivity that translates into employment growth. This refers to a situation whereby growth is accompanied by substantial employment generation as an outcome of productivity growth. This ensures that the opportunities presented by growth are broad-based and productivity gains are not entirely captured in real-wage increases but spread widely across a larger section of workers due to the extent of employment growth.

In sum, defining IG as a reduction in poverty by an absolute poverty line or the income of the poorest fractiles may miss important issues. Next, we consider the relationship between ST and IG. In the following section, we revisit the Lewis model and its distributional consequences for IG as outlined in Kuznets' seminal work and of others' since.

2.4 The Relationship Between Structural Transformation and Inclusive Growth

2.4.1 *Overview*

The discussion thus far has alluded to a relationship between ST and IG during the process of economic development without yet specifying a model. The purpose of this section is thus to situate ST and IG in a model of economic development. We do this to understand the relationship between ST and IG. We focus on the dual economy of the Lewis model as a heuristic device or an 'ideal type'. The model, developed by W. Arthur Lewis, envisaged capital accumulation through a transition driven by the labour movement from the traditional to the modern sector. The writing of Simon Kuznets and others following in the Kuznets tradition and using the Lewis model added the IG dimension by focusing on what happens to inequality during ST.

Why do we take the Lewis model of economic development? Why not another model of economic development? The answer to these questions is largely because the Lewis model of economic development is based on economic development by ST and thus ideally fits with the study of ST and further how IG interacts with ST. The Lewis model is appealing for the study within this book not only because of its focus on 'sectors' but because of its heterodox history and critique of neoclassical approaches that are indifferent to sectors and activities. It also covers the three dimensions of ST that are of interest (factoral, sectoral, and integrative ST). Palma (2005) refers to three schools of economic development theory.[15] The group within which Lewis sits is that which is premised on the notion that economic growth is both 'sector-specific' and 'activity-specific'. What binds this group together is that growth dynamics are dependent on the activities being developed and the capital accumulation effects of manufacturing. Thus, issues such as technology, externalities, balance of payment sustainability, and convergence with advanced countries are a function of the size, strength, and depth of manufacturing. The importance of manufacturing is predicated on the work of Kaldor (1967) who sought to explain the economic development of Western Europe through the development of manufacturing, which he argued was the engine of growth for every country at every stage of economic development. In terms of empirical support for the importance of manufacturing see Duarte and Restuccia (2010). Kaldor posited that: economic development requires industrialization because increasing returns in the manufacturing sector mean faster growth of manufacturing output which is associated with faster economic growth.[16]

The argument of this section is as follows: first, that the vision of Lewis provides the model of economic development that brings together both ST and IG because other models of growth place little importance on sector analysis. Second, that the Lewis model is best utilized as a heuristic device or 'ideal type' on the transition within which Kuznets' work on distribution dynamics can sit.[17]

[15] Palma (2005) identifies the neoclassical school, which is indifferent to both sectors and activities. The Solow convergence models (traditional and augmented), 'endogenous' models based on increasing returns, are examples of this school. Additionally, models based on market imperfections in technological change are a result of the production function. A second school is 'sector-indifferent' but 'activity-specific', which Palma associates with Roemer and the neo-Schumpeterians who argue that research and development matter but that there is nothing special about manufacturing in terms of Kaldor-effects. A third school is activity and sector specific and includes Lewis. Diao et al. (2017, pp. 3–4) seek to link the structural dualism of Lewis with the neoclassical model by arguing that the neoclassical model shows the growth process within the modern sector and the dual model shows the relationship among sectors.

[16] This is because backward and forward input–output linkages are strongest in manufacturing, and the scope for capital accumulation, technological progress, economies of scale, and knowledge spillover is strong. Further, there is a strong causal relationship between manufacturing output growth and labour productivity because of a deepening division of labour, specialization and learning-by-doing, and the scope for productivity gains is large due to economies of scale.

[17] Kirkpatrick and Barrientos (2004, p. 688) for example, referred to the Lewis model as 'an illuminating framework within which to discuss the reality of the process of development, not taking the homogeneity of its sectors literally, but looking behind this to uncover their internal workings and heterogeneity'.

While the Lewis model has faced criticisms, it is argued that the model remains useful as a heuristic device against which to compare the experiences of developing countries.

2.4.2 *The Lewis Model Revisited*

Arthur Lewis (see notably, 1954, 1958, 1969, 1972, 1976, 1979) provided one of the best-known and optimistic models of economic development in developing countries. Although sixty years old in its earliest iteration, the model remains relevant today to developing countries (see for contemporary discussion, Gollin 2014). Since Lewis's original work on the labour transition between sectors, much literature has been concerned with labour push-and-pull factors leading to various extensions of the model.[18] The dual model provides an ideal type, in the Weberian sense, for thinking about structural transformation and economic development with an emphasis on labour, which is the factor of production that dominates most developing countries.

Lewis argued that the driver of capital accumulation was a sectoral movement of the factor of production abundant in developing countries, labour, from the 'traditional' or 'non-capitalist' sector (of low productivity, low wage, priced to average product not marginal product, and thus with widespread disguised unemployment) to the 'modern' or 'capitalist' sector (of higher productivity, and where wages are set by productivity in the 'subsistence sector'.). Crucial is the existence of surplus labour in the traditional or non-capitalist sector.[19] Because of this wages are set just above subsistence across the whole economy, leading to the transfer of labour over time from traditional or non-capitalist to modern or capitalist sectors and the capture of labour productivity gains to capitalists as profits as these are the source of growth via reinvestment. The floor for wages is institutionally set at subsistence. Lewis (1954, pp. 151–2) posited that the transition of labour from the traditional to the modern sector was to be understood as follows:

> The key to the process is the use which is made of the capitalist surplus. In so far as this is reinvested in creating new capital, the capitalist sector expands, taking more people into capitalist employment out of the subsistence sector. The surplus is then larger still, capital formation is still greater, and so the process continues until the surplus labour disappears.

[18] See for discussion, Copestake (2003), Fei and Ranis (1964), Gollin et al. (2004, 2014, 2016), Harris and Todaro (1970), Kindleberger (1967), Ranis and Stewart (1999).

[19] Lewis believed in contrast to Asia that Africa had a labour shortage due to agricultural land availability. The constraint to growth in Africa was low agriculture productivity rather than manufacturing growth and required government intervention in agriculture (See Kanbur, 2016, p. 7).

When the surplus labour disappears an integrated labour market and economy emerge and wages will then start to rise. After which marginal productivity determines wages.[20] Lewis (1979, p. 211) later noted the 'wide range of specifications' to which his dual economy model had been characterized, which led him to reiterate the core elements as his saw them:

> The version I am using here has three characteristics. First, there are two sectors, hereinafter called 'modern' and 'traditional', such that the modern sector grows by recruiting labour from the traditional. Second, unskilled labour is paid more in the modern sector than in the traditional sector for the same quantity and quality of work. And thirdly, unskilled labour is initially abundant in the sense that at the current wage much more labour is offered to the modern sector than that sector wishes to hire.

The Lewis model was intended as a critique of the neoclassical approach in that labour is available to the modern or capitalist sector of an economy not in a perfectly elastic supply but upward sloping rather than flat, and with a distinction between surplus-producing labour and subsistence labour (the latter of which was a negligible source of net profits for reinvestment, which Lewis saw as the driver for growth).[21] Lewis also rejected the assumptions of neoclassical economists of perfect competition, market clearing and full employment and Lewis (see 1958, pp. 8, 18) made the distinction between productive labour, which produced a surplus, and unproductive labour, which did not:

> A transfer of workers from the latter [unproductive labour sector] to the former [productive labour sector] raises the national income, increases the total surplus over wages, and so makes possible further expansion... So long as unlimited labour is available at a fixed real wage, the share of profits in national income will increase. There are two reasons for this. First the share of profits in the capitalist sector may increase. And secondly the capitalist sector will expand relatively to national income.

In sum, in the Lewis model, growth is sustained by sectoral ST and the transfer of the factor of production abundant in developing countries. That is labour from low productivity to higher productivity sectors.[22] There were two sectors: (i) a modern or capitalist sector which is not necessarily synonymous with

[20] Lewis later (1979, p. 211) dropped the term 'surplus labour' for fear of the 'emotional distress' it causes to some and reiterated that 'the idea intended to be conveyed is that of an infinitely elastic supply of labour to the modern sector at the current wage'.

[21] As Lewis (1984, p. 132) put it,

> [A]ll one needed to do was to drop the assumption—then usually (but not necessarily) made by neoclassical macroeconomists—that the supply of labour was fixed. Assume instead that it was infinitely elastic, add that productivity was increasing in the capitalist sector, and one got a rising profits share.

[22] Lewis's thinking was influenced by his predecessors, notably Rosenstein-Rodan (1943, p. 202) who was concerned with similar themes such as the agrarian 'excess population' or 'disguised

urban or industrial or the private sector though these may be part of this sector, and (ii) a traditional or non-capitalist sector which is not necessarily synonymous with agriculture or the non-capitalist or public sector, though these may be part of this sector.[23] The sectors are not necessarily unified geographically.[24]

Those two sectors are different in terms of the 'rules' that apply in each: the rules of the modern or capitalist sector are competition and profit maximization and marginal productivity determines resource allocation; the rules of the subsistence sector are set by social conventions. The former is 'fructified' by capital or 'that part of the economy which uses reproducible capital, and pays capitalists for the use thereof' and the latter is 'all that part of the economy which is not using reproducible capital' (1954, p. 146). The former has higher wages and higher marginal productivity of labour than the latter and is capital intensive. The latter is lower wage, labour intensive, and has an oversupply of labour. Labour migrates and this migration sustains growth and economic development by raising productivity per worker. The capitalist surplus is reinvested in new capital and this expands the sector, which in turn provides more employment. This process continues until the surplus labour is used, or when capital accumulation is faster than population growth, or when the terms of trade between the sectors changes, or when new technology raises production in the subsistence sector. Wages in the subsistence sector start to rise as the Lewis 'turning point' is reached, at which point the supply of surplus labour is exhausted. This impacts on profits, the rate of reinvestment, and the capital stock.

Lewis did not ignore inequality. Indeed, Lewis (1954, p. 147) highlighted the high visibility of inequality, 'between the few highly westernized, trousered, natives, educated in western universities, speaking western languages, and glorying Beethoven, Mill, Marx, or Einstein, and the great mass of their countrymen who live in quite other worlds'.[25] Inequality was of importance to Lewis to the extent that it had an impact on output growth. Lewis generally discussed rising inequality in terms of functional distribution rather than

unemployment' in agriculture and the transfer of this low- or zero-productivity population to the industrial sector, some years prior to Lewis's own writing.

[23] Fields (2004) expresses a preference for the terms 'formal' and 'informal' sectors.

[24] As Lewis (1954, p. 147) puts it:

> What we have is not one island of expanding capitalist employment, surrounded by a vast sea of subsistence workers, but rather a number of such tiny islands... We find a few industries highly capitalized, such as mining or electric power, side by side with the most primitive techniques; a few high class shops, surrounded by masses of old style traders; a few highly capitalized plantations, surrounded by a sea of peasants.

[25] Lewis also wrote on horizontal inequality in terms of class, gender, and ethnicity (see Mosley et al. 2004, pp. 758–9 for discussion).

household or individual income distribution, as that was central to the model, and a rise in the share of capital drives growth but does not necessarily imply a change in the within-labour share. If there were a larger share of profits in national income this would mean more resources for capital formation but as Lewis (1954, pp. 157, 158) noted

> [t]he central fact of economic development is that the distribution of incomes is altered in favour of the saving class . . . All that the workers get out of the expansion is that more of them are employed at a wage above the subsistence earnings.

When the Lewis turning point is reached and surplus labour is exhausted wages would rise and the functional distribution of income would move in favour of labour though this would slow or end the transition. At which point labour markets would be unified not dualistic.

Lewis posited that the state could substitute for a capitalist class (where no such class was of a significant size) in order to deal with what he referred to as 'the sociological problem of the emergence of a capitalist class' (1954, p. 159). Further, the state needs to play a strong role in disciplining the capitalist class when it does exist, or guiding the emergence of such a class.[26] The role of the state was also important because during the Lewis transition inequality may rise and public policy intervention is needed because,

> the Gini coefficient may actually show a rise in inequality, since the share of national output accruing to the bottom 50 per cent may fall . . . To tax its developed sectors and subsidise its underdeveloped sectors is one of the most powerful ways that a government can use to ensure the benefits of development . . . The moral for policy makers is of course not to rely on trickle down to benefit the traditional sector, but to attack the problems of that sector directly
>
> (1979, pp. 212, 216).

Lewis (1976) presents an explicit framework to consider this relationship between growth and distribution, noting a starting point that,

> growth takes place in enclaves, surrounded by traditional activities . . . Development must be inegalitarian because it does not start in every part of an economy at the same time. Somebody develops a mine, and employs a thousand people. Or farmers in one province start planting cocoa, which will grow only in 10% of the country. Or the Green Revolution arrives, to benefit those farmers who have plenty of rain or access to irrigation, while offering nothing to the other 50% in drier regions (p. 26).

[26] Lewis (1955, p. 408) was critical of the state too, listing nine ways in which the state can harm the process of economic development through excessive laissez-faire as well as excessive control or excessive spending and failing to maintain order, plundering citizens, exploiting one class over another, constraining trade, neglecting public goods, and expensive wars.

Lewis (1976) discusses the relationship between economic development and distribution as one based on within *and* between sector inequality. He argues that the growth of the modern or capitalist sector, or the 'enclave sector' as he calls it in that paper, has good and bad impacts on the traditional sector (p. 27). Notably, the enclave may enrich the traditional sector by buying commodities and services from it; providing employment to those in the traditional sector; sending remittances; selling goods and services cheaper; and by developing infrastructure, public goods and, through an example of new ideas and institutions, the enclave sector can modernize the traditional sector. Whether development leads to widening inequality depends, he argued on whether the enclave is able to respond to the new economic opportunities (e.g. price changes or the demand for labour). In short, inegalitarian development is not the failure of 'trickle down' vertically from rich to poor but the failure to trickle along or spread horizontally the benefits from enclave to traditional sectors.[27]

Again, the role of the state is highlighted by Lewis (pp. 30–5) who posited that distribution in the enclave depends on the pattern of growth and a set of factors, many of which are 'susceptible to public control' (p. 35), notably the distribution of property, economic structure (in terms of firm size and the capital intensity of production and dependence on foreign resources) and the speed of growth which has the potential to alter 'the relative quantities of the factors of production, and the derived demands, and therefore the distribution of income'. Further, the traditional sector may see income stagnate because the enclave may be predatory (e.g. driving people off their land); products may compete with traditional trades; the wage rate in the enclave may be too high and raise the price of labour above its marginal productivity; because of geographical polarization (the enclave attracts 'best brains' and capital); because population growth accelerates due to improved public health reducing the death rate; and/or excessive migration from the countryside. Lewis concludes (1976, p. 29) that whether the enclave enriches or not the traditional sector 'probably depends most on whether the government coerces or helps the traditional sector, and on the nature of the enclaves' (meaning the modern or capitalist sector).

There have been various critiques of the Lewis model, many of which are of a 'red herring' variety as Ranis (2004, p. 716) puts it, meaning they are easily

[27] Lewis (1979, pp. 212–15), too, drew attention to several possible ways the modern sector might benefit the traditional sector: provision of employment; sharing physical facilities; modernization of ideas and institutions (Lewis cites new technologies introduced, girls attending school, land tenure systems changing, for example); and through trade (if the modern sector depends on the traditional sector for part of its needs, for example, for food or raw materials, the expansion of the modern sector will rely on the expansion of commodities in the traditional sector, but the traditional sector could be damaged by buying imports from the modern sector or abroad.

responded to or actually criticisms of Lewisians rather than the writing of Lewis himself. Many relate to the assumption of labour abundance in the subsistence sector (and thus the dominance of the wage from that sector across the economy), and the emergence of the urban informal sector, although Lewis's conception of surplus labour explicitly included the urban informal sector.[28]

It is clear Lewis (1954, p. 141) did not ignore the urban informal sector in the unlimited supply of labour concept:

> The phenomenon is not, however, by any means confined to the countryside. Another large sector to which it applies is the whole range of casual jobs—the workers on the docks, the young men who rush forward asking to carry your bag as you appear, the jobbing gardener, and the like. These occupations usually have a multiple of the number they need, each of them earning very small sums from occasional employment; frequently their number could be halved without reducing output in this sector.

Informality was taken a step further in Ranis and Stewart (1999) who developed a model of dualism within the urban informal sector between a dynamic sub-sector linked to the formal sector and a less dynamic 'sponge' (meaning highly labour absorbing) sub-sector.

There are other critiques of the Lewis model (see discussion in Fei and Ranis 1964; Harris and Todaro 1970; Minami 1973; Schultz 1964; Rosenzweig 1988; Todaro 1969). One relates to the oversimplicity of a two-sector model. However, as Basu (1997, pp. 151–2) notes '[T]he assumption of duality is merely for analytical convenience. If fragmentation—irrespective of the number of parts—in itself causes some problems and we wish to examine these, then the simplest assumption to make is that of dualism.'

Neoclassical economists would not accept that wages were set by any other mechanisms other than demand and supply. Contentions arising were related to labour use and agricultural productivity and the assumption of zero marginal productivity in agriculture (that said the Lewis model actually rests upon the elastic supply of labour itself).

Finally, there has been an incorrect view that the Lewis model takes little account of the integrative aspects of ST and open economies and thus contemporary globalization and global economic integration. This point is absolutely a misperception and based on the notion that the seminal Lewis (1954) piece outlining the basic Lewis closed economy model only contained a small section on an open economy. However, the role of external trade, and investment and finance are discussed in the 1954 paper and are highly evident in many

[28] This critique is really a critique of the Todaro model, which introduced the necessity of being physically in an urban area to be hired in a formal sector job.

other writings of Lewis, given his interest in primary commodity-exporting countries. The main focus in the original (1954) work related to integrative ST is where it is argued that the Lewis turning point of surplus labour exhaustion may be delayed by international migration and capital export. The closed economy versions of the Lewis model (the first and the second) were building blocks to get to the third model (the open economy model), which Lewis believed represented most developing countries. It is the third model, the one that explains the tendency for declining factoral terms of trade, which was a major concern for Lewis. Furthermore, an entire section is dedicated to critiquing comparative advantage based on his open economy model.[29] Elsewhere (Lewis 1976) a real concern of Lewis was—with great foresight—that primary exports dependency would eventually become a new dependency on a handful of manufacturing exports which would fall in value relative to import cost. Thus dependency on a few primary commodities whose relative price was falling vis-à-vis import needs, would be replaced with dependency on a few manufactures whose relative price was falling vis-à-vis import needs.

A set of contemporary challenges throws up greater levels of complexity. First, is that domestic labour migration may not be permanent but circular (back-and-forth) or 'commuting'. This means a worker may be active in both 'traditional' and 'modern' sectors. For example, non-farm rural income is generally estimated to be a substantial part of rural incomes, suggesting too that workers are active in and beyond the 'traditional economy' at a point in time (see Booth 2016; Wee and Jomo 2014). Second, that the contemporary scale of inter-sectoral resource flows via the growth of remittances further blurs the line between sectors with economic development and distributional impacts. Finally, that the Lewis transition can take a variety of forms beyond the anticipated one by Lewis and it is by no means guaranteed that the transfer will be from low to high productivity activities as flagged by MacMillan and Rodrik (2011). A transfer from low productivity agriculture to low productivity services has been the experience of many developing countries and a reversing of the Lewis transition has also been a phenomenon noted in a number of developing countries in 'premature deindustrialization'. In short, multiple pathways of ST are possible and not all are progressive.

If one focuses on four economic sectors alone, there are six potential modes of inter-sectoral ST: agriculture to non-manufacturing industry, agriculture to

[29] Kaldor (1967) also took the two-sector model to be applicable to trade between developing and developed countries through the export of agriculture products from the former, and import of manufactured goods from the latter. He argued that international trade could make developing countries poorer because liberalization would increase agriculture exports, which are produced at decreasing returns. These returns are not sufficient to compensate for the loss of manufacturing exports, which is a sector that produces increasing returns (this is essentially the same as the Prebisch-Singer hypothesis which is discussed in detail in Chapter 3).

manufacturing, agriculture to services, non-manufacturing industry to manufacturing, non-manufacturing industry to services, and manufacturing to services. To this one could add four modes of intra-sectoral ST.

Nevertheless, the Lewis model does provide a framework to situate the developer's dilemma and the inequality dynamics or tension between structural transformation and inclusive growth if one considers that structural transformation can take place in multiple ways. Lewis considered distributional dynamics in terms of the functional distribution of income and also the relationship between sectors as the discussion above highlights. Each mode of structural transformation is likely to have its own distribution dynamics as labour moves between or within sectors. The distribution dynamics of such movements were also of concern to Simon Kuznets whose seminal work we revisit next.

2.4.3 *Kuznets Revisited*

We next consider the contribution of Simon Kuznets, and those writing in the Kuznets tradition, in order to introduce inequality dynamics into a Lewis-type two-sector model. Kuznets focused, like Lewis, on the factor abundant to developing countries, that of labour and its sectoral transfer from rural to urban areas.

Often, one tends to find that in public policy discourse Kuznets' thinking is reduced to his famous curve alone. However, there is much more depth and many more nuances and caveats than are often recognized (see for more discussion, Kanbur 2012, 2017). Kuznets (1955) took a dual economy model somewhat like Lewis (though with a focus more so on urban–rural rather than modern and traditional sectors) though he posited that a labour transition from a rural sector to an urban sector would be accompanied by rising inequality in the early stages of development. In contrast, neoclassical economic theory would posit that the relative scarcity of factors determines inequality outcomes. The most important point to note regarding Kuztnets' seminal work is how tentative it is, and the number of disclaimers due to the scarcity of data available at that time. Kuznets builds theory through an abstract arithmetic model and then draws what he notes are very tentative conclusions. Kuznets' original thesis was based on time-series data for three countries (US, UK, and two states in Germany) plus point estimates for inequality in India, Puerto Rico, and Ceylon. He argued that inequality would rise in an 'upswing' and then fall later in the 'downswing' of what became known as the inverted-U or Kuznets curve.

Kuznets (1955, pp. 6–7) outlined two forces that would increase pre-tax and transfer inequality in the long term:

> The first group relates to the concentration of savings in the upper-income brackets... The second source... lies in the industrial structure of the income

> distribution. An invariable accompaniment of growth in developed countries is the shift away from agriculture, a process usually referred to as industrialization and urbanization.

The former of these two forces resonates with Lewis's view on the savings class and the latter to Piketty's (2014) focus on capital accumulation as the driver of rising inequality.[30]

Kuznets (1955, pp. 7–8) argued that inequality would rise as the inter-sectoral shift away from agriculture leads to income differences between sectors, and changes within each sector, as some of the population leave the more equal sector.[31] Inequality, Kuznets posited, is composed of inequality between and within sectors (urban and rural), and inequality tends to be lower in the rural sector (relative to the urban sector).[32] Thus, as the size of the more unequal urban sector increases, this will further add upward pressure on inequality and, given that during economic growth, productivity in urban areas is likely to increase faster than in rural areas, this will add even more upward pressure on inequality.

In short, inequality in the dual sector economy is an aggregation of (i) inequality in each sector (be that urban and rural or traditional and modern 'sectors'); (ii) the mean of each sector; and (iii) the population shares in each sector (Kanbur 2017). Thus, even the population shift itself could raise inequality as Kuznets (1955, pp. 14–15) himself noted:

> [E]ven if the differential in per capita income between the two sectors remains constant and the intra-sector distributions are identical for the two sectors, the mere shift in the proportions of numbers produces slight but significant changes in the distribution for the country as a whole.

Kanbur and Zhuang (2013) show how the between urban–rural and within urban–rural components of overall inequality can differ considerably between countries, and how the contribution of urbanization itself to inequality changes at the national level can also differ considerably between countries.

Although inequality may rise as a result of movement between sectors, that occurrence may be balanced or outweighed by what happens to the

[30] More specifically Piketty's theory is that rising inequality in the contemporary period is explained by slow growth (and hence a diverging of wages and returns to capital).

[31] Kuznets argued that the early benefits of growth go to those with capital and education but, as more people move out of the traditional sector, real wages rise in the modern sector and inequality falls. He argued that the poorest lost out more rapidly than other groups as income-expanding opportunities arose away from agriculture.

Kuznets argued that the only way to offset this was for the share of lower non-agriculture income groups to rise. He further contended that, in democracies, urban migrants would become politically organized, leading to redistribution.

[32] As Fischer (2014, p. 20) notes, Kuznets posited that 'underdeveloped' countries were more unequal than 'developed' countries (p. 20).

within-sector components and the shares of each sector. Initial inequality between and within sectors will also play a significant role.

Although largely rejected as a universal law in studies in the 1990s, the Kuznets hypothesis remains relevant to ST and IG as a backdrop to any discussion.[33] Piketty (2006) is broadly illustrative of critiques of Kuznets. He argues the following:

> The reasons why inequality declined in rich countries... do not have much to do with the migration process described by Kuznets... Inequality dynamics depend primarily on the policies and institutions adopted by governments and societies as a whole. (pp. 2, 11)

As Kanbur (2017) notes, this is unfair to Kuznets. Not only does Kuznets discuss countervailing forces (for example, the forces noted previously) but also institutional aspects are prominent for Kuznets (1955). For example,

> One group of factors counteracting the cumulative effect of concentration of savings upon upper-income shares is legislative interference and 'political' decisions. These may be aimed at limiting the capital accumulation of property directly through inheritance taxes and other explicit capital levies. They may produce similar effects indirectly [...]. All these interventions, even when not directly aimed at limiting the effects of capital accumulation of past savings in the hands of the few, do reflect the view of society on the long-term utility of wide income inequalities. This view is a vital force that would operate in democratic societies even if there were no other counteracting factors... Furthermore, in democratic societies the growing political power of the urban lower-income groups led to a variety of protective and supporting legislation. (pp. 8–9, 16–17)

There is resonance here with Polanyi's (1957) 'double movement' or the dialectical process of the expansion of marketization and the push back against marketization in a 'counter-movement'. Polanyi argued that liberal reforms seek to establish and expand a market society where all things are commodified, the economy is 'disembedded', and society is subordinate to the market economy. This triggers a reaction of 'counter-movement' whereby the creation of institutions such as labour law seeks to re-embed the economy in society.

Kuznets, in his seminal piece, said little about the integrative ST dimensions. There has been a set of contemporary scholars building new theory in

[33] Anand and Kanbur (1993a, 1993b) dismissed the Kuznets curve. Deininger and Squire (1988) found evidence of the curve in some countries and not others. Most recently, Gallup (2012) empirically posits an anti-Kuznets curve or non-inverted-U: inequality declines and then rises. Alvaredo and Gasparini (2015) do, very cautiously, identify a U-shaped curve using 2005 PPP data but the upswing of the curve is entirely in sub-Saharan Africa and the downswing is entirely in HICs.

Indeed, Kuznets himself only found a rising trend or upswing in the data he used, not an inverted-U (his downswing of the inverted-U was based on theory and a data simulation).

the Kuznetsian tradition, many of whom have focused on such integrative aspects of ST. Such scholars have developed theory with a focus on open economies and agrarian liberalization, the role of technology, as well as national aspects of domestic political economy and land distribution. For example, Galbraith (2011) argues that it is global forces that have driven the changes in national inequality since 1970. The key drivers of the changes in national inequality are world interest rates and commodity prices (and between-sector terms of trade). He argues that a commodity boom reduces inequality in countries with a dominant agricultural sector as it raises the relative income of farmers, and higher rates of interest are bad for debtor countries and this increases inequality. Galbraith presents an 'augmented Kuznets curve', or S-curve, whereby the curve rises, then falls, and then rises again.[34]

In a somewhat similar vein, at least in the sense of a focus on open economies, Lindert and Williamson (2001) argue that it is the shift towards market orientation (domestic to export) of agriculture and not the shift from agriculture to manufacturing and services that causes inequality to rise. Lindert and Williamson predict an initial rise in inequality. However, while Lewis and Kuznets envisaged a downswing, Lindert and Williamson argue that inequality continues to rise because income in the urban sector outpaces rises in income in the rural sector as agriculture shifts to market orientation.

In contrast, Roine and Waldenström (2014) suggest a new Kuznets curve based on technological developments starting not a sectoral shift of agriculture to industry but a shift from traditional industry to technologically intensive industry. If a given technology makes skilled workers more productive and there is an increase in the relative demand for those workers, the rewards accrue to a small proportion of the population who are skilled workers. Based on Tinbergen's (1974, 1975) hypothesis that the returns to skills are a competition between education and technology, the supply of skilled workers then determines whether or not their wages rise. Roine and Waldenström (2014) argue that the drivers of the Kuznets downturn were political and exogenous shocks.[35]

[34] Galbraith (2011) argues that national inequality tends to follow similar trends around the world and that there have been four phases over time: (i) a first period, from 1963 to about 1971, of relative stability in national inequality; (i) a second period from 1972 to 1980 when inequality declined slightly in much of the world due to the post-Bretton Woods inflationary boom based on extensive lending at negative real interest rates; (iii) a third period dated from 1982 to about 2000, consisting of sharply rising inequality due to the debt crisis, the collapse of many communist countries, and the liberalization of the 1990s which led to a fiscal squeeze and public sector retrenchment. There are some exceptions. China and India did not see the rise in national inequality until the 1990s and liberalization, because they did not liberalize their financial markets; (iv) a fourth period which began in 2000 and is one of modest declines in national inequality due to the slowing down of liberalization and the commodity boom.

[35] Lindert (2000) suggests that the factors compressing wages were institutional ones such as labour market regulation, trade unions, as well as the expansion of basic education.

Oyvat (2016) argues that it is agrarian structures—land inequality—that are deterministic. Consistent with Kuznets, he argues that migration is driven by higher urban incomes and this suppresses wages in the urban sector. If land inequality is higher, more people will migrate for lower wages as they do not own land or own small plots, and rural incomes are lower which will further depress urban wages.[36] Empirically, Oyvat argues that the level of land inequality has a significant impact on urbanization, intra-urban inequality, and overall inequality. The results suggest that land reforms or subsidies to rural smallholders would thus reduce urban inequality.

Acemoglu and Robinson (2002) discuss the political economy of the Kuznets curve in two models of late capitalism. The first is a high inequality, low output model that they call 'autocratic disaster'. In this model, inequality does not rise and political mobilization is too limited to address existing inequality. A second model is the 'East Asian miracle' of low inequality and high output where inequality does not rise in order to ensure political stability and avoid the discipline of democracy being forced on elites. They argue that when the process of industrialization does increase inequality, this leads to the political mobilization of the masses that are concentrated in urban areas and factories. Political elites thus undertake reform to ensure their continued position at the top. The extension of the franchise is the best option for elites as it acts as a commitment to future redistribution and thus prevents unrest.[37]

In sum, there have been various attempts at new theory-building on how income inequality evolves with economic development. As with Lewis, a set of contemporary challenges throw up greater levels of complexity. First and foremost is the experience of premature deindustrialization in developing countries.

ST has been associated with deindustrialization in the developed world. This typically means that there is a focus on the shrinking proportion of industrial or manufacturing activity in GDP, employment, or exports. A key question is what drives such processes and also if they matter (see for discussion, Rowthorn and Ramaswamy 1999; Singh 1977)? Such discussions were extended to developing countries in Palma (2005) and Rodrik (2015), though Singh (1977) and

[36] Oyvat argues that agrarian structures in Asia tend to have more owner-cultivators and tenants and thus small- and median-scale family farms rather than Latin America or sub-Saharan Africa, which tend to have high land inequality and large plantation structures that hire wage labour, and very small family farms. Thus, in Latin America and sub-Saharan Africa, the lack of sufficient formal employment opportunities for migrants generates an urban reserve army of labour in the urban subsistence sector, which depresses wages in the urban modern/capitalist sector.

[37] Examples given are those of the UK and France where extension of franchise led to changes in labour market institutions, mass education, and reduced inequality. The thesis of Acemoglu and Robinson (2002) is that capitalist industrialization increases inequality but that this induces a change in political regime towards more redistribution.

others have noted that shrinking shares are not necessarily a cause, but rather more a symptom of underlying structural economic problems.

This phenomenon, or what Palma (2005) and Rodrik (2015) labelled as 'premature deindustrialization' with reference to developing countries, is that developing countries have reached 'peak manufacturing' in employment and value-added shares at a much earlier point than advanced nations.[38]

Premature deindustrialization has two components. The inverted-U pattern of manufacturing shares versus GDP per capita shifts down and leftwards over time, making it harder for late developers to attain the benefits of industrialization that earlier developers saw. The first component is that 'peak manufacturing', in employment or GDP shares (or export shares), has been reached and the inverted-U curve is now on the plateau or even downswing of the curve. The second component is that that inverted-U curve is moving leftward over time. This means the point at which the inverted-U turns is, on average, lower in per capita income terms now than in the 1990s, which was already lower than in the 1980s (see Palma 2005).

What are the causes of the phenomenon? There are differing views. Rodrik (2015) links the phenomenon to trade liberalization over time and the impact of China's entry into manufacturing. One could also potentially add automation and technological change. Felipe et al. (2015) argue that premature deindustrialization is caused by the fact that large national increases in labour productivity were counteracted by a shift of manufacturing jobs to lower productivity economies.[39] They note that the global shares of employment and GDP in manufacturing have changed very little in the last forty years. What has happened is that international competition has spread what manufacturing there is across more countries.

Palma (2005) argues that there are several other potential hypotheses (which are not mutually exclusive) that could explain the phenomenon observed: (i) it is due to a statistical illusion caused by contracting out of manufacturing jobs to services (for example, cleaning or catering); (ii) it is due to a fall in the income elasticity of manufactures; (iii) it is due to higher

[38] See also Heintz (2009). See also Lewis (1979, p. 220) who notes that

> the surest way to run into trouble is to have 'de-industrialization' (industrial employment growing more slowly than the labour force), since this means that the reservoir of cheap labour will be filling instead of emptying. The political and social health of the community, no less its economic health, requires a continual transfer from the reservoir to the more productive sectors, rather than the relative expansion of the reservoir.

[39] So the average employment share in manufacturing that could be achieved has fallen over time, and countries have experienced deindustrialization earlier than they used to. In short, the changes in supply chains and the shift to lower productivity economies (for example, China) has spread manufacturing jobs more thinly, making it harder for individual countries to sustain high levels of manufacturing employment.

productivity growth in manufacturing; or (iv) it is due to outsourcing globally whereby manufacturing employment has fallen in OECD (Organisation for Economic Co-operation and Development) countries; (v) it is due to the change in policy regimes in OECD countries away from Keynesianism; or (vi) it is due to technological progress.[40]

Whatever the causes of premature deindustrialization, it is empirically visible though a question remains as to how or why it matters and if the service sector really is inferior to manufacturing output, employment, and exports. That said, in light of its visibility alone, the distribution dynamics of premature deindustrialization warrant further exploration.

2.5 Conclusion

The purpose of this chapter was to set out the conceptual points of departure in terms of ST and IG, and to situate the two in a model of economic development. We have thus discussed the concepts of ST and IG. We have revisited the Lewis model of economic development and the contribution of Kuznets and recent iterations.

To recap, this chapter has argued the following: (i) that ST and IG have tended to be approached in a reductionist sense and disconnected from each other. By defining down each to a more minimalist definition, one loses important aspects of each and of their interrelationship; (ii) that the vision of Lewis and Kuznets provides a two-sector model for connecting ST and IG that can be related to the sectoral, factoral, and integrative aspects of ST and the income, inequality, education, and employment aspects of IG. However, Lewis and Kuznets require contextualizing to the contemporary period in which a set of 'new' issues has gained prominence. Notably, multiple forms and dimensions of structural change, 'premature deindustrialization' and circular (back-and-forth) or 'commuting' labour movements; as well as non-farm rural income; the growth of inter-sectoral resource flows via remittances and the multiple dimensions of inclusive growth.

We have noted that Lewis focused on the inter-sectoral labour reallocation and related it to the functional distribution of income and inequality dynamics in terms of the relationship between sectors. Kuznets was concerned largely with the labour share in terms of the relationship between his sectors. Both were concerned with the sectoral aspects of ST as well as factoral ST.

The essence of Kuznets was that the labour transition could, unless governments intervene, be *unequalizing* if people move from the more equal sector

[40] Palma goes on to argue countries that have a commodity export surge or policy shift away from Keynesianism have an 'additional degree' of deindustrialization.

(which Kuznets took to be rural in developing countries) to the less equal sector (which Kuznets took to be urban) because of the differences in relative income and the relative population weighting. All else being equal, the Kuznets hypothesis will only hold if the rural sector is more equal or if governments do not intervene to neutralize the forces of inequality that were unleashed by ST.

On the other hand, the transition could well be *equalizing* if the rural sector is more unequal (or if governments intervene). However, it will depend on (i) where in the distribution of each sector the migrant starts out from and ends up in and (ii) on how equalizing the wage gain they get from the urban sector is overall, and furthermore, (iii) the extent of counterbalancing forces due to the movement of surplus labour from the traditional sector, which would lead the average income in that sector to rise and generate a pattern that could be equalizing.

In short, if developing countries seek economic development via ST and seek to make that inclusive form of growth then the Kuznetsian forces unleashed by ST require neutralizing. ST and capital accumulation tend to generate distribution tensions, these can be managed to some considerable extent by a focus on expanding public policy intervention. Specifically, addressing the urban–rural income divergence; the skilled–unskilled worker wage divergence; and the capture of productivity gains vis-à-vis capital and labour shares and the within-labour shares, and the extent to which productivity growth is translated into real-wage growth or employment growth. This would suggest ST with IG requires—counter-intuitively—highly activist rural and agricultural policy and public investments to constrain the urban–rural income divergence; large investments in public education to constraint the skilled–unskilled worker wage divergence; and state–capital–labour pacts to ensure substantial employment growth is the consequence of productivity growth.

In conclusion, this chapter has characterized ST as shifts towards higher productivity activities with aspects of that transformation that are: (a) sectoral, (b) factoral, and (c) integrative. The chapter has defined IG by income/consumption and capabilities, notably as (a) absolute poverty reduction with or without inequality of outcome reduction; (b) inequality of opportunity reduction and raised education levels; and (c) the direct inclusion in growth via employment growth. The chapter has also outlined the relationship between ST and IG using the Lewis model as a heuristic device/'ideal type', and revisited Kuznets and those writing since in the Kuznets tradition who have sought to include in their thinking such factors as agrarian structure, global integration, government regimes/policies, and technology/skills.

The discussion takes us to the essence of the developer's dilemma: If developing countries seek economic development via ST and seek to make that inclusive form of growth then the Kuznetsian forces unleashed by ST require neutralizing. There is the divergence between capital and labour and who captures productivity gains, the divergence within labour shares of workers in 'sectors' (urban versus rural for simplicity) and by skills (unskilled and skilled labour for simplicity). If developing countries seek to address the distributional tension between ST and IG then countervailing interventions—many of which Lewis noted in his own writing—are required.

Chapter 3 expands on these points and discusses theories of the broader drivers and impediments to the Lewis transition, their distributional consequences, and in particular why it is that developing countries have not followed the ideal-type pathway or transition that the Lewis model envisaged. The chapter also draws upon recent literature on the heterogeneity of late capitalism and provides a rationale for the analytical framework of this book, which is outlined and discussed as the culmination of the chapter.

3

Structural Transformation and Inclusive Growth

Theory and Heterogeneity

3.1 Introduction

In the previous chapters it was argued that developing countries are pursuing two developmental objectives that are in tension. The first, structural transformation—sectoral, factoral, and integrative—tends to put upward pressure on inequality. The latter, inclusive growth—be that poverty reduction with or without the reduction of income inequality or education expansion and employment growth—is best achieved with steady or falling inequality. It was also argued that structural transformation of developing countries has received too little attention in itself as well as being potentially in tension with inclusive growth. Part of the problem is that poverty and inequality have been, to some considerable extent, studied in a vacuum, separated from broader processes of structural transformation and economic development.

Chapter 2 outlined the conceptual points of departure on this developer's dilemma. Specifically, it discussed the meanings of structural transformation (ST) and inclusive growth (IG) and situated the concepts within a model of economic development. The chapter also discussed the distributional dynamics of economic development.

To recap, the basic thesis was that: (i) ST and IG have been defined in a reductionist way that disconnects them conceptually; (ii) the Lewis model of economic development and related thinking of Kuznets, and others writing in these traditions, can provide a useful model within which to situate ST and IG and consider the aspects of each in terms of sectors, factors and integration as well as reduction in poverty and inequality of outcome and education expansion and employment growth. Chapter 3 now reviews the theoretical literature on how the transition is accelerated or impeded, and lays the basis for the selection of the analytical framework of this book. The focus is on orthodox theory first and then heterodox theory as a reaction to orthodoxy. This survey of theory runs, in the main, from the late 1940s, and the emergence of structuralism, to the 1970s, at which point one lineage is pursued—the comparative capitalisms literature (which itself has several strands)—and notably the emergence of theory known as the Social Structure of Capital Accumulation. Throughout, the discussion draws on original sources and also interpretations and syntheses of the literature from others as noted. Those sources are referenced though, inevitably, one reads and is influenced by many readings across the area that may not be directly cited.

The Lewis model was a critique of orthodox neoclassical approaches to growth and industrialization in developing countries. The work of Lewis triggered a substantial response not only from orthodox scholars but also from heterodox scholars as they grappled in the 1960s and 1970s with the failure of the developing world to follow the pathway the Lewis model envisaged. Latin American structuralist, Furtado (1961, p. 122) put it starkly thus: first as a critique of orthodox theory and then as a failure of the Lewis model to explain underdevelopment and the inequality endemic in the developing world with reference to Brazil and 'modernisation without economic development':

> The Brazilian economy constitutes a very interesting example of how far a country can go in the process of industrialisation without abandoning its main features of underdevelopment: great disparity in productivity between urban and rural areas, a large majority of the population living at physiological subsistence level, increasing masses of underemployed people in the urban zones etc. The idea, implicit in the growth models or the genus started by Lewis, that steering the surplus [of] an undeveloped economy towards the industrial sector . . . would ultimately create an economic system of increasing homogeneity where the wage rate tends to increase in all economic activities . . . has been thoroughly disproved . . . Development satisfies the high levels of consumption of a small minority of the population . . . The study of underdevelopment must start with the identification of the particular types of structures created in the periphery of the capitalist economy by this system of international division of labour.

Lewis was thus a catalyst for an extensive period of theoretical ferment from the 1950s to the 1970s with many writers linking the failure of countries to achieve ST with unequal relationships between and within countries.

At the outset, it is worth recalling what the ferment was about. Theories sought to address how countries 'catch up', not only in per capita income but in terms of industrialization or transition from poor to rich nations. They were based around a set of questions: first, the point of departure. What is 'mal-' or 'underdevelopment'? Or what are the defining characteristics of underdevelopment (what does underdevelopment look like)? Second, what are the causal processes (mechanisms) that perpetuate underdevelopment and what are the future prospects for developing countries ('peripheries')? And relatedly, what is the hierarchy in the international order between advanced/ 'core' and developing/'periphery' countries? What is the role of international capital (foreign direct investment and finance capital) and what is its relationship with host economies and domestic capital? Third, what, if anything, can developing countries do to break free of the causal mechanisms that perpetuate underdevelopment? In particular, what is the role of the state in development—to lead or to follow? Orthodox and heterodox theorists through the 1950s and 1970s were ambitious in the scope of their theorizing, the former outlining prescriptions of how industrialization and ST can be achieved by developing countries, and the latter outlining why ST has not been achieved or cannot be achieved.

One issue is the extent to which countries differ in the nature of what kind of capitalism is inherited at independence and how it has historically evolved. Orthodox and heterodox theories have tended to see capitalism as one homogeneous mode (orthodox theory) or one global model with core and periphery components within it (much heterodox theory). Contemporary debates on comparative capitalisms in contrast have argued for a heterogeneity of capitalism in the North and South. The contemporary literature is considered and forms the justification for the analytical framework for this book.

This chapter reviews currents in orthodox and heterodox theories during the ferment of the 1950s to the 1970s in particular with a focus on modernization and neoclassical statements of comparative advantage on the one hand, and structuralism, dependency, and other theories of underdevelopment on the other. Such theories of structuralism, and dependency theory and underdevelopment hit their zenith in the policies of import-substitution industrialization (ISI) of the 1960s and 1970s.[1] This body of critical theories was largely dismissed in the 1980s as the limits of ISI became apparent and as East Asia industrialized, undermining any argument that ST was not possible in the periphery.[2] At the same time, the neo-liberalism or anti-statism that became practised by the 'Washington Consensus' was in ascendancy, further undermining the developmentalism of import-substitution, driven as it was by the state.

It is important to bear in mind that since many of these theories were originally developed, the global economy has changed in radical ways. Contemporary globalization has emerged as one within which there has been substantial growth and ST in some parts of the developing world. It is a

[1] Dependency theory emerged in part as a critique of the way ISI was being practised in Latin America (see for discussion, Fischer (2015)).

[2] Only in the most radical versions, such as that of Frank, was it argued ST was not possible in the periphery. Many others such as Furtado and Cardoso did not argue this.

world where industrialization itself has changed from building nationally owned infant industry (vertical integration) to attracting foreign direct investment and/or supplying global value chains (horizontal integration); a world within which many middle-income countries have large firms that have become transnational corporations; and a world within which financial markets have transformed from the end of the Bretton Woods system of fixed exchange rates to contemporary, 24-hour financial markets, and financial globalization.

The thesis of this chapter is that neither orthodox nor heterodox theories of ST fully explain the development of late developers because of the heterogeneity of contemporary capitalism. That said, heterodox theories, which coalesce around structural change, the nature of the incorporation of developing countries into the global economy, and in doing so respond to the work of Arthur Lewis, do retain conceptual usefulness not least in their focal point, 'developmentalism', or national economic development led by the state.

The chapter is structured as follows: Section 3.2 discusses the basis of orthodoxy theories. Section 3.3 discusses heterodox theories. In particular, it focuses on those theories that drove what could be called 'classical developmentalism' of ISI, practised across the developing world for much of the period from the 1950s to the 1970s. Section 3.4 then outlines the more recent literature on heterogeneity and comparative capitalisms, which forms the basis of the exposition of the analytical framework of this book. Section 3.5 concludes.

3.2 Structural Transformation and Inclusive Growth: Orthodox Theory

The purpose of this section is to review and discuss orthodox theory related to ST and the Lewis transition in the developing world. This section argues that orthodox theory does not satisfactorily explain ST in developing countries, and in fact pays relatively little attention to either ST or IG. In this section an overview is provided, then the key components of orthodox theory are considered.

Why are some countries poor and some not? How is the development of developing countries framed by history and/or hierarchy in the global economy? These have been questions for theorists of ST since and before the Lewis model. Orthodoxy theory—as defined here—is modernization theory and neoclassical economics, and in particular the concept of static comparative advantage, which lies at the core of orthodox theorizing.[3]

[3] Although Rostow seeks to provide an overriding theory, one could argue the core orthodoxy is neoclassical economics, especially as it re-emerges, as the combination of Solow growth models and Heckshser-Ohlin trade theory, with Samuelson's factor price equalization theory. However,

At the basis of orthodox theory is the relative abundance of natural resources and unskilled labour in developing countries, relative to advanced countries. Further, the problem was, or is, a lack of domestic savings in developing countries (not national and global structures), and an overly active state which prevents rather than facilitates development by choking off private sector capital accumulation, distorting prices, and wastefully subsidizing inefficient economic activity.[4] The focus on the role of savings and investment was dominant in the study of economics of the 1940s and 1950s. However, whilst savings were important to Lewis and others such as Kaldor, structures were also important. Notably, income distribution was a determinant of savings (and growth) and the state could facilitate saving via intervention in finance. Many scholars saw an important role for the state in intervening and facilitating a 'big push' mobilization of those savings and investments rather than the organic process modernization theory outlined (see, for discussion, Nurkse 1953; Mandelbaum 1945; Rosenstein-Rodan 1943; Leibenstein 1957).[5]

Modernization theory, as espoused by Rostow (1960) and others, was in evidence around the time Lewis and Kuznets were writing although much of Lewis and Kuznets (and Kaldor) theorising predates Rostow. Modernization theory is based in its well-known ideological Rostow iteration on the following premises: (i) economic development is linear in nature and characterized by a set of stages that take countries from traditional (agrarian subsistence) societies to modern, high-consumption societies; (ii) all developing countries will pass through the same stages that richer nations did in the 1700s/1800s; (iii) the journey can be sped up by higher savings rates and embracing Western investment, technology, and values (meritocracy and entrepreneurship) in developing countries; (iv) in keeping with Ricardo's comparative advantage, economic take-off is led by a small number of economic activities. In short, modernization theory is embedded within neoclassical economics: for instance, comparative advantage and free trade, in line with David Ricardo's and Adam Smith's classical thinking were seen as leading to specialization and extending the market internationally.

Rostow (1960) famously identified five stages of economic development: The starting point is a 'traditional society' of subsistence agriculture or a

there is no unified theory between these about the distributional consequences of growth. Solow is a one-good model and others are effectively one-good models, all with representative agents.

[4] Heterodox schools were unified primarily in the sense of critiquing this orthodoxy. They reacted to the subtitle in Rostow's (1960) iteration of modernization theory as a 'non-communist manifesto' at the height of the Cold War.

[5] At the core, driving the process of structural change, was the Schumpeterian (1942) concept of 'cumulative causation' (developed further by Myrdal 1957; Hirschman 1958; Kaldor 1966) meaning industrialization would generate future employment and income, and thus raise productivity, which in turn would generate future investment and growth.

hunter–gatherer society with limited technology. External demand for raw materials initiates economic change leading to the next stage or 'pre-conditions for take-off'. The emergence of commercial agriculture for export is part of this change and is facilitated by the spread of technology. Countries then 'take off' as urbanization increases and manufacturing emerges. A 'drive to maturity' follows out of diversification, and a rapid expansion of transport and social infrastructure (health and education). Finally, the 'age of mass consumption' emerges where the industrial sector is the most significant sector, where the primary sector is insignificant, and there is broad-based consumption of a range of consumer goods. Rostow, however, other than the importance of high saving and investment rates, did not outline a driver of change. Growth is presented as automatic and self-driven. Thus the causal process was to follow the perceived pathway of richer countries by mobilizing savings and investment, giving attention to a small number of economic activities, commercializing agriculture for export, and the developing of a manufacturing base. All this was to be achieved by adopting Western values, investment, and technology. Colonialism was not a substantive consideration in understanding the development of rich countries (nor a hindrance on poor countries). For orthodox theories, the only perceived hierarchy in the international order was that some countries had already gone through the process of modernization.[6] The role of international capital and the relationship with host economies and domestic capital were deemed to be positive, something Lewis was to become sceptical of (and Kaldor too).[7] There was no account of the Lewis transition of sectoral analysis per se. There was little or no account of distribution questions within countries, and thus any growth was assumed to be inclusive or it was thought that the exclusive growth of the economy was not a concern amid the imperative for economic development.

The neoclassical underpinnings of modernization theory—static comparative advantage—were to resurface in the 1980s within the anti-statist neo-liberal resurgence, and the anti-state or anti-developmentalism of, among others, Bauer (1981), Lal (1983), Balassa (1974), Krueger (1974a, 1974b), and Little et al. (1970). Such an approach neglects the whole history of colonialization, assumes that comparative advantage can be developed, and is based on a series of postulates (e.g. two countries, full employment, and so forth). The anti-statist and laissez-faire nature of much neoclassical thinking is something that the views of Lewis and Kaldor are impossible to reconcile with. In fact, the critique of modernization and neoclassical economic thinking is almost

[6] Contemporary modernization theory has focused on the political implications of economic modernization in terms of democratization (e.g. Inglehart and Welzel 2005). See for review and discussion Schlogl (2017).

[7] Lewis started as supportive, advocating 'industrialisation by invitation'. It was only later that he became more critical once he saw the results. The same was true of Prebisch.

self-evident: its linearity, its lack of specification of drivers, its belief in a self-fulfilling process of simply following a Western economic model, and its implied basis in liberal economics, free trade, and static comparative advantage. Furthermore, its premise that all countries gain in trade (something Lewis contested), and its limited role or even dismissal of the role of the state in development (which is contrary to Lewis and to Kaldor), and lack of attention to national inequality are all questionable assumptions that energized heterodox theories.

A contemporary attempt to reframe comparative advantage is that of Lin (e.g. 2012) who focuses on an iteration of comparative advantage through factor endowments. The state has a role to 'facilitate' industrial upgrading in keeping with the country's defined comparative advantage. Lin advocates an active government, providing state support that facilitates the private sector's expansion and pursuit of the country's comparative advantage. The state should coordinate investment for industrial upgrading and diversification as well as ensuring infrastructure development. Lin (2012, pp. 69–70), puts it thus:

> It is therefore imperative for a facilitating state in a developing country to identify and select new industries that are consistent with comparative advantage, use its limited resources to improve infrastructure for a limited number of carefully selected industries, provide adequate incentives for first movers, and coordinate private firms' related investments in those industries so that clusters can be formed successfully and quickly.

This kind of approach is also somewhat associated with Rodrik (see Hausmann and Rodrik 2003; Rodrik 2004) and Stiglitz (see Stiglitz and Weiss 1981; Stiglitz and Greenwald 2014) in terms of the role of the state in industrial policy and finance allocation. This is predicated on the state giving ST 'a nudge', as McMillan and Rodrik (p. 27), drawing from behavioural economics put it, in the 'right' direction. A critique, supplied in detail by Fine and Van Waeyenberge (2013), is that this approach ignores the history of colonization and assumes that comparative advantage can be developed. They argue that it is based on a series of fragile postulates as per standard theories of comparative advantage (e.g. two countries, full employment, and so forth). Wade (2011, p. 235) also notes, 'the underlying argument seems to be that we know that Japan and Korea succeeded in the given industries, therefore those industries must have been within their existing comparative advantage. It smacks of tautology.'

In sum, orthodox theory places integrative ST at the centre of analysis framed typically on static comparative advantage and—as noted before—sees little need to focus on sectoral or even factor ST in terms of movements of labour between 'sectors'. IG is assumed to follow growth for the most part.

In comparison heterodox theory places a similarly strong emphasis on integrative ST but with a more pessimistic outlook given the position of developing countries in the world economy and the immiserising role of integrative ST. Heterodox theory is further centrally concerned with sectoral and factoral ST and the Lewis transition even if it views the Lewis model as too optimistic. IG is not to be taken as given in heterodox theory. Indeed, domestic distributional questions may hinder ST and ST may occur with much of the population remaining marginalized.

3.3 Structural Transformation and Inclusive Growth: Heterodox Theory

3.3.1 *Overview*

The purpose of this section is to review and discuss heterodox theories related to ST and the Lewis transition in the developing world. The argument of this section is that although the global economy has radically changed since many of the theories of structural transformation were outlined, the concepts of periphery, underdevelopment, and dependent—although perhaps subordinate rather than dependent—development and developmentalism remain insightful and useful concepts. In this section an overview is provided, then the key components of structuralism, dependency, monopoly capitalism, and world systems theory are revisited.

Lewis and Kuznets were sources of interest for many heterodox theorists. Some like Lewis did not reject capitalism outright. Others did. The unifying theme of heterodox theory, it can be argued, is not the rejection of capitalism but the unambiguous centrality of the state in late development that is inherent in the concept of 'developmentalism' as an intentional strategy of national economic development. This is in keeping with the role of the state framed by Polanyi (1957 [1944]) as 'the handmaiden' and 'the regulator' of capitalism, who wrote not of developing countries but the industrialization of Europe and the social and political upheavals in England in particular, as the demands of the new, emerging mercantile class on the state which evolved as demands to protect their capital. In short, the expansion of capitalism and market systems is predicated on the expansion of the state as a regulator or handmaiden.

The concept of developmentalism beyond the state as handmaiden or regulator can, however, be a slippery one (see discussion in Ferrari Filho and Fonseca 2015). It can refer to a set of economic policies and strategies for late development, or a set of ideas that evoke different visions of and for the developing world. The unifying aspect is one of state-led national strategies or projects of late, national economic development, which are ST-based and which have a socially transformative aspect in terms of labour markets, public policy, and IG.

The origins of developmentalism lie in late 1949 and the early 1950s though the discussion was of 'industrialization' rather than 'developmentalism' which, as a concept, more visibly emerged in the 1960s around decolonization. 'Developmentalism' is often associated with Prebisch though one can find echoes in the early development economists and the role of the state, notably in the writing of Lewis and others. Lewis (1954) argued that it was the state who had the power to mobilize capital and finance. Gerschenkron (1953, 1962) argued that the state would need to lead late industrialization. Rosenstein-Rodan (1943) and Nurkse (1953) also argued that the private sector would be unwilling to accept the risk.

These debates stimulated the discussion of the ideas. However, it became evident that industrialization in Latin America had produced modified underdevelopment and the persistence of dual economies and marginalized populations, raising substantial questions for the optimism of the Lewis model of economic development.

Developmentalism needs to be defined tangibly. We take developmentalism to mean an elite-initiated and orchestrated attempt at broad-based national economic development within which the state is like the conductor of an orchestra. By this we mean that the state instructs the agents, and those agents obey that instruction—the conductor sets the tempo, instructs who should do what, and manages the different parts of the orchestra in a collective endeavour. Such a definition is broadly in keeping with Chang (1994, 2008, 2010) and Storm (2017) and the analysis of Kohli (2004) and Vu (2010).

Chang (1994, 2008, 2010) argues that the very concept of a developmental state is defined by what happened in East Asia. Chang thus offers the following definitions of such a state as: 'a state which can create and regulate the economic and political relationships that can support sustained industrialization' (1994, p. 183) and 'a state that derives political legitimacy from its record in economic development, which it tries to achieve mainly by means of selective industrial policy' (2010, p. 1).

Storm (2017, p. 1) defines 'developmental' or 'activist' or 'entrepreneurial' states (in the absence of a domestic entrepreneurial class) as those which go 'against capitalist logic and static comparative advantage' to provide strong 'sponsorship' and 'directional thrust', and are somewhat autonomous from rent-seeking classes (landlords and financial rentiers).[8] Storm (2017, p. 1) identifies the question of developmentalism as 'what governments can do to

[8] Mandelbaum (1945) was one of the first to argue that late industrialization required 'directional thrust'. He also argued that lack of demand due to income inequality was a barrier to industrialization.

foster industrial development within the constraints and contradictions imposed by domestic political (class) alignments and the global capitalist order'.[9] Thus, underlying any concept of developmentalism is a question that Kanbur (2016, p. 10) refers to as Edmund Burke's 'eternal question of political economy'. This question is, specifically, what ought the state take upon itself to do? What Keynes referred to as (1926, pp. 287–91) the 'agenda' and 'non-agenda' of government.

3.3.2 *Structuralism and Developmentalism*

Structuralism is the body of theory that gave birth to a widespread challenge to orthodoxy theory and static comparative advantage in particular. The Lewis model stimulated a considerable reaction, as did the work of Kaldor.[10] In some ways Lewis gave stimulus to structuralists in the sense that the structure of the economy or the existence of the dual economy and the marginalization of populations was one that orthodox writers said little about. The Lewis model, however, was classical. One might link the emergence of structuralism with Rodan, Nurkse, Singer, Seers, and of course Prebisch. Hirschman also called himself a structuralist. Although modernization theorists such as Rostow did talk about industrialization, and modernization, writers tended to talk about

[9] In contrast, Doner et al. (2005, p. 334) define developmental states in a more institutional way as,

> complexes of particular types of bureaucratic agencies and public–private-sector linkages. The bureaucracies in question are Weberian in nature: recruitment is by competitive exam; promotion is by merit; remuneration is competitive with rates in the private sector; tenure in office is long; sanctions for corruption are clear and effective; and leadership occurs through a 'pilot' agency that 'stands outside and astride' individual ministries. Incentives in these bureaucracies encourage the development of independent organizational perspectives and the alignment of broader organizational goals with individual incentives. But developmental state bureaucracies go beyond the Weberian ideal by promoting linkages with private actors, particularly business and, ideally, labor as well.

[10] Kaldor's argument, as per Lewis, is that as a result of the productivity rates between sectors differing so substantially, the transfer of labour and production is a major source of productivity gains and thus economic growth. However, in an open economy Kaldor argued that imported food weakens the link between urban food demand and domestic food production and, in this case, the balance of payments (and thus foreign exchange) may replace agricultural productivity as a constraint. Kaldor posited that in open economies, the self-sustaining cycle of industrialization, productivity growth, higher incomes, growing investment and demand, and greater industrialization may never get going because movement of labour may be into informal services rather than manufacturing employment, as the demand for those goods may also be imported. Indeed, in many developing countries, it is the informal service sector which expands rather than manufacturing because of higher income elasticity in marketed services, and because lower productivity in services allows employment to expand faster than in manufactures (and services are less tradable and thus grow as domestic income grows). The informal service sector may be good at employment creation, but the long-run productivity gains are much less than those produced by manufacturing and, in an open economy, the demand for services could be from overseas and thus produce growth elsewhere.

dual economy as an expression of the stages of growth; the difference is that structuralists attributed it to the nature of integration into the international economy, among other things. Furthermore, the structuralists discussed the international economy in considerable depth, just as they did the international distribution questions, and the national distribution questions that concerned Kuznets.

Structuralism is associated with (in some cases strongly and in other cases less so) various scholars including Prebisch (1949), Singer (1950), Furtado (1956, 1961, 1971), Myrdal (1968, 1970) and Sunkel (1966, 1972, 1989, 1993). Structuralism was influenced by early development economists, not only Lewis and Kaldor, but also Kalecki, Keynes, Nurkse, Schumpeter, and Veblen and classical political economy.

Important aspects of structuralism resonate with these early development economists, such as, on the ST side, chronic balance-of-payments deficits, and on the IG side, unemployment, underemployment, and unequal income distribution. The dual economy concept is echoed in their thinking and although credited to Prebisch-Singer, it was Nurkse (1944) who identified the terms of trade constraint that shaped structuralist thinking (the elasticity of demand of commodities versus manufactured goods). Furthermore, both Lewis and Kalecki predicted that manufacturing exports would replace primary commodity exports, but that manufacturing exports would function similarly to the primary commodities they replaced, in that export prices would fall and the terms of trade would decline.[11] Kalecki wrote this after many of the foundational structuralists had made similar arguments.

Structuralist theorists were interested in the structure of production, and national and international demand, as well as the place in the global economy that developing countries found themselves in as a result of history and colonialism in particular. ST was a core aspect and a major difference to neoclassical economists to whom the sectoral composition of output, employment, and exports is not a relevant concern as noted.

Chenery (1979, p. xvi) outlined the differences between a structuralist and a neoclassical approach thus:

> Economic development can be viewed as a set of interrelated changes in the structure of an economy that are required for its continued growth. They involve

[11] Kalecki, in particular, had a profound impact on Latin American structuralism. One route was via Kalecki's (1976) demand constraint which is as follows: industrialization leads to rising demand for basic goods such as food, but the supply of such goods is inelastic in the short term: thus, food prices rise, which raises wage costs and thus production costs, and reduces profits. Furthermore, as food prices rise, more of the household budget must be spent on food, dampening demand for non-food items such as manufactured goods, which could stall the industrialization process. The poorest would be worst hit as food costs make up a high proportion of their household budget. Thus, governments need to control prices of basic goods.

> the composition of demand, production, and employment as well as the external structure of trade and capital flows. Taken together, these structural changes define the transformation of a traditional to a modem economic system.

Chenery (1975, 1979) argued that the sources of growth were not just capital accumulation, an increase in labour quantity and quality, increased intermediate inputs, and total factor productivity (TFP) as the neoclassical approach outlined, but also reallocation of resources to higher productivity sectors, economies of scale and learning by doing, and the reduction of internal and external bottlenecks.

At the basis of structuralism is an asymmetry between advanced nations and developing nations that has led to a 'centre' (of advanced nations) and a 'periphery' (of developing countries). Fischer (2015, p. 701) sums up 'peripherality' as follows:

> Peripherality...is not merely spatial; it is an assessment of structural modes of integration into the world economy via the dissemination of technological and industrial development, and associated factors such as finance and ownership. Within these specific dimensions—which are vital to wealth and power in the global economy—centres generally emit and peripheries generally receive.

Peripherality was the central issue for the structuralists, and its causes and consequences. For example, Chenery (1975, 1983) outlined how the structuralists understood peripherality in terms of developing countries not being on the same trajectory as advanced nations in the 1700s/1800s, but being on a different pathway altogether. In contrast, Prebisch or Furtado, identifies the last quarter of the nineteenth century as the key moment of integration that had a profound impact on the structure of economies, and that produced growth for a while, until the 1930s.

Structuralists sought to identify specific rigidities and lags in ST in developing countries, and explore how the structure of their economies impacted the availability of policy choices and forms of ST possible. Although structuralism has a shared intellectual history with dependency theory (see Section 3.3.3) it is distinct in that it advocates policies for pursuing development within the global capitalist system, rather than breaking free of that system altogether, though that is a caricature of dependency theory, based on the most extreme version of Frank or a few others.

Saad-Filho (2005) notes the key features of structuralist thinking. The following, in particular, are central to note:

- Structuralist thinking provides a central role for the state in industrialization;
- Market failures are the norm and are caused by structural factors in developing countries;

- The periphery tends to export primary products, whose prices tend to fall over time, but import manufactures whose prices tend to remain constant; thus, the periphery's terms of trade will decline over time. International trade benefits the core because of the periphery's declining terms of trade (the Prebisch-Singer thesis). The terms of trade (the ratio of unit prices of exports to imports in a country) can improve if exports increase in value and lead to a trade surplus.[12]

The latter point is very much associated with structuralists and was labelled the Prebisch-Singer thesis. To overcome this, structuralists advocated state-led ISI focused on manufacturing with state subsidies, cheap credit, infant industry protection, exchange rate controls, and the use, not only of state-owned enterprises but also foreign direct investment. This is a simplified characterization, but of course many of these were common policy tools that we accepted at the time, and countries were industrializing through necessity in one way or another.

Prebisch (1949) outlined his thesis on the price relationship between raw materials and manufactured goods and how it turned against developing countries, leading to foreign exchange shortage, problems with affordability of capital goods (which were imported), and debt service. His explanation was focused on the business cycle and factoral aspects. He discussed monopolistic labour and goods markets in advanced nations, and competitive markets in developing countries.[13]

Singer (1950) also outlined, using different data, the terms of trade hypothesis. He argued that this could not be explained by orthodox comparative advantage theory. He noted, as all structuralists did, that the structures of developing economies are quite different to those of the advanced nations and they hold different roles in the global economy as a result. Resonating with Lewis, Singer argued that the dualism of the world economy is evident within peripheral economies where there exists a small enclave economic sector where the primary-export sector predominates, which is typically owned by foreign capital and has high productivity. That sector sits alongside, and is only weakly connected to, a relatively inefficient agricultural sector producing for domestic consumption.

[12] Lewis and Prebisch talked about declining factoral terms of trade. Prebisch had three arguments for why terms of trade tended to fall, of which the Prebisch–Singer hypothesis is one. See for discussion, Fischer (2015).

[13] The impact of this was that improvements in the productivity of exports of developing countries benefit advanced countries as prices fall. Conversely, improvements in productivity of advanced nations leads to higher wages and profits in advanced economies. Prebisch outlined three further features of developing countries: the first was the marginalization of poorer populations in developing countries; the second was the consumption patterns of elites in developing countries, which followed elites in advanced countries; finally, there were inflationary and balance-of-payments deficits leading to chronic macroeconomic instability.

Singer argued that unequal terms of trade emerge because the advanced economies benefit disproportionally from technical progress (smaller amounts of raw material per output unit are needed) and as real income rises, the increase in demand for manufactured goods is more than proportional. In contrast, the low-income elasticity of demand for raw materials and food leads to falling prices as a structural phenomenon. Singer correlated the deterioration of the terms of trade to the fall in the unit values for exports (primary commodities or manufactured goods) of developing countries relative to the unit values of the exports of advanced nations, as well as the higher proportion of primary commodities in the total exports of developing countries.[14]

Sunkel (1966) and Furtado (1956, 1971) further developed structuralist thinking. Sunkel (1966) argued that the structural causes of Latin America's underdevelopment were—resonating with Lewis—due to: the high concentration of land and other asset ownership; differential productivity levels in the export and domestic sectors; a monopolistic industrial structure; financial instability due to the structure of trade; a shortage and misallocation of 'social overhead capital' meaning infrastructure such as roads and energy; and low levels of education due to much of the population living in the non-modern sectors. Sunkel also wrote substantially about the effects of foreign direct investment and transnational corporations on the domestic economy.

In a similar vein, Furtado (1956, 1971) concluded that, if productivity is the engine of growth, the main distinction between rich and poor countries is that rich countries are those which can generate growth via technological innovation whilst poorer nations grow via assimilation of existing technology. For Furtado, underdevelopment is an autonomous historical process. Underdevelopment is visible in a labour oversupply and imported capital-intensive technology, which further perpetuates inequality. He argued that the answer was agrarian reform and the redistribution of income, and that to achieve this, a strong state with popular support would be needed.

Myrdal (1968, 1970) also made important contributions to structuralism. Myrdal was involved with the earlier group of development economists in the 1940s. He also made various contributions in the 1950s (Myrdal, 1956, 1957a, 1957b).

Myrdal's major theoretical contribution to structuralism was in the 1950s with thinking on the interplay of 'backwash and spread effects' in global and regional economies, and in circular and cumulative processes, which

[14] He noted that one could emphasize more intra-South trade and investment but autarky would not be a solution because developing countries already have large trade/GDP; a shift towards manufacturing could lead to weak growth in the North, and diminished export markets and increasing export volumes would only reduce prices further; financial support could help but would merely postpone and intensify the problem whether it was bank lending or foreign investment.

exacerbated polarization. The backwash effect was that as one area of a country develops, labour migrates to it, as does physical capital. That leaves a backward area that is worse off by the movement than before the movement. Thus, growth in one area is to the detriment of another. In contrast, the spread effect is when development in one area spreads to neighbouring areas.

Myrdal's well known Asian Drama (1968), was much more radical and pessimist than his earlier work. In that book he argued that the structural problem of underdevelopment lies primarily in the mass poverty and characteristics within developing countries. In rich countries, savings are the engine of investment and thus growth. However, in South Asia, the region of this study, mass poverty constrains this. In South Asia, growth would need to come from increased consumption of the masses rather than from savings and investment. He argued that consumption needed to rise first and then investment would follow. He maintained that international aid could bring high-tech industries, but that they formed enclaves because they require high-skill labour, which often came from overseas as it was not available domestically. The solution for Myrdal was the traditional sector, which should be kept and modernized with technology to produce for the domestic market, thus raising consumption and labour productivity.[15]

Critiques of structuralism came from within structuralism initially (e.g. from Furtado and Sunkel). Notably, the underdevelopment of the periphery is not entirely due to the global economy and trade relations, but much more so due to domestic social structures within the periphery. The more sophisticated structuralists (and dependency theorists), including Cardoso and Furtado, did argue that domestic structures were important, so they had already pre-empted that critique. In contrast, the criticism of structuralism from a neoclassical perspective was largely anti-state (see Bruton 1981, 1998), positing that there is no problem in specializing in primary exports and that the Prebisch-Singer thesis is inconclusive and empirically flawed.[16] Structuralism, even if it does trigger some growth, is based on unsustainable growth as it is an inefficient subsidy of capital-intensive manufacturing which is not the comparative advantage of developing countries. Critics argued that state-led development has been inflationary due to large fiscal deficits and import-

[15] Myrdal also argued that inequality had slowed down development, thus greater equality was not contradictory to promoting growth and welfare. Indeed, he stated that education and health provision would lay the basis for sustained rapid economic growth and equality of opportunity. However, he thought this was unlikely as political power is held by small elites or oligarchies that prevent reform and the advancement of the interests of the masses.

[16] In terms of the Prebisch-Singer thesis, declines in the terms of trade were challenged because some primary products, notably oil, exhibited different trends, especially so in the 1970s. Conceptually, the Prebisch-Singer thesis was critiqued on at least two points: the difficulties in distinguishing primary products and manufactured goods; and that international commodity prices are complex (e.g. there are various types of coffee, not just one) and misleading as they are, at best, indirectly related to the farm-gate prices that the producers receive (Saad-Filho 2005).

substitution, given its basis on imported technology and foreign capital, and thus had led to the deterioration of the balance-of-payments situation.[17]

In sum, structuralism, as a body of theory, identified the causes of underdevelopment as based largely, though not entirely, within international trade relations though some of the more sophisticated theorists did discuss how domestic structures were also critical. The failure of the Lewis transition in developing countries was due to the place in which developing countries found themselves in the contemporary global economy. Structuralism proposed departing from existing relations via state-led ISI and foreign investment that would help in the industrialization endeavour. This would lead to inclusive growth where the benefits would reach the poorer parts of the population.

3.3.3 *Developmentalism and Dependency, Monopoly Capitalism, and World Systems Theory*

Dependency theory, monopoly capitalism, and world systems theory are a further set of theories that have, to a greater or lesser extent, some intellectual history with structuralism and, to differing degrees, sympathy for the idea of developmentalism in terms of the scope for national economic development. These theorists have much less sympathy with, though were influenced by, Lewis among others. There is a focus on domestic social structure and national distribution as important issues; thus, there is some linkage to Kuznets in a broad sense. If we take dependency theory first, the primary difference between dependency theory and structuralism is that, whilst structuralists, as Lewis, were optimistic that the periphery might achieve structural change and industrialization through trade and through ISI, dependency theory—in its various iterations—was much more pessimistic. It argued that trade relations are the very cause of the perpetuation of underdevelopment and that, in terms of rising inequality, import-substitution has made matters worse.[18]

[17] Hirschman's (1968) critique of ISI was influential and was as follows: ISI is based on a set of stages and gets 'stuck' after the easy early successes without moving into the exporting stage. Further, ISI tends to induce capital- and import-intensive industrialization dominated by large companies and is unequalizing (see also Chenery et al. 1974).

[18] Dos Santos (1970) argued that there were various types of dependence and each form of dependency corresponds not only to the international economy but also to the internal structures of production, capital accumulation, economic reproduction, and corresponding social and political structures. Dos Santos outlined three kinds of dependence: colonial dependence which was trade- and export-oriented and in which the colonial state dominated economic relations by trade and production monopolies; financial–industrial dependence which is characterized by the domination of big capital from the hegemonic centres, and their expanding investments in primary sectors in developing countries for consumption in the centre; and a technological–industrial dependence which shaped the post-Second World War era, based on multinational companies who invest in developing countries.

Dependency theory, however, is not one cohesive body of theory but contains several strands. Palma (1978) posits that dependency theory has three distinctive strands demarcated by the extent to which capitalist development of the periphery is viewed as possible: first, he identified a lineage of dependency theory evolving from structuralism. This stance reflected optimism that self-reliant development was possible with the state guiding industrialization and a nationally minded business class. Second, a lineage critical of structuralism as demonstrated by Cardoso and Faletto (1979) who, though less optimistic than the first lineage, viewed the development of developing countries as possible. Third, he identified a lineage of neo-Marxist thinking—associated with Frank (1966, 1972), Baran (1957), and world systems theory—that was highly pessimistic of the possibility of development in the periphery. According to Frank, contemporary underdevelopment was the historical product of global relations between the 'metropolis' (the rich countries) and 'satellites' (developing countries) that were connected by the extraction of economic surplus from satellites by the metropolis. Baran argued that this was positive in the sense that it would make, at a later date, socialism possible.

What unifies dependency theory is the centre's exploitation of the periphery via economic surplus extraction and transfer to the centre; the concentration of foreign capital in primary sectors which has largely benefited international capitalists, and facilitated net capital outflow from developing countries and indebtedness; and foreign capital that creates a local elite with interests tied to foreign investors and with influence over policy.

Dependency theory, although neo-Marxist in certain strands sat/sits uneasily with classical Marxism. Marx and Engels believed that capitalism in the advanced nations would spread industrialization to the developing world. Neo-Marxists in the US 'monopoly capital' school (drawing on Frank's dependency theory lineage) included Baran (1957), and Baran and Sweezy (1966).

The main features of the monopoly capitalism school were that a new form of capitalism had emerged and modern capitalism was dominated by monopolies, and that this leads to rising inequality. Monopolies also tend to slow technological progress, and lead to economic stagnation and insufficient demand or under-consumption in developing countries, thus causing militarism and imperialism.

Baran (1957) argued that underdevelopment was based on the history of colonialism and plunder which was, post-independence, replaced with 'neo-imperialism', which used 'unequal exchange' to extract surplus from the developing world by the developed world.[19]

[19] Baran's (1957) main argument was that economic backwardness is primarily due to external causes, notably imperialism in the colonial and semi-colonial eras. For him, imperialist powers seek

Warren (1973, 1980) took a different view. He critiqued Lenin's theory of imperialism, where imperialism is the final, decadent stage of capitalism, and an obstacle to industrial development in developing countries. Warren argued that imperialism is progressive because it develops the productive forces of developing countries. In this way, colonialism, and thus the spread of capitalism, is a powerful engine for social change as it can destroy pre-capitalist systems. Capitalism acts as a bridge to socialism as imperialist capitalism creates the conditions for its own destruction in spreading capitalist relations of production in the non-capitalist world.

Another body of theory, linked in some way to dependency theory and the monopoly capitalism school, is world systems theory. This also introduced heterogeneity in a further concept of 'semi-periphery' and, to some extent, turned dependency theory on its head, in that it argued that a country's position in the hierarchy determines its trade rather than vice versa. World systems theory rejected nation states as an analytical category and emphasized that all countries were enmeshed in the global economy and ranked in the hierarchy.

Seminal works are those of Wallerstein, Arrighi, and Emmanuel. Wallerstein (1979), recognizing the nuances and graduation of some countries between categories, developed the concept of semi-peripheralism. Based on this, there were three positions in the capitalist world economy that countries could hold: core, semi-periphery, and periphery. Arrighi (1990) posited that the semi-periphery gains, not when they exchange with the core, but when they exchange with the periphery. Wealthier countries could buy more labour contained in goods and thus exploit other countries more. However, unequal exchange is only one mechanism that reproduces these positions. Emmanuel (1972) developed the mobility of capital as an explanatory variable for why the distance between countries grows over time. Surplus value is higher in advanced countries than in the periphery ones. Given capital mobility, profit rates will equalize in between levels in the rich and poor countries. Thus, the size of the centre's surplus value will increase and the periphery's will fall. If the costs of production are the same in core and periphery countries the unit value of exports will rise in the centre and fall in the periphery. In short, capital mobility will lead to transfer of value from the periphery to the core as well as changing the terms of trade, and this will block prospects for industrialization in the periphery.

Critiques of dependency theory, monopoly capitalism, and world systems theory focus on the fact that they fail to consider sufficiently how agency in

to sabotage economic development in developing countries because of the risks that it poses for rising wages in advanced economies. Thus, foreign capital restricts the growth of developing countries by, for example, importing manufactures that destroy local handicrafts.

the periphery and centre may shape the relationship between them. Critics also note that dependency theory and the monopoly capital school do not define or explain well how monopolies arise, how they shape the reproduction of industrial capital and income distribution, and point out that there is little to account of state regulation or competitors entering the market. Finally, they note that the concept of 'dependency' is vague and cannot be defined.

Brenner's (1977) critique was damning, asserting that these theories fail to consider the way in which class structures emerge from class struggle and determine the course of economic development or underdevelopment. In doing so, these heterodox theories failed to transcend the economic determinism of modernization theory and neoclassical economics.

One can sum up the contributions of dependency theory, monopoly capitalism, and world systems theory as follows: first, there is a focus on an integrated global economy where the centre and periphery have specific roles but are dependent on each other. One could thus make some comparisons with Lewis. Further, contemporary dependency is merely an evolution of a history of dependency since colonialism. Second, there is the creation of a social structure in developing countries led by a 'comprador elite' or 'lumpenbourgeoisie' that exploits the population of developing countries for the benefit of the centre and the elites themselves. Finally, surplus extraction is due to unequal exchange and profit remittances by foreign investment, debt repayments, and capital flight. These lead to a growth pattern based on primary exports and luxury goods, which is an observation that Lewis would have recognized.

There is, however, a fundamental question as to whether there is one form of national-based capitalism or one form of capitalism in advanced and one in developing countries (as per dependency theory or monopoly capitalism theory), or one form of capitalism that is global and within which all countries are interconnected albeit in a hierarchical way (as per world systems theory and which Lewis appreciated too). In consequence, contemporary debates have not focused on one, but on multiple forms of capitalism, and have emphasized the heterogeneity of capitalisms with two or three core types of capitalism in terms of institutional arrangements or 'varieties' of capitalism.

3.4 Comparative Capitalisms and the Social Structure of Capital Accumulation

3.4.1 *Varieties of Capitalism*

The purpose of this section is to give an overview of the most recent theoretical contributions on the heterogeneity of capitalism. The heterogeneity of capitalism is not something that Lewis, Kuznets, nor the orthodox or heterodox theorists discussed in any significant depth. On the basis of the heterogeneity of capitalism, an analytical framework for this book is outlined.

The basis of both orthodox and heterodox theories previously discussed, that there is one mode of capitalism common to all countries or one mode common to developing countries, is difficult to sustain. Research on comparative capitalisms is a body of work that has emerged since the Cold War and seeks to account for the heterogeneity of capitalism. The enquiry has an evolution in two largely unrelated streams. The first, within business studies, is often labelled as the 'varieties of capitalism' literature. It has sub-variants (see discussion in this section). The second stream, within social policy studies or political sociology has been labelled as the 'welfare capitalisms' or 'welfare regimes' literature. Here we review both. These contemporary literatures, together with the heterodox theory previously discussed, lay the foundations for the analytical approach of this book.

A body of literature that emerged from business studies is referred to as the varieties of capitalism (VoC) literature. It focuses on private firms as the central actors in capitalist economies and the institutional systems that shape their behaviour. The VoC literature has three variants: first, 'classical' (meaning first order) or VoC (developed in particular by Hall and Soskice 2001); second, a variant known as 'national business systems' (associated with Whitley 1991, 1999); and, third the 'varieties of institutional systems' (proposed by Fainshmidt et al. 2016). These theoretical frameworks seek to capture the diversity of institutional contexts.

In their seminal work, Hall and Soskice (2001) identified just two varieties of capitalism focusing solely on advanced nations: a liberal market capitalism with competitive market arrangements (the exemplar they cite is the US) and a coordinated market capitalism which is less competitive in nature and instead based on strategic interactions and collaborative arrangements. It is characterized by institutional arrangements that coordinate firm behaviour and by the regulatory regime for labour markets and corporate governance (noting exemplars of Germany or Japan), rather than institutional arrangements based on competitive firm behaviour.

Hall and Soskice's classical exposition of the varieties of capitalism is based on the differential institutional characteristics across countries governing or regulating: (i) financial markets (equity and credit markets); (ii) human capital (and the 'coordination' of labour); and (iii) corporate governance and ownership concentration. Hall and Soskice (2001) outlined how they believed institutions are socializing agencies promoting a set of norms, power arrangements, and a matrix of sanctions and incentives, by which the behaviour of actors is shaped. Thus, they take a relational view of firms as developing relationships with society in, for example, industrial relations (to manage wage demands), vocational training and education (to secure the skills needed for production), corporate governance (to access finance on favourable terms), inter-firm relations (to ensure technology transfer, standard-setting, research and development collaboration), and employees (cooperation and competence).

Hall and Soskice argued that it is the way that firms address these spheres which differentiates economies between the two ideal types of liberal market economies (LME) and coordinated market economies (CME). The former is heavily based on market relationships whilst the latter is heavily based on non-market relationships. Hall and Soskice posited that in LMEs, profitability is essential to survival due to the structure of financial markets and thus access to capital. Further, market share is maintained by flexible labour laws. In CMEs, in contrast, firms can survive with declining profitability because they have access to capital independent of their level of profitability. Market share is maintained by the long-term employment strategies of the state. They note that in much of Europe employment protection is high, but stock market capitalization is low. In contrast, in the US, UK, Canada, and Australia, the opposite is the case as employment protection is weaker and stock market capitalization is higher. They argue that there may be variations in the short term, but in the long run both types of capitalism can lead to reasonable economic performance. However, they argue that the latter, CME, has come under pressure due to financial globalization since the late 1980s.

Hall and Soskice do not ignore inclusive growth. They note that the two ideal types differ drastically in terms of the level of income inequality produced, the nature of employment in terms of hours worked, and the security of employment. In social policy, LMEs are characterized by liberal welfare states based on means-testing, low benefits, and flexible labour markets. On the other hand, in CMEs, the welfare state often provides pensions and benefits (for example, for unemployment). Their exposition thus resonates with a parallel literature that has evolved in tandem, the 'welfare capitalism' literature.

Welfare capitalism literature is a parallel literature in social policy and political sociology. This body of work evolved from the seminal work of Esping-Andersen (1990, 1999) and in particular the typology of welfare capitalism, which was focused solely on advanced countries. Esping-Andersen (1990, 1999) argued that there are three types of specific welfare capitalisms: liberal, corporatist–statist, and social democratic welfare regimes. In the first regime, the poorest receive modest benefits (e.g. in the US) through targeted programmes and cash benefits as a minimal security provision. In the second regime, corporatist–statist, rights to welfare are institutionalized as part of the state–citizen relationship in terms of employment protection and corporatism. Benefits are linked to employment and dependent on previous income or tax contributions, and different groups receive different benefits. In the third regime, the social democrat welfare regime, it is organized labour that is integrated into a social security regime. Benefits are universalistic and financed by higher taxes and not linked to employment.

The VoC and welfare capitalism approach have been expanded to consider developing countries over the last decade. There has, not surprisingly, been a stronger focus on the state, given that until relatively recently it was assumed that the taxonomy of Hall and Sockice, or Esping-Andersen, was hard to apply to developing countries. This was due to the limited extent of private sector development, and the stronger role of the state (evident in many developing countries), endemic market imperfections, weak institutional arrangements and the, at best, fledgling welfare state, as well as endemic or structural unemployment and insecurity.

The VoC literature has evolved to take more account of the role of the state in developing countries and in 'varieties of state capitalism'. A sub-variant of VoC, known as 'national business systems', is associated with Whitley (1991, 1999). National business systems added the role of the state in indirect intervention in the private sector, focusing on state capital, knowledge capital, levels of trust, and family ownership patterns. Whitley's (1991, 1999) framework identified four institutional dimensions that, collectively, interact and coalesce on the form of the model of capitalism or the 'national business system'. These four dimensions are i) the activities of the state in spending and regulating; ii) the financial system, equity markets, and allocation of capital; iii) human capital in terms of skill development, and the 'control system' in terms of trade unions and collective bargaining; and iv) national cultural norms in trust relations in perceptions of corruption levels (as the inverse of trust) and 'authority relations'.[20] Judge et al. (2014) used fuzzy set analysis to then identify six models of capitalism applying Whitley's approach empirically: three associated with more equitable and three with less equitable 'configurations' of capitalism. The former are more typical in OECD countries, the latter are more typical in developing countries. They find that more equitable capitalism is associated with lower 'power distance', better education and training systems, and higher state expenditures.

A sub-variant of VoC, known as 'varieties of institutional systems', proposed by Fainshmidt et al. (2016) also seeks to capture the diversity of institutional contexts. The varieties of institutional systems taxonomy expanded the lens to include a wider variety of types of states. It classified states as 'regulatory', 'welfarist', 'developmental', or 'predatory', drawing on Whitley (2000), and Carney and Witt (2012). The regulatory state is one in which the state protects

[20] The concept is drawn from cultural psychology. Power distance cultural norms assess how, in 'low power distance' societies, authority figures can be challenged whilst in 'high power distance' societies, authority figures are less likely to be questioned.

property rights and enforces rules but does not significantly participate in economic activity beyond that; a welfare state is one in which the state protects and promotes the well-being of the population via redistribution mechanisms; the developmental state is that which has a substantial economic role in terms of long-term national economic development and is active in, for example, industrial policy; and the predatory state is one that is characterized by weak institutions, limited market competition, and elites who monopolize power. They posit that there are the following six types of capitalism in the developing world: state-led (e.g. India, China, Malaysia, Indonesia, and Thailand), fragmented with fragile state (e.g. Angola, Egypt, and Ethiopia), family-led (e.g. Brazil, Mexico, and Nigeria), centralized tribe (covering many Middle East countries such as Iran, Saudi Arabia, UAE), emergent liberal market economies (such as Chile, Singapore, South Africa), and two categories covering Eastern Europe and the former Soviet Union and labelled, 'collaborative agglomerations' and 'hierarchically coordinated'.

In a related vein, Musacchio and Lazzarini (2012, 2014) have sought to push forward-thinking in terms of state capitalism in the developing world. Their main argument, somewhat echoing Polanyi (1957), is that state and market, or state and private are intertwined. Musacchio and Lazzarini (2014) argue that this manifests itself in minority or majority state ownership, for example, part-privatized, publicly traded, state-owned enterprises (SOEs), or financial support to private firms, through sovereign wealth funds, holding companies, or even development banks. Different SOE patterns then frame development trajectories and they argue for two new ideal types: the state as majority investor and the state as a minority investor. Musacchio and Lazzarini (2014) identify four varieties of capitalism as follows: private ownership, the state as a majority shareholder or investor, the state as a minority shareholder/investor, and the state as an entrepreneur (meaning the state owns and manages SOEs within the bureaucracy of the state).

In social policy and political sociology, Esping-Andersen's work has been expanded to developing countries by Wood and Gough (2006; see also Gough 2000), who present an empirically grounded theoretical framework for the comparative analysis of 'meta-welfare regimes', and in doing so develop a taxonomy of regime types to compare developing countries. In contrast to OECD nations, in developing countries, the welfare outcomes of the population are formed by basic institutional conditions such as the nature of markets, the legitimacy of the state, the extent of societal integration, and the nature of integration into the world economy. In other words, they are shaped by the institutional responsibilities for welfare of state, market, household, and community, and by the stratification system or the existing distribution of power and various assets. They note three types of meta-regime in developing countries: first, actual, or potential welfare state regimes as those with high state commitment and relatively high welfare outcomes; second, informal security regimes which are contexts whereby people rely on non-state relationships to meet security needs—in such situations, poorer people often trade informal security for longer-term vulnerability and dependence; and third, insecurity regimes, which are contexts whereby there are gross insecurities, conflict, and political instability.

Finally, in a critical vein, and in keeping with the tradition of heterodox theory, Ebenau et al. (2015) developed a 'post-VoC' approach which focuses on the dynamics and tensions of capital–labour institutions, and which discusses how different varieties of capitalism corrode the existing domestic political settlement between classes. They combine institutional dynamism with capital–labour tensions which allow them to analyse how the common goal of different capitalist models (profitability and the search for new markets) can corrode the viability of internal settlements between classes. This is much in keeping with a further political economy/sociological literature known as the social structures of capital accumulation (see Section 3.4.2).

In short, there is then a rich set of literature which has evolved in tandem in different disciplines on comparative capitalisms, and which has been extended to developing countries in recent years. The literature on welfare capitalisms in social policy sits alongside a literature on varieties of capitalism in business studies and comparative capitalism studies. Each seeks to make sense of the heterogeneity in capital accumulation regimes and welfare regimes. In doing so, they break from the study of capitalism inherent in heterodox theory, and in Lewis, Kaldor, and Kuznets. They also point towards the importance of detailed empirical case studies and 'thick description' to understand the dynamics of capitalisms and historical trends, the regularities and, echoing Lewis, Kaldor, and the heterodox theorists, the structures, and systems. This analytical framework is called the 'social structures of capital accumulation'. Its focus is on investigating the social structure—the institutional arrangements—that support a wave of capital accumulation under capitalism. We discuss this next as the culmination of the theoretical discussions of this chapter and the framework for the book henceforth.

3.4.2 *The Social Structure of Capital Accumulation as an Analytical Approach to the Study of Heterogeneous Capitalisms*

The social structures of (capital) accumulation approach originally evolved in the 1970s. However, in the last decade or so there has there has been a considerable shift and evolution in the approach.[21]

[21] See, for example, the two-volume reference works of seventy-two articles, McDonough et al. (eds) (2014).

We briefly introduced this as the analytical approach for this book's discussion of South East Asia in Chapter 1. This analytical approach is distinctive in the sense that it is, or seeks to be, an interdisciplinary, non-reductionist, methodologically mixed approach.[22]

The approach is consistent with pursuing detailed empirical comparative case studies that are inductive and empirical (as per Kuznets and the approaches of the structuralists), and capture historical trends, regularities, structures, and systems set in a 'thick description', which can explain the context in time and as part of a country's history, not as a rational response to scarcity, but as substantivism in the Polanyi (1957 [1944]) sense.

The approach seeks to avoid reductionism in terms of materialism and the mechanistic thinking evident in some heterodox thinking. The approach aims to be a more nuanced, non-deterministic, account of history, which has led to an association with French regulation theory, and an interest in new forms and tensions of capitalism, and how capital accumulation is stabilized or regulated (see, for example, Aglietta 1976; Boyer and Saillard 1995). The seminal work is that of Gordon (1978, 1980) and Gordon et al. (1982).[23]

Like much of the heterodox theory discussed so far, the analytical approach draws key concepts—such as crises, class conflict, and historical materialism—from Marx and those writing about structuralism, and other heterodox theories discussed previously. That said, a core aspect of the analytical approach is in direct contradiction to orthodox Marxism; specifically, the regenerative power of capitalism.

The influences of Keynesianism, post-Keynesianism, institutionalism, and long-wave theory are as equally as visible as Marx if not more so.[24] Most notably, the analytical approach is predicated on the regenerative power of capitalism.

[22] It shares some intellectual history with heterodox theory and evolved originally in a similar time period to monopoly capitalism, as both were a response to understanding the crises of capitalism in the late 1970s and early 1980s. The difference with monopoly capitalism and the approach is the concern with how capitalism reincarnates for a new wave of capital accumulation following a crisis. In contrast, the concern of monopoly capitalism was the 'fundamental crisis' or demise of capitalism.

[23] Other influential works were those by Reich (1997), Kotz (1994), Kotz et al. (1994).

[24] The extent of the influence of Marxism is disputed and whether the approach has moved towards Marxism or away from it over time is questioned (see discussion of Kotz 1994, 2016). Inspiration for Gordon's seminal work came from the imperialism theory of Hilferding (1981 [1910]), Lenin (1985 [1917]), and Mandel (1964), which is one link to the monopoly capitalism school.

Gordon et al. (1982) did make use of the circuit of capital in analysing the capital accumulation process as originally outlined by Marx (1885). Specifically, capitalists seek to make profits by investment of their money capital, which is required for production; the labour process occurs and then the products of labour are sold and this is converted back into money capital. Each stage requires institutions that support these processes and together that is what constitutes the social structure of capital accumulation.

Keynesianism provides the concept of investment and investment is viewed as the stabilizer of the social structure. Institutionalism provides the idea of the embeddedness of economies in society and history and social institutions, as per Polanyi, are the basis of an economy. Long-wave theory also provided inspiration, notably, Kondratieff (1935), who argued that there were long waves of fifty to sixty years of economic super-cycles, or K-waves.[25] Kondratieff hypothesized that cycles were composed of expansion, stagnation, and crisis. He considered rising prices and low-interest rates to characterize the expansion. Waves were driven by technological innovation. Kuznets (1930) too, hypothesized waves or 'demographic' or 'building cycles' of fifteen to twenty-five years. He argued that these were due to demography and migration, which led to construction booms. Finally, Kitchin (1923) hypothesized a cycle of forty months based on information time lags, the impact on firms' decision-making, and the impact on commodity inventories which run down in periods of market saturation.

In short, the analytical approach is concerned with the medium- to long-term cycles or waves of capitalism. A cycle consists of capital accumulation, growth, stagnation, and crisis. The crisis leads to a new wave. The approach is interested in the causes of periods of capital accumulation and crises. The approach is based on the idea that capital accumulation is predicated on institutions (economic, political, ideological, or cultural) that are compatible and together support a wave of capital accumulation. Any period generates class conflict—notably between classes but also within classes, and/or market saturation, which leads to stagnation and crisis, leading to a new social structure being established and a new wave of capital accumulation.[26]

The extent to which global neo-liberalism is a new social structure of capital accumulation is a contemporary intellectual fault line; as is the necessity for capital accumulation to define a social structure of capital accumulation (it is argued that a social structure of capital accumulation may not be associated with capital accumulation and is, rather, a source of institutional stabilization of between and within class conflicts).

Wolfson and Kotz (2009) outline two types of institutional structure, echoing the previous discussion of varieties of capitalism and welfare capitalisms previously. Kotz noted a 'liberal institutional structure' and a 'regulationist institutional structure' or 'constrained market'.[27] A set of dimensions is given

[25] Mandel (1964) also took up Kondratieff's thinking.

[26] The approach has tended to focus on the nation state as the unit of analysis. However, the limitations of this became clear in terms of the emergence of neo-liberalism and globalization. The approach has evolved much in the study of the US. There are some applications to developing countries, though these are few. For example, India in Harriss-White (2003).

[27] Wolfson and Kotz (2009) note the historical tendency for social structures of capital accumulation to alternate between liberal and constrained markets in keeping with Polanyi (1957 [1944]) who noted how the establishment of a liberal economy sought to separate markets

for difference: how conflicts between and within capital and labour are stabilized; the role of the state in the economy; and the dominant ideology. The former is more laissez-faire; the latter is more interventionist. The former is where capital has a stronger position; the latter is where capital–labour relations are more cooperative; the former is where capital–capital relations are intense; the latter is where capital–capital relations are more muted; the former is one of a dominant ideology of free markets; the latter is one of an interventionist state. The likely economic problems and potential crises will then differ depending on whether a social structure of capital accumulation is a liberal or constrained market. The latter will see profits squeezed whilst the former may be more likely to experience inadequate aggregate demand or overcapacity.

In sum, the focus on the social structure of capital accumulation is best described as an approach or an analytical framework. It will be used in the second half of this book to approach the study of South East Asia. It is an approach which seeks to explain the institutional basis for episodes or 'waves' of capital accumulation. In doing so, it is predicated on a history of heterodox thinking that runs through much of the preceding discussion.

3.5 Conclusion

The purpose of this chapter was to revisit orthodox and heterodox theories of ST and the Lewisian transition. The chapter has also set out the basis for the choice of analytical approach to comparative capitalisms to be applied to the study of South East Asia in the following chapters. We thus discussed both orthodox and heterodox theories of ST, considered the contemporary literatures on comparative capitalisms, and used this as the basis for outlining the analytical approach or framework for the second half of the book.

Overall, the chapter has argued the following: the approach of both orthodox and heterodox theory is to focus on integrative ST though the former is more optimistic and the latter more pessimistic of the outcome for developing countries. The former, orthodox theory, however, places little or no emphasis on sectoral and factor ST and the Lewis labour transition (nor the Kuznetsian upswing hindering IG). In contrast, heterodox theorists have been acutely aware of the importance of sectoral and factoral ST, even if they felt as equally acutely that the Lewis model was too optimistic. Heterodox theorists also

from the society in which they are embedded. This, however, created instability and immizeration for some and was thus opposed by an opposite movement. In contrast, the opposite movement sought to embed the market economy within society and to regulate capital.

placed considerable attention on aspects of IG in terms of the role of income distribution in hindering ST and the fact that ST could take place without IG marginalizing much of the population.

It was argued in this chapter that orthodox theory is of limited use in explaining contemporary development because it is characterized by a deterministic, 'natural', pathway followed by richer countries. In a similar vein, heterodox theory is also too deterministic, and lacks an account of variation in late capitalisms. That heterogeneity, and the incorporation of concepts from heterodox theories, such as the focus on struggles between or within classes or groups leading to outcomes, and concepts such as subordinate development and understandings of peripherality—the adverse incorporation into the global economy of developing countries—provide a further basis for the forthcoming focus on the social structure of capital accumulation. The strength of the social structure of accumulation as an analytical approach is that it recognizes the regenerative power of capitalism and the waves of capital accumulation. Finally, it recognizes the framing of national capital accumulation within global capital accumulation as per the structuralists and the work of other heterodox theorists.

In conclusion, this chapter has focused on theories of economic and social transformation that include orthodoxy in modernization theory; static comparative advantage; heterodoxy in structuralism and developmentalist theories; and contemporary debates on comparative capitalism and its heterogeneity. It has proposed an analytical framework based on cycles of expansion, stagnation, crisis, and renewal as a new social basis emerges.

The developer's dilemma remains the core distributional tension at the heart of economic development. The pursuit of ST may be hindered by unequal distribution of income. ST also unleashes tensions between capital and labour shares (to follow Lewis), between sectors (such as urban and rural, to follow Kuznets), and between workers (such as skilled and unskilled). We would argue that the social structure of capital accumulation can only be sustained if there is IG and a set of public policy interventions that seeks to neutralize the Kuznetsian upswing.

In what follows in Chapters 4, 5, and 6, we consider how MIT addressed the developer's dilemma. We focus on three waves of ST and capital accumulation, and label the social structures of capital accumulation respectively by their modality of developmentalism, specifically as 'classical developmentalism', 'two-tier developmentalism', and a nascent, revivalist or new developmentalism. In the first, the state's orchestration of economic activity is direct and crude, typically in the form of SOEs, orchestrating agencies, import-substitution, and domestic industry-building. After a crisis, it was replaced by a new social structure of capital accumulation, which was a regeneration of capitalism in a 'two-tier developmentalism', meaning continued protection for domestic capital but selective liberalization to international capital. This mode of developmentalism was evident in the 1980s in South East Asia and up to the mid 1990s. Again, after further crises, this model was replaced and a new social structure of capital accumulation, which can be labelled 'new developmentalism' emerged.

4

Great Transformations

Classical Developmentalism in South East Asia

4.1 Introduction

In the previous chapter the discussion of Lewis and Kuznets was extended into a broad range of heterodox theory, culminating in the discussion of heterogeneous and comparative capitalisms, and the discussion of the analytical approach to be utilized. Central themes are those of developmentalism and the role of the state in economic development and distribution dynamics.

In this chapter, as well as in Chapters 5 and 6, we consider that role of the state as Polanyi's (1957) handmaiden and regulator, protector of the emerging domestic capital class, and the 'double movement' between marketization and pushback in South East Asia.[1] We identify three waves of ST and capital accumulation, each shaped by a specific variety of developmentalism, separated by the crises of the mid to late 1960s, the early to mid 1980s and the crises of the late 1990s.

In a heterodox and notably structuralist tradition, we argue that each wave of ST and capital accumulation, and the variety of capitalist developmentalism that shaped it, holds within it a specific modality of global incorporation, which acts as the trigger and driver of ST, and also contains the seeds of its eventual crisis. In short, we are arguing that, whilst domestic social structures make possible a wave of capital accumulation, it is global capital accumulation that triggers, drives, and frames what is possible. This, thus, resonates with Lewis and heterodox theories, such as structuralism, that place emphasis on the dynamics of global integration. The immediate cause of the demise of a

[1] Specifically, Polanyi (1957), writing with reference to Europe, refers to the 'great transformation' in the following ways: as the disembedding of the economy from society, by processes of commodification of 'fictitious commodities' (land, labour, and money), or to the emergence of post-war welfare states.

wave of ST and capital accumulation is changes in the global economy, meaning changes in global prices of commodities, relative exchange rates, and relative interest rates in particular. In short, the discussion builds on the conceptual and theoretical discussions of the preceding chapters in the sense that those concepts and theory inform our discussion.

The focus of this chapter is the first era of developmentalism or what can be called 'classical developmentalism' in South East Asia. This encompasses the launching of the Lewis transition of labour, output, and exports away from low productivity agriculture and towards the higher productivity manufacturing sector and industrialization under the substantive protection of the state. The second era of developmentalism or 'two-tier' developmentalism is the focus of Chapter 5. This encompasses a rapid acceleration of the Lewis shift away from low productivity agriculture, though under selective liberalization of international capital alongside protection of domestic capital. The third era of developmentalism or a nascent, 'new developmentalism' is the focus of Chapter 6. This encompasses what could be called a post-Lewis shift away from manufacturing, somewhat prematurely, under a resurgent handmaiden who is much more protective of domestic capital.

In this present chapter, regarding the first wave of ST and capital accumulation, the drivers, orchestration, and social base for ST are respectively, the oil boom, classical developmentalism, and the raising of rural living standards. In Malaysia, the period of classical developmentalism begins with the crisis of 1969 and ethnic riots that led to the ascendancy of institutionalized developmentalism under the guise of the New Economic Policy. This policy sought to respond to the distributional tensions and created a large range of state-owned enterprises (SOEs) and state agencies with the goal of promoting national economic development and indigenous capital. This was a response to the perceived internal threat of communism.

In contrast, in Indonesia the period begins with the hyperinflation crisis of the early to mid 1960s under President Sukarno, which led to rising social tensions. There followed bloodshed that preceded the institutionalized developmentalism of the New Order state led by General Suharto. The spread of sympathy for the communist party in Indonesia was a major factor prior to the coup. The goal of strengthening indigenous capital was central though many of the SOEs and state agencies pre-dated the New Order era.[2]

In Thailand, the period begins with the 1968 social tensions, which led to the reintroduction of elections. The military won the elections in 1969 and mass protests and a communist rural insurgency followed, though the latter was confined to the Southern region. The 1970s, then, were a period of evolving

[2] For example, the nationalization of Dutch companies in the late 1950s and the nationalization of US and UK companies was initiated by Sukarno in the early 1960s.

political settlement following another election, a new constitution, and a longer period of democracy from the late 1970s onwards. As with Malaysia and Indonesia, the strengthening of domestic capital, protection against foreign dominance, and the institutionalization of developmentalism in a set of national agencies were evident.

The purpose of this chapter is as follows: to revisit this first era of classical developmentalism and industrialization in South East Asia from the late 1960s to the early to mid 1980s. The chapter argues that (i) the outcomes were impressive in terms of structural transformation and inclusive growth, and the end of classical developmentalism in South East Asia was due to global forces and the mode of global incorporation. The regeneration of developmentalism into the next iteration was a national response to the crisis that these global changes caused; (ii) in keeping with much heterodox theory and Polanyi, the key drivers were: the handmaiden or conductor role of the state and its core developmentalist agencies. The latter were important in managing distributional tensions to address the Kuznetsian upswing of inequality that ST unleashes. Specifically, the focus on agriculture and rural development ensured a social basis—improvements in welfare for the rural masses—that compensated for democracy. Agricultural development also supported industrialization as Kaldor (1967) envisaged.[3] It is important to note, the absence of structural intra-elite conflict facilitated ST and IG in the region. That said, there was a high price in terms of human rights violations, the curtailing of political opposition, and political freedoms.

The social basis was yet more strengthened by cheap and stable food prices which meant that the large productivity gains were not translated into large real wage rises, but instead into employment growth and rapid capital accumulation, in many ways as the Lewis model foretold. That said, to achieve this, a Faustian pact between the state and labour was reinforced, when necessary, by repression. At the same time, continual education expansion redistributed the future by addressing the skilled/unskilled wage differential (something Kuznets would have noted) and ensured that the forces of rising inequality were neutered; and (iii) the era of classical developmentalism was predicated on the following social structure of capital accumulation: a political settlement that limited intra-elite conflict through building a consensus on national development that would be based on nurturing indigenous capital,

[3] Kaldor (1967) argued that industrialization requires a basis in agricultural modernization to ensure the food supply and that labour will transfer to manufacturing. As manufacturing grows, productivity across the economy will rise even in agriculture and services through positive spillovers such as technological knowhow and complementary markets in services. Kaldor argued that the agriculture and industrial sectors are not only connected by the Lewis labour transition (the elastic supply of labour is due to industry wages exceeding agriculture wages), but also because agriculture creates autonomous demand for the manufacturing sector.

whilst ensuring that development was broad-based enough to ensure a social base to capital accumulation.

This chapter is structured as follows: Section 4.2 sets out the broad debate on classical developmentalism in the period across East Asia. Section 4.3 then considers the empirical experience of South East Asia. Section 4.4 provides a characterization of the period in terms of the social structure of capital accumulation and Section 4.5 concludes.

4.2 Classical Developmentalism

The purpose of this section is to outline the broad debate on the nature of capitalist developmentalism in East Asia and to set the scene for the forthcoming discussion of classical developmentalism in South East Asia. The arguments of this section are: (i) strategies for ST and IG from the late 1960s to the early to mid 1980s were driven by an unambiguous handmaiden or developmental state; (ii) the nature of that developmentalism as 'market-friendly' or 'getting prices right' or the opposite is in many ways a red herring as the state and market are—to echo Polanyi—inseparable. Rather, capitalist developmentalism sought to primarily strengthen the size and position of domestic capital vis-à-vis other societal forces and vis-à-vis international capital. This was done via state ownership or quasi-state ownership, though precise control over decisions was more complex as state bureaucrats sat on the boards of public and private companies, and had in some cases ownership stakes in companies. In this section we outline the contours of the specifics of classical developmentalism in the East Asia debate, discussing the contributions of Alice Amsden and Robert Wade in particular, and then turn to South East Asia.

East Asia, both North and South, has been an intellectual battleground for developmentalism and the role of the state in development. The debate fault lines lay between those who saw East Asia as 'market-friendly' (Bhagwati 1978; Krueger 1983; Lal and Rajapathirana 1987; World Bank 1991, 1993) and those who identified the East Asian economies as state planning-based, neo-mercantilist, and protectionist, and linked rapid growth to state intervention (see for discussion, Amsden 1989; Bello and Rosenfield 1991; Wade 1990; Yusuf and Peters 1985). Within the latter, the state was the central factor in economic growth. The latter identified a set of factors that drove rapid capital accumulation in East Asia as follows: strategic economic planning managed by government, exemplified by five to ten-year plans; government targeting of specific industries for development, and generous subsidies to private enterprise to support these industries through directed and subsidized credit or 'financial repression'; planning of the shift from the development of consumer goods industries to intermediate goods and capital goods so as to build economic depth; reserving the domestic market for local entrepreneurs by maintaining tight restrictions on imports and foreign investments whilst aggressively winning and dominating export markets; and, Keynesian-style manipulation of macro-economic mechanisms.

This 'prices wrong/right' debate was essentially triggered by the World Bank's (1993) report on the East Asian 'miracle'. This report itself was a product of international battles between Japan, who wanted the role of the state in development recognized, and the USA who saw this as a challenge to the market-friendly 'Washington Consensus' at that time, which was immediately after the end of the Cold War (see for discussion, Wade 1996). The World Bank (1991, 1993) argued that East Asian countries were primarily 'market-friendly' with limited price distortions, though with qualification. The East Asian success was attributed to the following: good 'fundamentals' of macro-economic stability, high human capital investment, effective and secure financial systems, limited price distortions, openness to foreign technology, and agricultural development; selective interventions of export push, financial repression, directed credit, and selective promotion; and institutional factors such as technocratic insulation and a high quality civil service (World Bank 1993, p. 88). In short, a set of 'functional' state interventions was identified as they addressed market failures.

The debate on East Asian developmentalism thus became framed around the notion of whether either list of state interventions above (Bello's or the World Bank's) were instrumental in getting prices 'right' (see, for example, Page 1994; World Bank 1993) or in getting prices 'wrong', meaning the state deliberately allocated resources in a way that was contrary to market signals (see, for example, Amsden 1989, 2001; Wade 1990, 2014). The argument that the state was getting prices 'right' or 'wrong' is difficult to sustain given that there were no reference markets against which to compare reality, even in the abstract sense. More fundamentally, as Polanyi (1957 [1944]) discussed in considerable detail, states and markets are non-separable; markets require states to exist and thus to ask if developmentalism—a central role for the state in capital accumulation—is getting prices wrong or right is an impossible question to answer, not only because there is nothing to compare to, but also because prices are set by the interaction of the market and the state.

Fine (2013) argues that there are two stylized schools within the developmental state literature: an economics school that focuses on what the economic policies were that led to economic development and how those policies were non-orthodox (e.g. protectionist trade policies, directed credit and so forth); and a political school that focuses on how the state is organized and how economic development requires a state that has relative or embedded autonomy, meaning it is independent rather than captured by special interests.

Amsden (see 2001) would fall into the economic school and provides one of the most cited examples of the 'getting prices wrong' school, though to frame it as getting prices wrong is too reductionist. Indeed, underlying her argument is a 'reciprocal control mechanism' between state and domestic capital. She noted the commonalities across North and South East Asia, specifically that the developmental state was predicated on four functions: development banking, local content management, selective seclusions (i.e. opening of some but not all markets to foreign interests), and national firm formation.

Amsden's reciprocal control mechanism had the following components (2001, p. 9): a sensor (to detect what to control); an assessor (to compare what is happening with what should happen); an effector (to change behaviour); and a communications network (to transmit information between sensors, assessors, and effectors). She argued that this mechanism in practice is a set of state institutions that imposes a principle of reciprocity—rather than giveaways—whereby economic agents gain subsidies in return for monitorable results. For example, in Thailand, Amsden (2001, pp. 23–8) notes that Thailand's Board of Investment (BOI) was one agent of industrial promotion. The BOI gave a range of support to industry, including tax breaks, tariff protection, subsidized credit, and protection from competition, which were exchanged for performance requirements on export targets, local content requirements, national ownership minimums, and investment obligations with deadlines. The BOI had contracts specifying which were expected. Contracts or licences were withdrawn for failure to meet those conditions. The 'control mechanism' in Thailand was managed by the highly educated civil service. In short, Thailand subsidized manufacturing, and recipients of the subsidies faced performance requirements that were redistributive in nature to ensure social stability.

Amsden also argues that relatively low-income inequality was important in Thailand and elsewhere in East Asia. This is because greater income inequality (across classes, race, or geography) generates a society that is fractured and thus one where it is difficult to mobilize support for national business enterprises and firm-specific national skill-building. She links relatively low-income inequality to land abundance in Thailand, and the nationalization of natural resources in Malaysia (Petronas' exclusive rights to Malaysia's oil) and Indonesia (Pertamina has a similar special status) which prevented state capture by private wealth. At the same time, the fact that bureaucrats and politicians held equity shares or sat on company boards led to a further reciprocal mechanism.

An example of the political school is that of Evan's (1995) concept of 'embedded autonomy', meaning 'a concrete set of connections that link the state intimately and aggressively to particular social groups with whom the state shares a joint project of transformation' (p. 59) but at the same time the state has 'the ability to formulate collective goals instead of allowing officeholders to pursue their individual interests' (p. 45). Jenkins (1991) for one argued that East Asia's growth was due to an 'autonomous' state, meaning that the state has some degree of autonomy from class politics, therefore conflict between classes is temporarily settled, and thus the state is able to discipline both capitalists and workers.

An example of thinking that fits both the economic and political school is that of Wade's (1990) account of North East Asia's 'governing the market' which has a Polanyi and structuralist undercurrent. Wade (1990) asked: what explains the cross-country differences in industrial performance? He critiques the neoclassical position that efficiency in resource use was the principal driver of growth ('getting prices right'). In short, the neoclassical argument was that East Asia did well because markets worked and East Asia got prices 'right' so there were fewer price distortions. There are two variants of the view that Wade discusses with reference to East Asia: first, free market theory that goods and factor markets were freer; second, a 'simulated free market' theory where there were some distortions but these were offset by other market distortions, which led to a neutral impact overall on resource allocation. Wade contrasts these views to his 'political economy' approach of 'governed market' theory, where capital accumulation is the driver of growth and a different composition of investment occurs due to government action, and an authoritarian and corporatist state. Wade uses the concepts of 'government followership' (p. 299) to characterize East Asian industrial policy: the government claims success but success is really due to the private sector. Wade (2014) refers to this as 'market with state' rather than market versus state. Wade argued that the 'hardness' or 'softness' of states is important. Drawing on Myrdal's terms, Wade notes (p. 337):

> Soft states do little more than register the demand of social groups or at most resist private demands. Hard states... are able not only to resist private demands but actively shape the economy and society. They are able to exert more control over the direction of the effects of their interactions.

Wade argues that Taiwan and Korea are examples of hard states. What he means by a hard state is that there is a sense of community among key senior powerholders which leads to little elite conflict in economic advancement and an 'appreciation of the national situation', meaning a shared agreement on the imperative for national economic development (p. 340). More recently, Wade (2014) outlines the development state Mark I and II. He argues that a capitalist state or a developmental state Mark I can no longer create an autonomous industrial base due to (i) the global rules of the World Trade Organization (WTO) and (ii) the contemporary ownership by transnational corporations (TNCs) of much of the global value chains, which makes entry harder for new companies. However, a development state Mark II is still possible because (pp. 793–4) global rules such as those of the WTO do little to constrain certain policies such as competitive devaluations, investment incentives, trade finance, and export taxes. Thus, the state can still act strategically about what foreign investment to attract, or make use of non-incremental jumps in the product and technology space.

Wade (2014, p. 796), concludes that,

> The short answer to why the East Asian capitalist developmental states took the form they did is that (a) their societies faced external enemies capable of overwhelming the whole society, generating wide acquiescence to state discipline; and (b) the owners and managers of capital consented to state direction in exchange for tight control over collective labour, in response to episodes of labour unrest early on. The famed 'embedded autonomy' of the East Asian developmental state came out of co-determination between these external security threats, class relations, and . . . state capacity.

Wade's focus, and to a significant extent Amsden's, is on North East Asia. This begs the question: is South East Asia different? Booth (1999), for one, discusses the differences between North East and South East Asia's industrialization. She argues that the similarities in North and East Asian industrialization are high levels of investment, export expansion, and insulated bureaucrats. However, there are important differences in terms of the abundance of land and natural resources, disparities in income, as well as horizontal inequalities such as ethnicity and regional disparities. South East Asia also has weaker post-colonial education systems, much slower post-primary education expansion, and a differing in the nature of government economic intervention and regulation.

Doner et al. (2005, pp. 12–13) discuss the similarities and differences between North East Asia and South East Asia and argue a thesis of the centrality of 'systematic vulnerability' in the sense of restive popular sectors, extreme geopolitical insecurity and the severe resource constraints that shaped North East Asia. They argue South East Asia is quite different because systematic vulnerability was never faced by elites in MIT thus power was retained with much less ambitious state-building. They contrast the 'developmental states' that emerged in North East Asia with the 'intermediate states' of South East Asia, based on an analysis of institutions (the state bureaucracy and state-business relations) (see in particular on pp. 349–55). They argue that South East Asia is characterized by 'broader coalitions' with more pressure for extensive 'side payments' (elites provide goods and services that only have value for coalition partners such as the New Economic Plan (NEP) in Malaysia or BULOG in Indonesia) though not in competition with security spending. In contrast, North East Asia is characterized by 'narrow coalitions' with less pressure for such side payments.

In South East Asia, although Malaysia, Indonesia, and Thailand had different starting historical points and thus differing levels and structures of output, there is evidence of some core elements of 'classical developmentalism'. These are as follows:

1. A largely cohesive elite that cohered around anti-communist ideology and ensured political domination or elimination of popular forces.

Rock (2017) puts it thus: following the destruction of the left, a set of leaders with political coalitions set out on nation-building with a wish to create an indigenous capitalist class (see Robison 1986; Jomo 1988; Hewison 1989). These were conservative elements of the military, business, and state bureaucrats who had eliminated any threat to their power from civil society or trade unions and other alternative groups often through bloodied means. In short, elite in-fighting was minimal or superficial (i.e. between individuals) rather than structural (i.e. between groups). Indeed, by the 1970s, a political settlement was in place in Malaysia and Indonesia following the major crises of the late 1960s (although this took longer in Thailand); in each of MIT, a developmentalist leader emerged: Mahathir Mohamad in Malaysia (and prior to Mahathir, Tunku Abdul Rahman, Abdul Razak Hussein and Hussein Onn), Suharto in Indonesia, and Sarit Thanarat and later Prem Tinsulanonda in Thailand. In each case there was a political coalition of anti-communists who had excluded or destroyed opposition from the political left, workers, farmers, religious fundamentalists, and students, and defined what it meant to be Malaysian, Indonesian, or Thai through unifying national developmentalist ideologies (the Pancasila principles of national unity in Indonesia which included political moderation and pembangunan—development/modernization; Rukunegara in Malaysia which was based on respect for rulers and special rights for indigenous Malays and Islam; and in Thailand the centrality of respect for the nation, monarchy, and Buddhism).

Rock (2017) argues that growth was built on clear winners and losers. The former, once in power, committed to nation-building projects, typically centre-right coalitions of the military and business and bureaucratic elites, and in the case of Thailand, the monarchy.

The nature of political dominance, though, differed across MIT. Thailand swung back and forth between democracy of a kind and direct military rule. In Malaysia and Indonesia, forms of managed democracy prevailed.

In 1960 in Thailand Sarit took power in a military coup, ending battles between different groupings within the Thai state. Sarit established the national planning agencies—the National Economic Development Board and a Fiscal Policy office in the Ministry of Finance. Like Suharto and Mahathir and others, Sarit espoused a nationalist-capitalist ideology and built a political coalition to back it by limiting or even destroying the role of popular forces. In Thailand, military governments were interspersed with short-lived democratic governments and power was located in the bureaucracy.[4]

In Indonesia and Malaysia a small number of political parties was created to manage and ensure the winning of elections, and make election rules. In Indonesia, GOLKAR became the political party of the New Order; in Malaysia, UMNO (United Malays National Organization) and its alliances; and in Thailand the conservative Democrat Party. In Indonesia, opposition parties were silenced and political critics imprisoned. However, much was done in the form of softer control, for example, the Indonesian military was visible in every village and district as the largest employer and a provider of public services, and civil society organizations were drawn into GOLKAR structures, which were designed to turn out to the vote for Suharto.

In Malaysia, outright gerrymandering was used, as well as state control of the media, and a set of national security legislation including an Internal Security Act, a Sedition Act, and an Official Secrets Act shaped political control (see Rock, 2017). Further, UMNO officials controlled many government projects and used this to support local UMNO officials.

2. The state's central role, directly and indirectly, explicitly and implicitly, in orchestrating finance and production via state-planning agencies, state production units (notably SOEs), and directed cheap credit.

In Malaysia, the key agencies were the Central Bank, the Ministry of Finance, and the Economic Policy Unit of the Prime Minister. In Indonesia, equivalent agencies were the planning agency, BAPPENAS, the Ministry of Finance, and the Central Bank again. In Thailand, there was the planning agency, the National Economic Development Board, the Office of Fiscal Policy in the Ministry of Finance, the BOI, and the Bureau of the Budget.

This demonstrates the state commitment to building and protecting a domestic capitalist class that requires the management of global (and national) competition's potentially destructive impact on infant industry. In each country the process of economic development led to the domination of a small number of large companies. In Malaysia, the government pursued trusteeship—building with the state the capital to latter hand to a Bumiputera (indigenous Malay) class of capitalists. In Indonesia a small group of cukong (Indonesian capitalists) and Sino-Indonesian business people had close relationships with Suharto and his family and received privileges (such as monopolies, government contracts, subsidized credit, and tax exemptions) in return for growing the economy. In Thailand, constraints on the Chinese capitalists

[4] Khan (2010) argues that the period from the 1970s onwards in Thailand was one of 'vulnerable authoritarianism' in which an authoritarian military dominated politically weak capitalists. The country then evolved into a structure of 'competitive clientelism' with moderate to high capability and more powerful capitalists from the early to mid 1970s whereby industrial policy induced rapid growth.

were curtailed and government supported a private sector and favoured a small group of Sino-Thai capitalists, through tax exemptions, tariff protection, and subsidized credit.

In sum, there existed in each of MIT a state that in every way provided 'directional thrust' as Lewis proposed to late industrialization. In doing so, further resonating with Polanyi, it was a state that expanded the interests of the domestic capitalist class by nurturing and protecting domestic capital from international competition, as the structuralists argued would be necessary. In the following sections, we discuss the empirical experience of Malaysia, Indonesia, and Thailand (MIT) in the period. We then turn to the social structure of capital accumulation in each country.

4.3 Classical Developmentalism in South East Asia: The Empirical Experience

The purpose of this section is to reassess, with the latest data, the outcomes of classical developmentalism in MIT. We consider the first signs of a Lewis transition in the shift of labour and economic activity; the attempt to address a Kuznetsian upswing in inequality; and the constraints outlined by heterodox theory in relation to the global economy. This section argues that the outcomes of ST and IG in MIT under classical developmentalism were impressive. With reference to a Lewis-type transition, we note dramatic declines in agriculture employment shares and equally dramatic rises in shares of manufacturing employment and value-added. There were rapid rises in manufacturing productivity but overall growth is driven by physical capital accumulation. With reference to Kuznets, we observe some clear signs of attempts to address rising inequality unleashed by ST. Inequality was flat over the period in Malaysia and there was only a slight rise in Thailand in terms of top income shares of gross national income (GNI), though the poorest half of the population were not squeezed; the expansion of primary education curtailing skilled/unskilled wage differentials; and inclusive growth in the employment sense in agriculture in Indonesia and Thailand, and in manufacturing and services across MIT is evident. With reference to heterodox theory, and structuralism in particular, we see ST which includes large rises in manufacturing and fuel exports driven by natural resource rents in Malaysia and Indonesia, foreign direct investment (FDI) in Malaysia, and external debt across MIT.

This section involves the consideration of ST and then IG. We use the Groningen Growth and Development Centre (GGDC) 10-Sector Database (version 2014) developed by Timmer et al. (2015), which provides a long-run, comparable dataset on value-added and employment for ten economic sectors covering thirty-three developing countries over the period since the 1950s.[5] The GGDC can be used to consider ST over time in developing countries. Data on IG is drawn from the World Bank's World Bank PovCal and World Development Indicators and the UNU-WIDER World Income Inequality Database.

Limitations of the PovCal dataset are discussed in Edward and Sumner (2014, 2015) and specifically are the usual caveats to poverty and inequality data in terms of the use of purchasing power parity (PPP) conversion rates for poverty estimation; the setting of poverty lines which take no account of the differing cost of education and health across countries; the comparability of expenditure and consumption surveys; and the poor capture of expenditure/income among the richest, to name just some of the most important limitations. Additional limitations of the GGDC dataset to those noted above by Fischer (2014) are identified by Diao et al. (2017, pp. 4–6) who note the following: (i) the data broadly include all employment regardless of formality or informality, but the extent to which the value-added data do so depends on the quality of national sources (see Timmer et al. 2015); (ii) the quality of data from developing countries is questionable; (iii) the measurement of labour inputs is not by hours but the number of employees in a sector: thus seasonality might lead to an underestimation of labour productivity in agriculture, for example, though it is noted that Duarte and Restuccia (2010) find a correlation between hours worked and employment shares in a set of twenty-nine developed and developing countries; and (iv) if labour shares differ greatly across economic activities, then comparing average labour productivity can be misleading.

First, let us consider the experience of MIT in the period in terms of sectoral ST.

If one takes the GGDC data for the period 1971–85, overall gross domestic product (GDP) growth rates were typically above 5 per cent per annum, sometimes substantially higher. Further, growth rates per capita were typically above 3 per cent per capita per annum. Two points are worth noting though: first, the volatility of growth rates that is evident in the data; and second, the overall downward trend of growth rates over the 1971–85 period. In short, growth rates were slowing over time. Whilst growth was strong overall, it was at the same time volatile from year to year, and on a downward trend over the period, as the highest growth rates were towards the beginning of the period.

[5] We also make use of the World Bank's *World Development Indicators* (October 2016 version) and the UN Population Division's *World Population Prospects* (2015 Revision). Sector aggregation is as follows: 'Agriculture' = agriculture, hunting, forestry, and fishing; 'Non-manufacturing industry' = mining and quarrying, electricity, gas, and water supply, construction; 'Manufacturing' = manufacturing; 'Services' = wholesale and retail trade, hotels and restaurants, transport, storage, and communication, finance, insurance, real estate, and business services, government services, community, social, and personal services.

In the sectoral growth rates for 1971–present, considerable volatility is also evident (see Figure 4.1). However, over the period, per capita growth rates in agriculture, where much of the population resided at that time, were reasonable at around 2–3 per cent per capita on average, albeit volatile. Growth rates in the manufacturing and non-manufacturing industry were very impressive (though the latter were highly volatile). Growth rates in manufacturing during the classical developmentalism period were often at or above 10 per cent per capita per annum, pointing towards rapid capital accumulation. Service sector growth was reasonable over the period as well.

One consequence of diverging growth rates at sectoral level is ST. Figure 4.2 shows the sectoral structure of GDP and employment relative to GDP per capita. One can also assess the relative labour or capital intensity of production by the position of the value-added and employment curves.

The figures show that over the period there was a decline in shares in agriculture, albeit gently, and a clear rise in manufacturing as a share of output and employment across MIT. The value-added increase in manufacturing shares in Malaysia and Thailand was more gradual. In contrast, the value-added increase in Indonesia was substantial and rapid at much lower levels of GDP per capita. Figure 4.3 shows the decomposition of growth by sector. The total change in growth equals 100 per cent. The figures show the rise in importance over time of manufacturing and services from the early 1970s

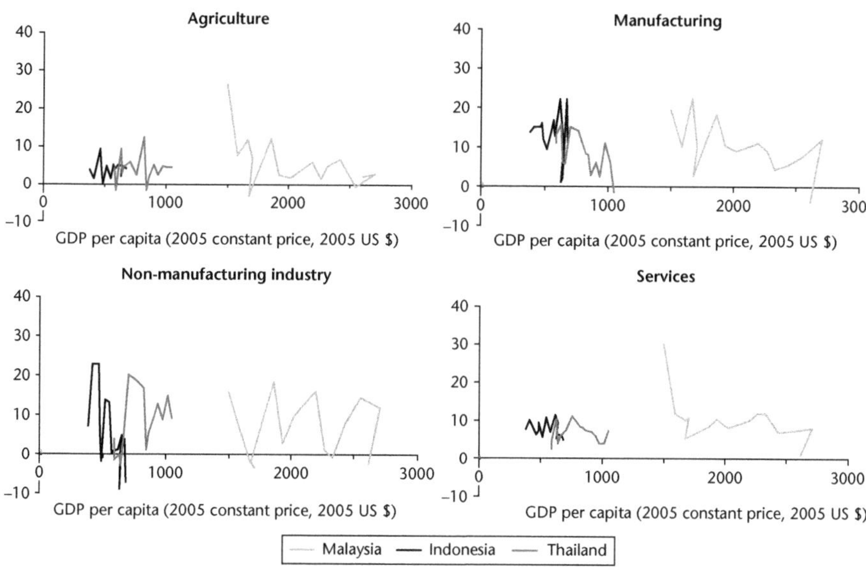

Figure 4.1 Sectoral growth rates (five-year moving average), 1970–1985 (or available years)

Source: Author's calculation based on Timmer et al. (2015).

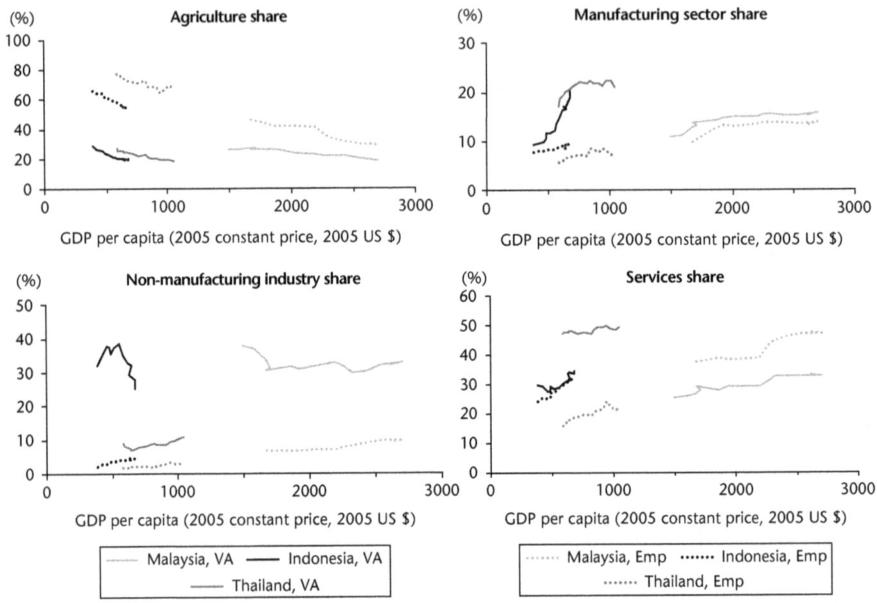

Figure 4.2 GDP and employment shares, 1970–1985 (or available years)
Source: Author's calculation based on Timmer et al. (2015).

onwards in Indonesia. They also show a rather gentler growth in the importance of manufacturing in Thailand and Malaysia where, earlier, the service sector was much more significant.[6]

Next, let us consider factoral ST. If we consider demography across South East Asia, Malaysia, Indonesia, and Thailand all followed similar demographic patterns (see Figure 4.4). Dependency ratios in each country had peaked in the 1960s and then fell rapidly (to what will be a turning point around 2020). As a result the working age population drastically increased in relative and absolute size in the 1970–85 period. Lewis would have noted that this ensured a substantial and expanding supply of surplus labour throughout the 1970s and into the 1980s. Indeed, Amsden (1995), with specific reference to South East Asia, argued that the importance of falling death rates meant many countries industrialized with an 'unlimited' supply of labour as per the Lewis model. Specifically, in the 1970–85 period Malaysia, Indonesia, and Thailand

[6] These growth decomposition estimates are based on the method of Anand et al. (2014) with one difference: Anand et al. (2014, p. 22) assume, as did Kaldor (1957), that the labour share is constant at two-thirds across all countries and all years. This is based on Cobb-Douglas (1928) who argued empirically (based on the USA) that labour shares are static. However, these estimates presented here and in other chapters take labour shares from the latest Penn World Tables rather than make the assumption that labour shares are two-thirds.

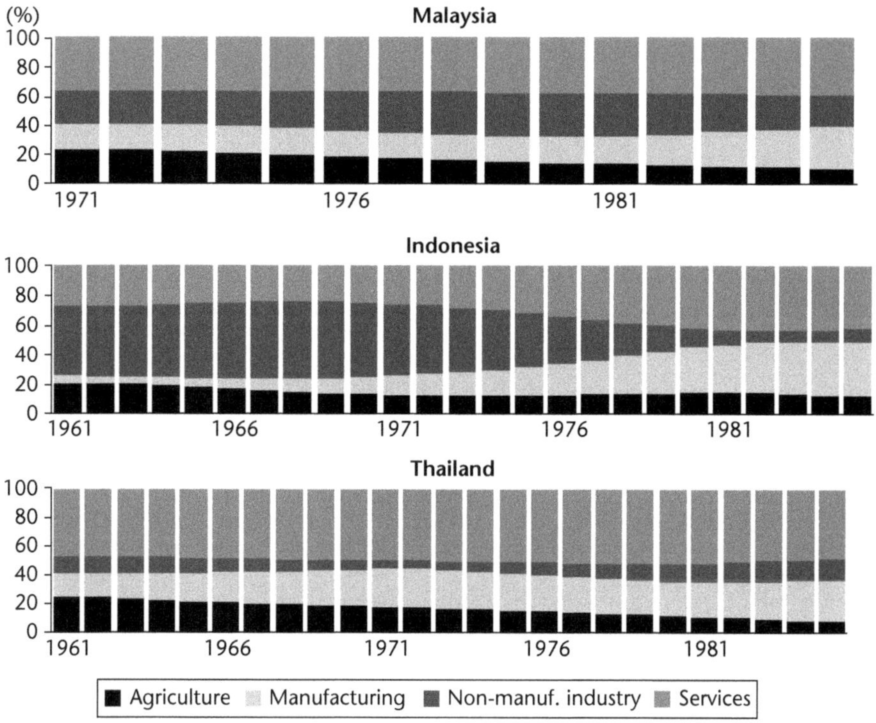

Figure 4.3 Growth decomposition by sector, 1960–1985 (or available years) (change in growth = 100.0)

Source: Author's calculation based on Timmer et al. (2015).

experienced rapid falls in the age dependency ratio (see Figure 4.4). This was especially the case in Malaysia (where it fell over the period of 1970–85 from 93 per cent to 72 per cent) and Thailand (where it fell from 90 per cent to 63 per cent). Whilst it fell less in Indonesia, the fall was still substantial (87 per cent to 74 per cent). Underlying these were declines in mortality rates. This was also the period in which urbanization began to take off. Malaysia's population urbanized rapidly (from a third to a half of the population), whilst Indonesia and Thailand experienced urbanization of a more modest scale though still seven to nine percentage points in this period.

Lewis and Kuznets would have pointed out here how inequality would depend on also relative labour productivity. Figure 4.5 shows labour productivity by sector. The figure shows that there was a substantial increase in labour productivity during the period across MIT in both manufacturing and services. Labour productivity growth in agriculture was weak in Indonesia and Thailand but substantial in Malaysia.

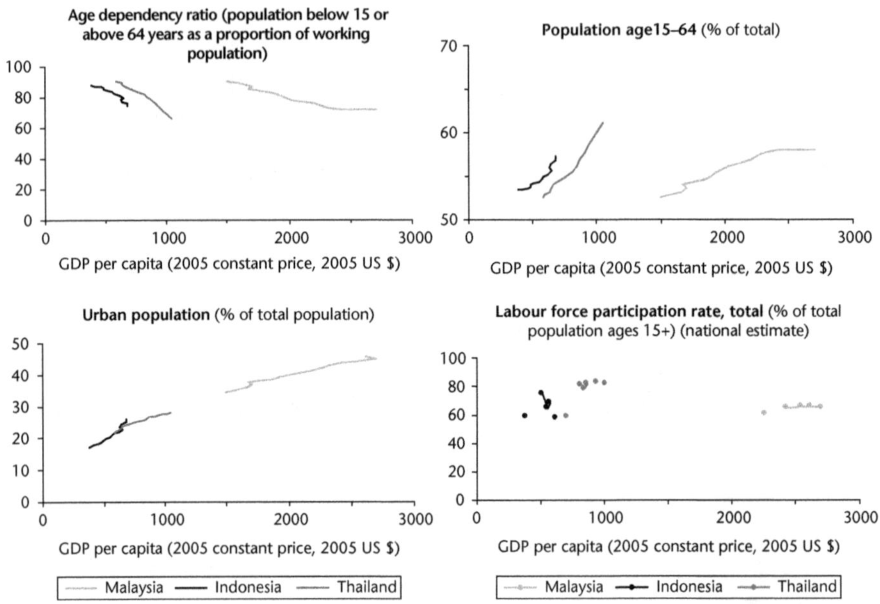

Figure 4.4 Demographic and urbanization trends, 1970–1985 (or available years)
Source: Author's calculation based on World Bank (2017).

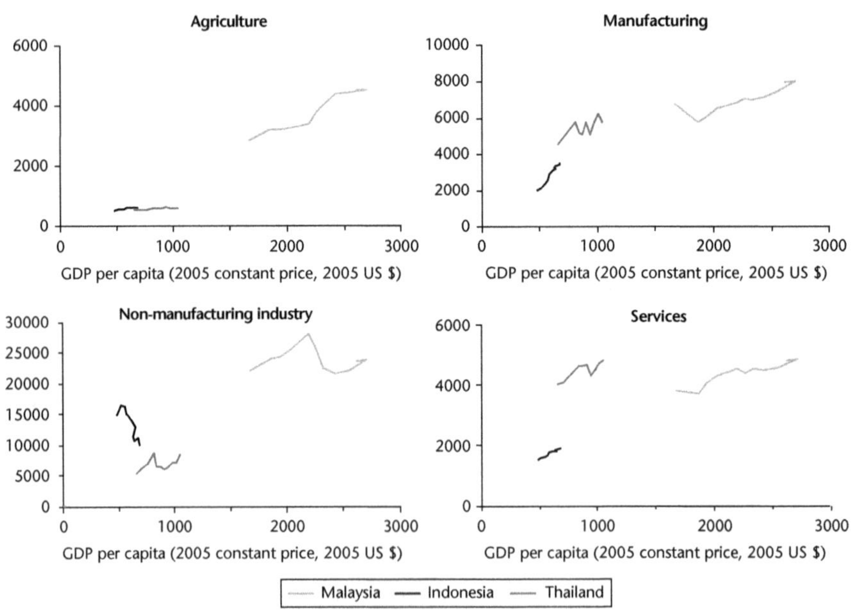

Figure 4.5 Labour productivity, 1970–1985 (or available years)
Source: Author's calculation based on Timmer et al. (2015).

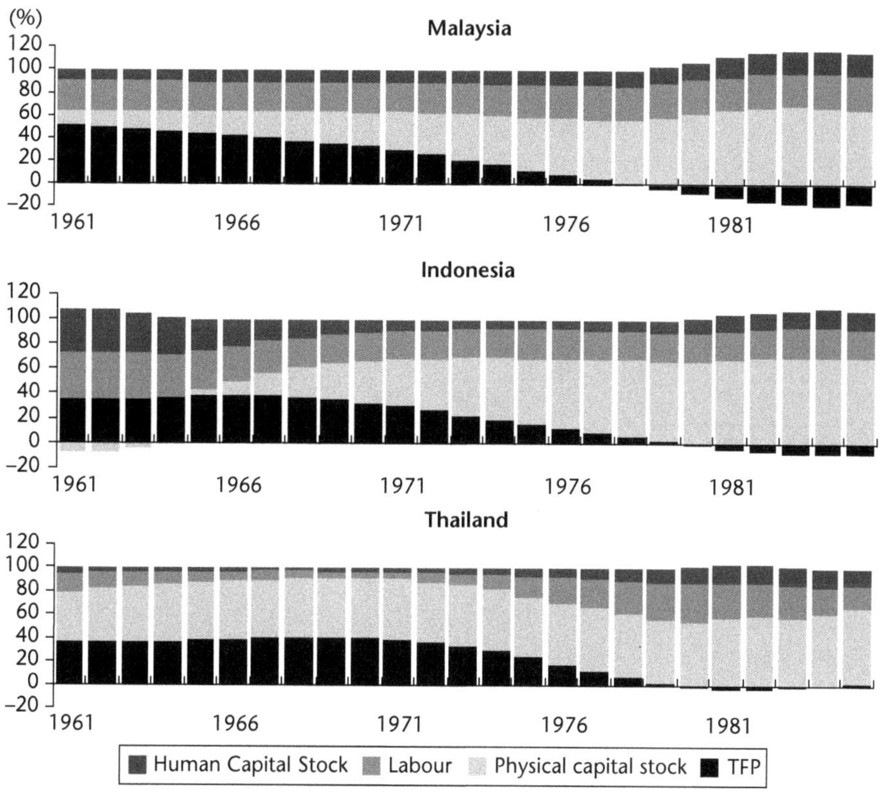

Figure 4.6 Growth decomposition by factor, 1960–1985 (or available years) (change in growth = 100.0)

Source: Author's calculation based on Timmer et al. (2015).

Figure 4.6 decomposes growth by factor (change in growth = 100.0) and shows the importance of total factor productivity (TFP) growth in MIT in the 1960s, giving way to capital accumulation and labour inputs driving growth from the 1970s onwards.[7] This is significant as it would suggest rising labour productivity was matched with falling capital productivity.

Finally, we consider integrative ST as the structuralists might have done. Figures 4.7 and 4.8 respectively show the composition of exports and imports, including the trade balance for MIT for the period. The transformation of the export structure from one of agriculture raw materials, ores, and metal towards manufactures was rapid. The speed of the change in the shares of manufactures in exports was phenomenal. Import composition also changed radically over a short period. Most notably, imports of manufactures fell dramatically in

[7] The usual caveats with TFP calculations apply. TFP is calculated as a residual and the methodology is thus contentious. See Storm and Naastepad (2005) for discussion with reference to East Asia.

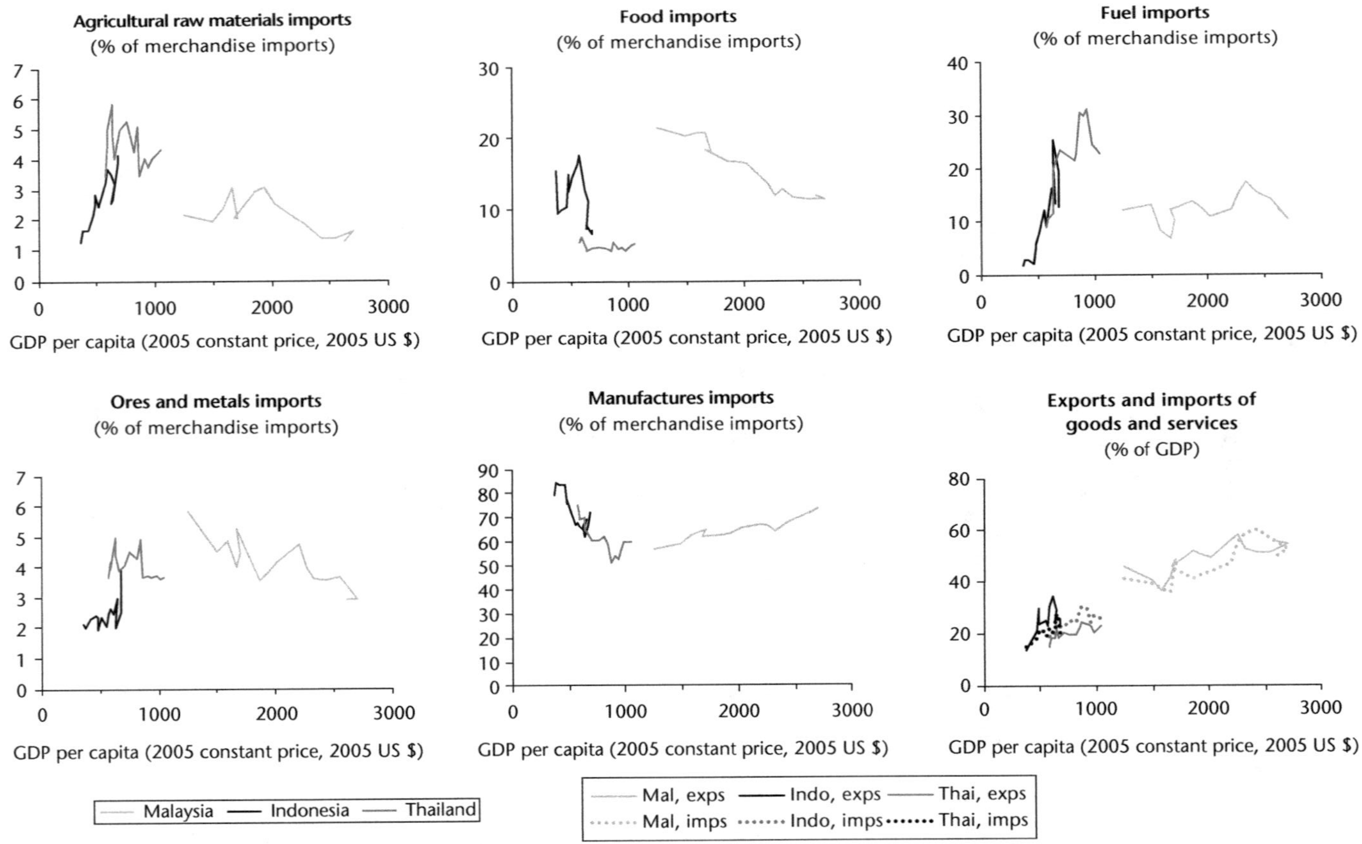

Figure 4.7 Composition of imports, 1970–1985 (or available years)

Source: Author's calculation based on Timmer et al. (2015).

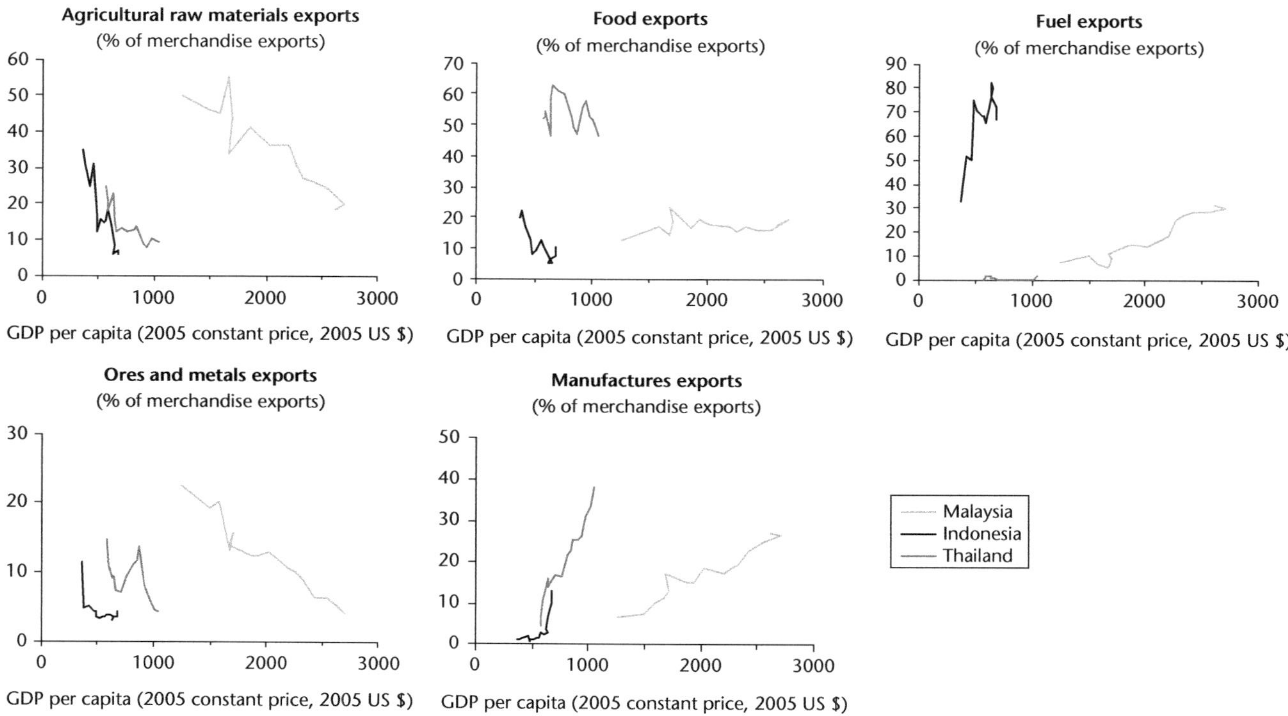

Figure 4.8 Composition of exports, 1970–1985 (or available years)

Source: Author's calculation based on Timmer et al. (2015).

Indonesia and Thailand though they actually rose slightly in Malaysia. Food imports also fell dramatically in all three countries due to domestic food production increases. Indonesia and Thailand experienced large increases in the significance of fuel imports, demonstrating the emerging vulnerability to oil price movements.

The figures show the trade shares and patterns by country. Indonesia was comfortably in trade surplus. Exports were greater than imports of goods and services until the end of the period where the comfortable trade balance suddenly evaporated. Malaysia was also in surplus for much of the period, although a substantial deficit emerged towards the latter part of the period. In contrast, Thailand was in trade deficit for the whole period. In short, the shift in export structure did not bring unambiguous trade surpluses by the end of the period in the way one might have expected.

Figure 4.9 outlines sources of finance. Four central sources of financing for development in the period under consideration were natural resource rents (important for Indonesia and Malaysia), overseas development assistance (important for Indonesia in the early period), international capital in the form of FDI (important for Malaysia), and external borrowing (important for Malaysia, Indonesia, and Thailand).

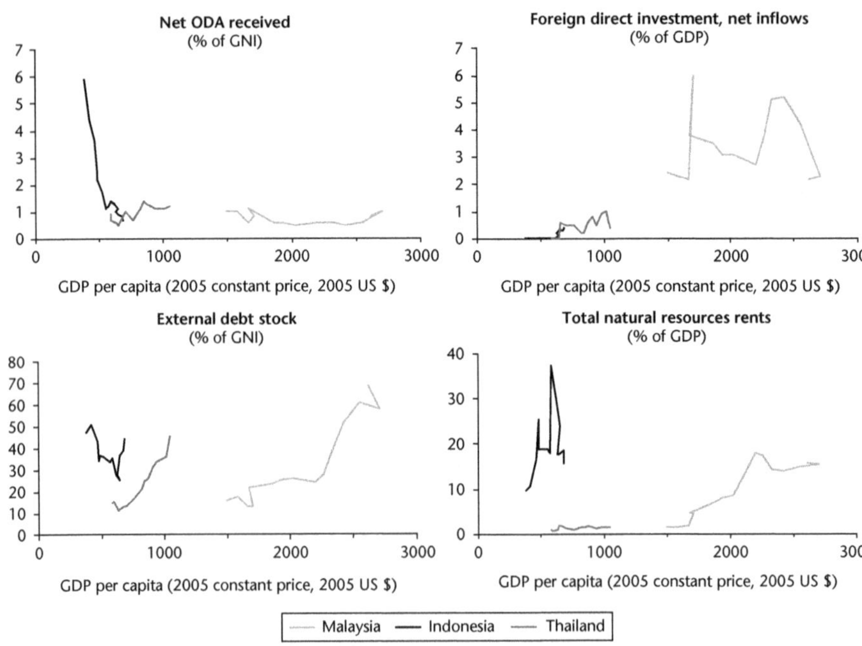

Figure 4.9 Sources of development financing, 1970–1985 (or available years)
Source: Author's calculation based on World Bank (2017).

The mix between the four sources of finance differed across time and country. Natural resource rents data are only available from 1970, but one can see very large rents in Indonesia and Malaysia. In Indonesia, over the period, those rents amounted to 20 per cent of GDP, peaking at almost 40 per cent of GDP in the late 1970s. In Malaysia, the level was lower than Indonesia but still almost 10 per cent of GDP annually over the period (peaking at almost 20 per cent in the late 1970s). The vast majority of these rents in Indonesia and Malaysia were from oil—approximately three-quarters of the total in both cases. In Thailand, natural resource rents were much less significant, amounting to just 1–2 per cent annually of GDP.

Aid was important to Indonesia only (see Figure 4.9) where it averaged 4–6 per cent of GNI in the late 1960s and early 1970s. In contrast, official development assistance (ODA) as a proportion of GNI was much less significant in Thailand (but had been important before this period), and in Malaysia, aid amounted to 1 per cent of GNI throughout the 1960s, 1970s, and early 1980s. In Thailand, as a proportion of gross capita formation, aid was as high as 10 per cent in 1960 though this fell to a fairly insignificant average of 4–5 per cent a year from the mid 1960s through to the mid 1980s. Similarly, Malaysia's ODA inflow in the 1960s was slightly lower than Thailand as a proportion of gross capital formation, and continued at a similar level of 3–5 per cent right up to the late 1990s. In Indonesia, in the late 1960s, ODA amounted to a staggering 30–40 per cent of gross capital formation annually. This fell to Malaysia and Thailand-type levels for the decade after Suharto came to power through to the late 1970s as oil prices rose and as oil production came online and replaced ODA. To put this into context, in the late 1960s and early 1970s, Indonesia received ODA inflows, which would be among the highest (as a proportion of gross capital formation) in the contemporary developing world.

Finally, international capital inflows in the form of FDI and external borrowing data are available from 1970. FDI inflows to Malaysia were significant—in the order of about 4 per cent of GDP annually, on average. In contrast, FDI inflows to Thailand and Indonesia were negligible in the period at about 0.5 per cent of GDP annually or less in the case of Indonesia. External borrowing was essential to all three countries. External debt began at a higher level in Indonesia and fell before growing in the mid 1980s. In Malaysia and Thailand external debt stocks were low at the beginning of the period but grew drastically. Malaysia's and Thailand's external debt stock grew from just over 10 per cent in the 1970s to almost 50 per cent of GNI by the mid 1980s in the case of Thailand, and almost 70 per cent of GNI in the case of Malaysia.

In sum, the period of 1970–85 was one in which development was financed significantly by ODA at the outset in Indonesia. In Malaysia, FDI was important at the outset of the period. In both Malaysia and Indonesia there was a shift to natural resource rents, notably oil rents in the mid to late 1970s. In contrast, Thailand had substantial ODA inflows prior to the period here that fell to low levels, and had little in the way of resource rents or FDI inflows. External borrowing was an essential source of finance across all three countries. All of this made MIT vulnerable to changes in the global economy.

Next, we turn to distribution questions and to IG. We consider the various dimensions of IG as Kuznets might have done: poverty reduction with/without reductions in inequality of outcome; and changes in inequality of opportunity and employment. How inclusive was growth by different dimensions of IG? If we take changes in consumption first—changes in poverty and inequality—one is hindered by the fact that there are no $PPP poverty data for comparability across countries until the end of the period. There are poverty rates by national poverty lines but these—as one would expect—differ in consumption baskets, $PPP values, and so forth, making comparison problematic. In terms of inequality, Malaysia's inequality data is for income, and Indonesia's and Thailand's are for consumption, making direct comparisons across all three countries also problematic. Figure 4.10 presents the available data.

Poverty rates at $2.50 per day—the average poverty line across all developing countries in 2011 PPP$, as estimated by Hoy and Sumner (2016)—were already below one in ten people by the early 1980s in Malaysia (see Figure 4.10).

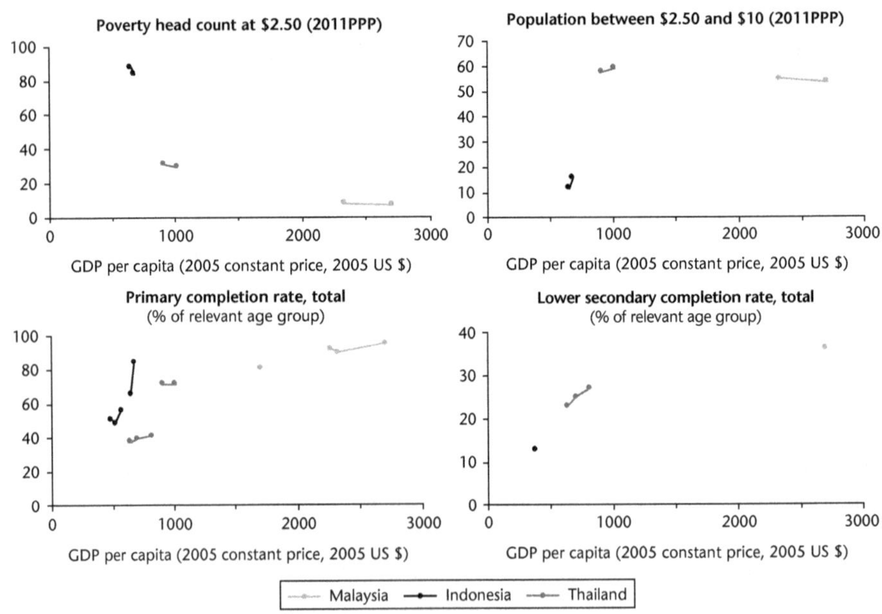

Figure 4.10 Poverty, insecurity, and inequality of opportunity, 1970–1985 (or available years)

Source: Edward and Sumner (2016) and World Bank (2017).

However, they were higher in Thailand at about 1 in 3 of the population and much higher in Indonesia where almost 9 in 10 of people lived below $2.50 per day. At $10 per day—a poverty line developed by López-Calva and Ortiz-Juarez (2014) and associated with low probability of falling back into poverty—even Malaysia and Thailand had notable poverty counts. At $10 per day, poverty affected two-thirds of Malaysians, 90 per cent of Thais and 99 per cent of Indonesians. Poverty at $2.50 per day was falling in the early 1980s in each of MIT. However, poverty counts at $10 were barely changing.

Figure 4.10 also shows changes in inequality of opportunity. If we consider inclusive growth through changing capabilities and as equalizing opportunities, data on primary and secondary school completion rates can give some sense of this. Primary schooling completion in the period in the early 1970s was estimated in MIT respectively as 81 per cent, 51 per cent, and 38 per cent. In short, by the early 1980s Malaysia had made considerable progress and this grew to over 90 per cent of the age cohort. Indonesia also made progress, though from a much lower base, as primary schooling completion rose to 85 per cent in the early to mid 1980s. Thailand also had a very low base—just over a third of the cohort completed in the 1970s—but this rose to approaching three-quarters by the early 1980s. Progress on lower secondary completion is harder to discern in this period due to data limitations. Estimates suggest that Malaysia had achieved almost 40 per cent completion rates at lower secondary by the early 1980s. In contrast, Indonesia had just 13 per cent in the early 1970s. Thailand was inbetween.

Figure 4.11 shows inequality of outcome and fiscal redistribution. It is important to note that this household survey data underestimates the real extent of income inequality because it does not capture well top incomes (see discussion of Korinek et al. 2006). This is evident when one considers taxation data (see Alvaredo et al. 2017) or estimates of the impact of untaxed income on national inequality measures (see Cobham et al. 2016). Furthermore, estimates of asset inequality suggest much higher levels of inequality.[8]

Figure 4.11 shows that, although MIT had somewhat similar net Ginis, net shares to the top 1 per cent differed from 12 per cent in Indonesia to 5 per cent in Thailand, and Malaysia was in-between these. Further, the data suggest that the fiscal systems of MIT made little difference in the period to levels of consumption/income inequality. The net shares to the poorest half of the population are actually highest in Indonesia despite the above and lower in Thailand and lowest in Malaysia in the period. Towards the end of the period

[8] For example, Credit Suisse (2016) estimated that the top 1 per cent of the Thai and Indonesian population holds 58.0 per cent and 49.3 per cent of those countries' assets, respectively, and estimates an asset Gini for Malaysia of 80.0; and 84.0 for Indonesia and 85.9 for Thailand. On inequality with reference to Malaysia, see in particular Khalid (2014). With reference to Indonesia, see Leigh and Van der Eng (2009).

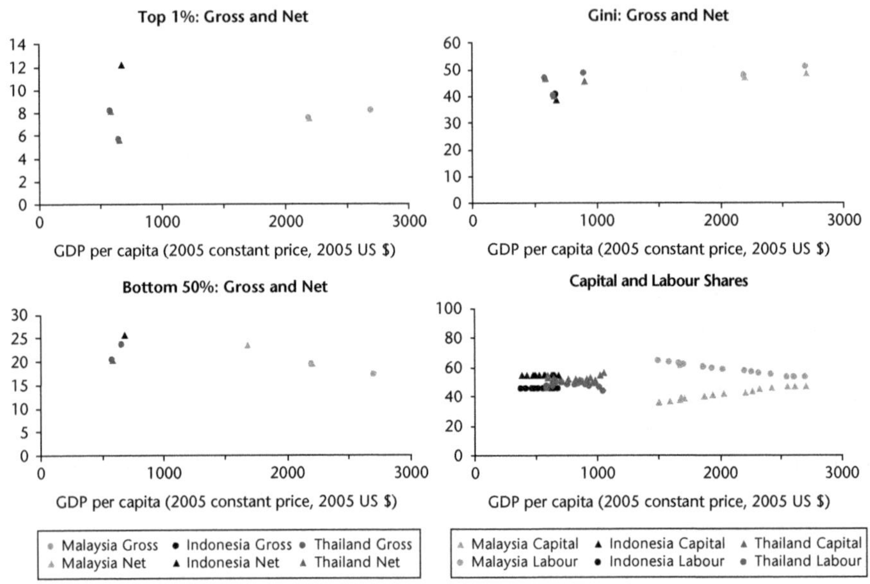

Figure 4.11 Inequality of outcome and fiscal redistribution, 1970–1985 (or available years)

Note: Inklaar and Timmer (2013) assume labour shares remained constant or if missing years linearly interpolation and a set of rules are used (see pp. 20–21).

Sources: Inklaar and Timmer (2013); UNU-WIDER (forthcoming).

labour shares are about the same level in MIT though static in Indonesia over the period, and more or less steady in Thailand but dramatically shifting in Malaysia over the period in favour of capital.

The GGDC dataset shows that in Indonesia and Thailand, much of the job creation was in the agriculture and service sectors with manufacturing starting to become more significant in employment creation only at the end of the period. However, in Malaysia it was services that were the source of most job creation, with agriculture being insignificant and manufacturing only being significant up to the mid 1970s. Figure 4.12 investigates the relationship connecting ST and IG. This is the relationship between employment growth and value-added growth.

Heintz (2009) notes how labour productivity improvements may have a negative impact on employment growth, in that employment growth will weaken if, as Kaldor noted, output is not stimulated by productivity rise, or if the GDP growth rates fall behind the productivity growth rate.[9]

[9] It is Kaldor's second law, also known as the Kaldor-Verdoorn law, which contains a tension of particular importance to ST and IG. The Kaldor-Verdoorn (respectively, 1966 and 1949) coefficient is the employment elasticity of growth. The more manufacturing grows, the more productivity grows across the whole economy because manufacturing provides capital goods across the

The declining employment elasticity of GDP has been extensively researched and linked to globalization and competitive pressures to reduce labour costs. As exports become a larger proportion of GDP this is likely to exacerbate the situation. Heintz (2009) examines employment growth and the productivity growth rate in thirty-five countries between 1961 and 2008 and finds that increases in productivity slow down the rate of employment growth, and that this pattern is getting stronger over time. In the 1960s, a one percentage point increase in the growth rate of productivity reduced employment growth by just 0.07 percentage points. However, in the 2000s that same one percentage point increase in the growth rate of productivity reduced employment growth by a substantial, 0.54 percentage point.

Several possible explanations are as follows: (i) it could be that increases in productivity over time are reducing the employment elasticity of growth; (ii) it could be that the proportion of wage labour is increasing; or (iii) it could be that increases in real wages, employer's social contributions, or strengthening labour institutions are raising unit labour costs and dampening employment creation, though this is ambiguous in empirical studies.[10]

Storm and Naastepad (2005) argue that East Asian countries were unique in the sense that they avoided any productivity–employment trade-off where productivity gains lead to slower employment growth or even negative employment growth, in a unique way that is not visible in the data in any other developing country with data in their dataset (twenty-four countries) for the 1950–2003 period. They do find a weak negative correlation between productivity growth and employment that is not statistically significant, but

economy. Kaldor argued that increases in manufacturing employment raise agriculture productivity (as labour migrates) and because the manufacturing sector is the only sector with static and dynamic returns to scale due to new processes. In contrast, the neoclassical position on growth and employment is based on Okun's (1962) law, which states that changes in the GDP growth rate and rate of unemployment have a negative association. This was critiqued for not accounting for changes that could be due to changes in labour force participation (see Basu and Foley 2013). Kaldor's (1966) interpretation of Verdoorn (1949) is that output growth induces improvements in labour productivity (assuming an elastic labour supply) and not vice versa. In contrast, the hypothesis of neoclassical models, such as Solow, is that productivity growth is due to technological progress. Verdoorn's argument was one of cumulative causation where demand rather than supply determines the rate of capital accumulation. From this basis, Kaldor (and later Thirlwall) developed models where the growth of exports leads to specialization, which then leads to increases in productivity and skills improvements. This then causes resources to move to the export sector. Thirlwall (1979) added that the rate of economic growth will not exceed the rate of growth of exports to the income elasticity of demand for imports. In short, he argued that there is a balance of payments constraint on growth.

[10] A meta-review of 150 studies of labour institutions (Betcherman 2012) covering minimum wages, employment protection regulation, unions and collective bargaining, and mandated benefits with an emphasis on studies in developing countries, found that in most cases effects are either modest or work in both directions in terms of productivity. Distributional impacts are much clearer though—equalizing effects on workers covered, but unequalizing effects on workers outside coverage. It may also be that most minimum wages are set where impacts on employment and productivity are deliberately limited.

if the set of East Asian countries in the dataset (China, Malaysia, Singapore, South Korea, Taiwan, and Thailand) are removed the association becomes statistically significant. In short, the trade-off does not apply to the East Asian countries but is evident in all other countries.[11]

Sen (forthcoming) seeks to explain the extent to which the manufacturing sector does provide employment opportunities. He argues that the extent of employment creation in manufacturing is a function of a scale effect (how big the increase in manufacturing output is), a composition effect (whether the increase in manufacturing is labour or capital intensive), and a labour intensity effect (whether the increase is due to labour productivity) and the relative strength and direction of these three effects (whilst the scale is positive, the composition effect and the labour intensity effect may be positive or negative).[12]

In terms of MIT, Figure 4.12 shows the sectoral relationship between value-added and employment in the period. The figure is concerned with employment creation per unit of GDP value-added. Specifically, the horizontal axis is the log of value-added (GDP, $m) and the vertical axis is the log of employment (thousands of jobs). Of importance is the trend in observations (the line of best fit) either as converging or diverging from the dotted line. Indeed, the gradient of the line of best fit itself, is of significance in terms of the relationship between output expansion and the number of jobs created.

What does the MIT data say? Figure 4.12 shows that growth was employment-rich in agriculture, where much of the population worked, in Indonesia and Thailand over the period. The opposite is the case in Malaysia. In manufacturing and services as well, Indonesia and Thailand were close to the dotted line in the earlier part of the period although diverging and Malaysia experienced job-rich growth in manufacturing and services.

In sum, structural change and inclusive growth in South East Asia in the period of classical developmentalism was impressive and rapid. It was also

[11] If one takes the latest GGDC dataset and divides 1960–2010 and considers the periods of 1960–85, 1985–95 and the 1995–present period, one can see different patterns suggesting globally that the regimes of capital accumulation were different vis-à-vis the productivity growth and employment growth relationship. One also finds that the line of best fit for developing countries weakened between 1960–85 and the 1985–95 period, and then strengthened again in the 1995–2010 period. The South East Asian countries, MIT, are notably above the line of best fit for developing countries in the 1960–85 period and 1985–95 period. However, they are much closer in the 1995–present period. The data show that growth in labour productivity is associated with a declining rate of employment growth in East Asia.

[12] Sen argues that the variation in manufacturing employment growth relates to trade, labour institutions, and human capital variations across countries. He finds that trade has a positive effect on employment via scale and composition, but a negative effect via labour intensity. Human capital is positive through scale but negative through labour intensity. And labour institutions have no effect via scale and composition and a negative effect through labour intensity.

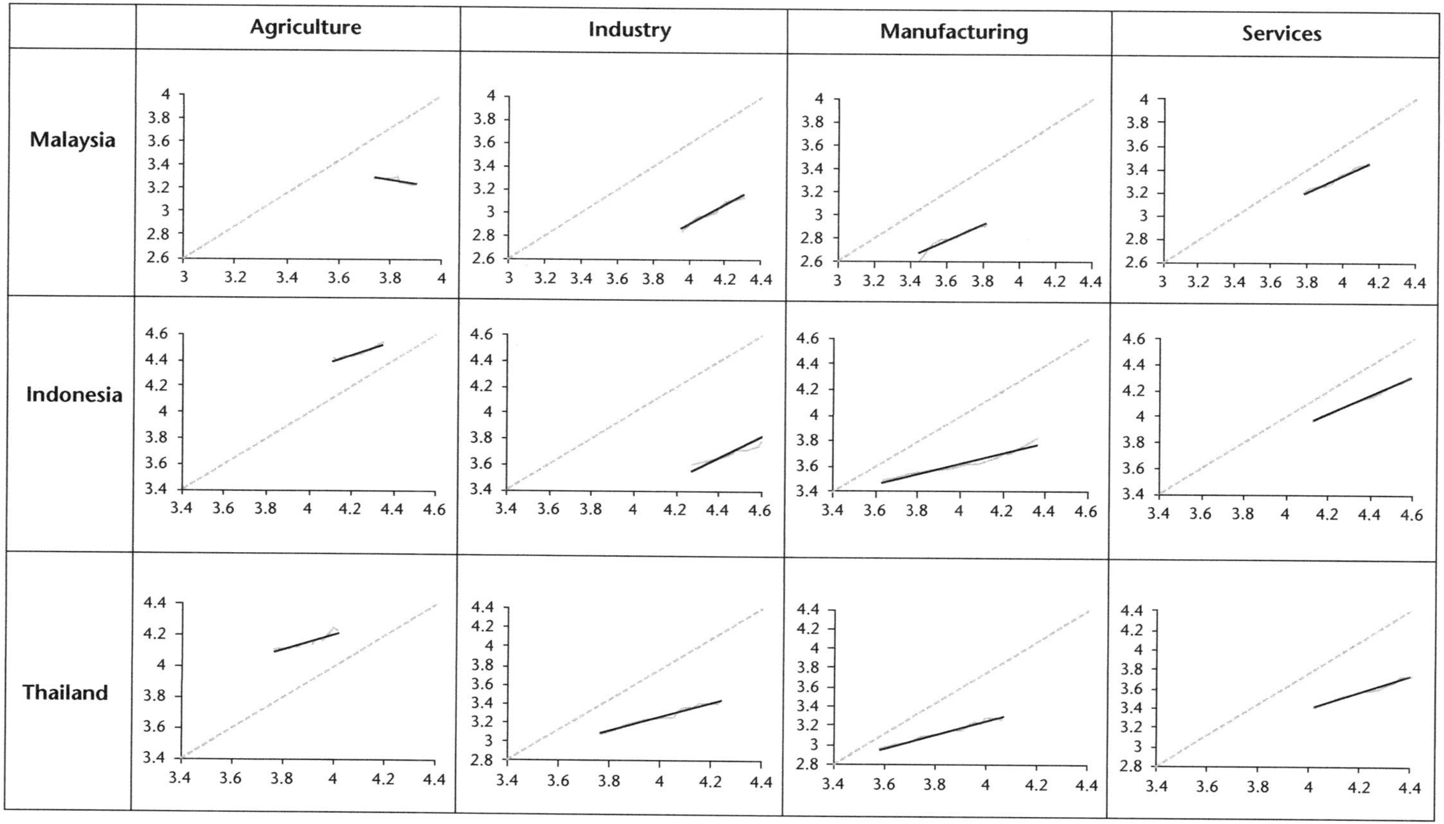

Figure 4.12 Value-added versus employment growth by sector, 1970–1985 (or available years)

Source: Author's calculation based on Timmer et al. (2015).

achieved without substantial increases in income/consumption inequality. How can we explain this? In the following section, we consider the social structure of capital accumulation and welfare in MIT.

4.4 Classical Developmentalism in South East Asia: The Social Structure of Capital Accumulation

4.4.1 *Overview and Context*

The purpose of this section is to address these questions: what was the social structure of capital accumulation from the late 1960s to the early to mid 1980s and how did that differ between MIT? We take the early to mid 1980s as the cut-off because of the crisis that ensued around that time and which led to the end of the era of classical developmentalism. The timelines should not be taken as hard cut-offs: rather, indicative points in history.

We are interested in the variety of developmentalism and the social structure of capital accumulation, which means the role of the state in the ownership or regulation of capital, and the modalities of global incorporation.

The argument of this section is that the era was one of classical developmentalism. MIT achieved substantial ST and IG in this period. The key contours of classical developmentalism were a state–private capitalist pact for national economic development that was broad-based to ensure a social base amid worries about the spread of communism in MIT. Public investment was at the forefront in the form of SOEs and state agencies that acted to orchestrate development. Domestic capital was heavily protected from international competition. In terms of IG, inequality did not rise dramatically as one might expect as capabilities were expanded in terms of educational attainment and employment growth.

4.4.2 *Malaysia*

Malaysia gained independence in 1957. In 1963 Singapore and Sabah, Sarawak joined the federation of Malaysia. Singapore seceded in 1965. In Malaysia, classical developmentalism emerged full force in the period under discussion, though was evident prior to that period.[13]

The 1960s were a period of industrial policy and the impact of the colonial legacy (colonial policies had discouraged local industry). In the 1960s/1970s

[13] Sources for this section and parallel sections in Chapters 5 and 6 are: Alavi (2002), Gomez and Jomo (1997), Hill (2012), Jomo (1986, 1990, 1993, 1994), Jomo and Edwards (1993), Jomo and Wee (2014), Jomo and Tan (1999), Khay Jin (2010), Khoo (1995, 2003, 2008, 2010), Mohd (2010), Ricklefs et al. (2010), Rigg (2015), Robison (2012), Salleh (2010), Sen and Tyce (2017), Tan (2014).

the state was instrumental in plantation agriculture and mining. Exports constituted tin, rubber, palm oil, wood, petroleum, and gas. In this phase 1 of industrialization that Tan (2014) refers to, import-substitution industrialization (ISI) was introduced based on high effective rates of protection (via tariffs, import duties, and quotas) and economic development was based on the attraction of FDI with tax breaks. In the 1960s, the Federal Industrial Development Authority (later renamed the Malaysian Industrial Development Authority) was set up. ISI was strengthened and expanded with finance from this agency, which was established to coordinate investment, and from Bank Bumiputera, which was established to assist Malays so they could participate in commerce and industry. However, provision of credit was not restricted to only Malays.

At Independence, Malaysia was ethnically divided. Political consolidation in the late 1960s (following the political crisis of 1969 and ethnic riots) led to the New Economic Policy of 1971, which was largely about the promotion of Malay capitalists and to some extent there was an aim to marginalize Chinese and Indian capitalists or at least redress the balance between these groups. The NEP had two declared objectives: to eradicate poverty and to restructure society so that ethnicity was less correlated with economic function.

The social structure of capital accumulation was based on an elite consensus, which was visible in the ruling coalition in terms of ethnic political patronage, led by UMNO, and the beneficiaries of the NEP were within the coalition including not only UMNO, MCA and MIC, and not only Malays (even if that was the intention). The consensus was for the pursuit of national economic development in the face of the perceived domestic communist threat. Thus, economic development was to be broad-based to ensure rising living standards, and domestic capitalists were to be supported and strengthened in a state–capital pact and protected. The NEP aimed to eradicate poverty (see later discussion) by restructuring society to achieve equality for Malays vis-à-vis non-Malays though this was worded as reducing the identification of ethnicity with economic function.

Tan (2014) characterizes the period from 1970 onwards as one where Malaysia pursued FDI but with an emphasis on manufacturing exports (following the Investment Incentives Act of 1968) and within the New Economic Policy. The Free Trade Zones Act was introduced to promote the labour-intensive export industry.

Tan notes the emergence of an urban Malay middle and business class, which led to a shift towards more state support. Tan argues that this was a class created under colonialism with state protection, and their demands were established at the Bumiputera Economic Congress in 1965 and 1968 and as a consequence of the race riots of 1969. Bank Bumiputera was established in 1965 and MARA (the Council of Trust for the Indigenous People) in 1966, as the Rural Industrial Development Authority before the race riots. Labour-intensive FDI was attracted to manufacture exports in free-trade zones. Malaysia attracted much FDI as it acted as an intersection for the global value chains of Japanese and the US electronics (semi-conductors and hard disk drives). At the same time, the NEP transferred assets to state agencies and to individuals with preferential treatment. The Industrial Coordination Act of the mid 1970s required companies to have 30 per cent Malay equity, and lending was directed to priority sectors and types of companies by the Credit Guarantee Corporation. The two largest banks were taken into state ownership and, together with Bank Bumiputera, were used to direct credit to the 700 SOEs set up at the same time. In fact the number of SOEs grew from just ten in 1957 to over 1000 by the mid 1980s. These SOEs were favoured in government procurement and financing, and in return met employment quotas to ensure redistribution of opportunities towards the Malay population.

The roles of the state were substantial beyond simply direct ownership of SOEs. Khoo (2010) notes that the Malaysian state was a provider of opportunities (to Malay nationals or Bumiputera in business and government roles), a regulator of business (both domestic and foreign), a major investor (public resources were used to set up SOEs that controlled the 'commanding heights' of the economy), and a trustee of Malay economic interests (equity was held 'in trust' for the Bumiputera).

The role of the state in Malaysia was nowhere else clearer than in the emergence of import substitution.[14] There was a further shift in the 1980s' heavy industrialization programmes (focusing on iron, steel, cement, petrochemicals, ship-building, small-engine building, and a national care project) as the emphasis of the latter ISI phase.

Central to developmentalism in Malaysia was the NEP, which was introduced following the social and ethnic tensions of the late 1960s. The NEP established the following policies, quotas and targets: first, that 30 per cent of capital be Malay and other Bumiputera by 1990. The policy required all companies beyond a certain size to meet this goal in their own capital via assistance to established firms; second, modern sector employment quotas were to match the ethnic structure of the population; third, ethnic quotas were to be met for tertiary and professional education; fourth, there was to be price and non-price positive discrimination for Bumiputera companies; fifth, there was to be price support and subsidized inputs for poor households, especially those in agriculture. Various state agencies led the NEP, notably, Bank Bumiputera, the Urban Development Authority (UDA), Perbadanan Nasional Berhad (PERNAS, or National Corporation), Permodalan Nasional

[14] The late 1950s–60s were the initial phase of ISI. The late 1960s then saw a shift to export-orientated industrialization (EOI) and a latter ISI phase of building heavy industry.

Berhad (PNB, or the National Equity Corporation), Amanah Saham Nasional (ASB, or the National Unit Trust Scheme), and the state economic development corporations (SEDCs).

As Kuruvilla (1995) notes, the NEP was successful in its own terms. The Malay share of corporate ownership rose from 2 per cent to 30 per cent between 1970 and 1990. Firms gained import protection, tax breaks, and government contracts in return for employment quotas. The 1976 Industrial Coordination Act gave the Ministry of Trade and Industry absolute power to direct and control industry by issuing licences linked to NEP compliance. In the same year, the Petroleum Development Act gave the state control over petroleum and related industries without compensation. In the late 1970s there was a massive campaign to expand private domestic and foreign investment though incentives, infrastructure, tax breaks, and labour law changes.

Alavi (2002) provides one of the most systematic accounts of the period for Malaysia. Alavi identifies four sub-periods within the thirty-year period of ISI in Malaysia. Phase 1 was that of ISI during 1957 to 1970 in which simple consumer goods and domestic market-orientated production were emphasized. This was followed by a decade, from 1970 to 1980, which emphasized an export-orientated strategy based on incentives and free-trade zones. The exports of electronics and textiles played a key role. The 1980s was a decade of mixed ISI and export-orientated industrialization.[15] Protection via tariffs was a major policy tool used throughout. Alavi shows that between the 1960s and the end of the 1980s, effective rates of protection in Malaysian manufacturing were high.[16]

In short, there was a central role for the state in the protection of domestic capital, and the regulation of international competition.

In terms of the welfare or IG components of the period, Khoo (2010) and Jin (2012) both note that, as part of the NEP, there was a major focus on agriculture and rural development through irrigation programmes and the introduction of green revolution technology (high yield varieties of rice developed in the late 1960s). They note that these increased job creation because of the labour-intensitivity of agricultural work. In the 1970s, rural poverty was linked to small landholdings and a lack of extension services. The new Federal Land

[15] The former was based on heavy industries, intermediate, and capital market goods, and consumer durables for domestic markets. The latter was based on resource-based industries and export promotion.

[16] Alvari's conclusion is that industrialization strategy, though successful in structural change, was subject to rather more fluctuations than it may have appeared. Although a primary commodity-driven economy shifted to a manufacturing growth-driven economy, dependency on two primary commodities (tin and rubber from large-scale plantations) was replaced with a dependency on two manufacturing sub-sectors (textiles/apparel and electronics) as sources of foreign exchange. Furthermore, a dependency on the importation of consumer goods has shifted to a dependency on the importation of intermediate and capital goods.

Development Authority (FELDA) provided landless farmers with land and the Integrated Agriculture Development Programme (IADP) provided both poor and small landholders with support programmes. As Rock (2017) notes in considerable detail, agriculture was an essential political tool for co-opting rural support. Each of MIT sought to provide the staple foodstuff—rice—at stable and reasonable prices. In Malaysia in 1965, the Federal Agricultural Marketing Authority was set up and tasked with developing SOEs in agriculture markets. In 1971, the National Padi and Rice Authority (LPN Lembaga Padi dan Beras Negara) was established to ensure fair and stable prices and sufficient supply of rice to meet all needs and ensure rice buffer stocks. LPN developed storage, milling facilities. Farmers were given fertilizer subsidies, price support schemes, water, and credit subsidies.

Jomo (2003) links some limited contribution to poverty reduction in the 1960s and 1970s to land reform programmes and the expansion of land under cultivation. He notes that although there was no major land reform programme of the type in North East Asia, new agricultural land was distributed via the land development schemes of the FELDA, the Federal Land Consolidation and Rehabilitation Authority (FELCRA) and the Rubber Industry Smallholders Development Authority (RISDA). As Kuznets may have noted, any land reform would also make income inequality lower in rural areas, and this would influence whether there was increase in inequality as labour moved out of agriculture and rural areas.

Furthermore, the NEP deepened rural development, poverty reduction, and inter-ethnic redistribution via a set of state agencies and ministries such as Bank Bumiputera, MARA, and PERNAS, who were established to raise the living standards of the indigenous population. One vehicle for this was large public investments in rural infrastructure. At the same time, as noted previously, the green revolution increased rice cultivation through double-cropping, new seeds, fertilizers, pesticides, and agricultural practices which raised yields and rural incomes.

In the 1980s, poverty eradication was pursued more programmatically via the 'Programme for the Eradication of the Hardcore Poor', a project enacted to repair houses and build new homes to resettle the poor in new villages with amenities, and a Village Improvement Programme. Such poverty eradication programmes were integrated into the NEP economic plans. NEP plans typically included rural development programmes, education and employment programmes, and asset redistribution programmes. The NEP took the Malaysian state into a highly interventionist phase, framing development as a nationalist-capitalist project. As part of the NEP, the rural landless were drawn into large state-managed land schemes. Further, education (universal primary and secondary education), health services (e.g. maternal and childcare), and other public utilities and infrastructure were improved in rural areas. Finally, there were various income protection schemes such as pensions, compulsory savings funds, and transfers to specific vulnerable groups.

Although the designer of the NEP, Prime Minister Tun Abdul Razak, referred to it as 'nationalist socialism', labour and leftist sentiments were weakened by the NEP's focus on redistribution and full employment. Furthermore, at key moments, labour movements were repressed through the promotion of in-house company unions, diffusing worker militancy and fragmenting existing national industry unions. There was refusal to introduce minimum wages or enforce labour law in free-trade zones. Labour representation was minimal on the high-level consultative councils.

In short, the welfare component of the period was substantial and production-orientated. There was heavy state involvement in the rural and agricultural economy via public investments and interventions to ensure staple food prices remained stable and low and this likely contributed substantially to material standards of living.

4.4.3 *Indonesia*

In Indonesia, classical developmentalism also evolved in the period under discussion.[17] As with Malaysia, the social structure of capital accumulation was based on elite cohesion and a consensus on national economic development in the face of the spread of domestic communism. The social base was thus one of improving standards of living in rural areas where much of the population lived. The state was the main economic actor via SOEs and state agencies, and tasked with protecting and strengthening domestic capital. A military general, Suharto, led the country from the mid 1960s to the late 1990s in what was called 'the New Order'. Robison (1986, 2009) outlines the features of the New Order as entrenchment and central authoritarian rule by the military, the appropriation of the state by the military officials, and the effective exclusion of all political parties from decision-making.[18] In short, an economic and political alliance grew between military capitalists, state capitalists, ethnic-Chinese capitalists, emerging indigenous capitalists, and foreign investors. From the point of view of the masses, the end of Sukarno's

[17] Background sources for this section and parallel sections in Chapters 5 and 6 include: Booth (2016), Dick (2002), Hadiz (2004), Hill (1996, 2002), Thee (2012), Ricklefs et al. (2010), Rigg (2015), Robison (1986, 1990, 2009, 2012), Van Zanden and Marks (2013).

[18] Robison details the relationship between military and private businesses in terms of companies and joint ventures with both domestic and foreign capital. The military businesses included companies nationalized by the military in 1958, assets confiscated, and privileged access to licences and contracts. As a result of military businesses, the military had a shared interest in capital accumulation and labour control. Furthermore, the political domination of the military strengthened the position of ethnic-Chinese capitalists who became major beneficiaries of the Suharto era in trading monopolies, and a wider range of contacts and supplies for SOEs and state projects.

administration had left instability and hyperinflation which Suharto's government successfully curtailed.

The period from the early 1970s to the early 1980s was one of an unambiguous developmentalist state (albeit following laissez-faire policies in the mid to late 1960s). Accommodation was reached with ethnic-Chinese capitalists alongside the protection and extensive support provided to domestic businesses to expand the indigenous capitalist class. Further, the strategic management of international capital via joint venture, local sourcing, and export requirements, albeit with an open capital account for profit remittances by FDI, was critical. ISI was pursued with export-orientated industrialization. SOEs were substantial in size and number, and as ODA financing gave way to oil income, infrastructure spending was initiated and subsidized credit to companies and exporters was possible.

In the decade of the 1970s and into the early 1980s the agents of the developmental state were noteworthy. For example, the Ministry of Trade and Industry set policy and was highly interventionist. It pursued complex restrictive and discretionary investment procedures and licensing. Substantial power resided within the Investment Coordinating Body within the ministry.[19] SOEs, key agents of the developmental state, drove growth during the period. SOEs in Indonesia included the banking sector, natural resource sectors, infrastructure and SOEs in production (including cement, steel, and petrochemicals); and state corporations organizing processes of storage and distribution (such as rice procurement and distribution). Most of these enterprises were inherited from the Sukarno years and were sizeable. The major beneficiaries of the period were senior bureaucrats and technocrats trained in US economic faculties (for example, the 'Berkeley Mafia'), senior military officers, ethnic-Chinese businesses, and, as they grew, indigenous business groups.

The relationship between international capital and the developmental state was complex as there were various forms of joint venture utilized. In Lindblad's (2015) review of the role of FDI in Indonesia's economic development since the 1960s, Lindblad notes that Sukarno's hostility to FDI and the nationalization of Dutch companies in the late 1950s was followed by the nationalization of US and UK companies in the early 1960s and was replaced with a radically different policy position by Suharto from the mid 1960s onwards. New laws as early as 1967 established a highly liberal FDI regime. However, protests in the early to mid 1970s against Japanese FDI led to a more restrictive regime in 1974 whose most notable requirement was that a foreign investor had to enter into joint ventures with indigenous partners whose equity must be above 50 per cent within a decade. At the same time, tax

19 The allocation of import and distribution licences was an important part of the patrimonial network between the state and the Indo-Chinese business community.

incentives were curtailed and foreign firms were pressured into training indigenous staff. The 1970s oil boom meant that Indonesia did not need foreign capital to the same extent as it might have.

In terms of international trade, Pangestu et al.'s (2015) review of Indonesian trade policy since the mid 1960s is instructive and consistent with a more restrictive regime. Trade policy in this period included promotion of strategic industries via subsidies and directed lending, promotion of local content, import licensing, and a currency devaluation in the late 1970s. Imports were restricted and ISI policies attempted wherever possible. Exports were mainly resource-based and the SOEs had monopoly rights to import. Additionally, new SOEs were created in strategic industries, notably cement and fertilizers. There was extensive use of tariff and non-tariff barriers to protect industries. The latter included administrative procedures, restrictions on entry via licensing, and the closure of some sectors to private companies or foreign companies, or both.

The trade regime, in the late 1970s shifted due to the fall in oil prices. A very large number of goods had their import tariffs reduced by half, import taxes were also cut by half, and an export subsidy was introduced in the form of an export certification scheme. In the early 1980s, tariffs and import taxes were reduced again in the General Agreement on Tariffs and Trade (GATT) round. However, at the same time there was an increase in protectionism by quantitative restrictions on imports, an 'approved importer' scheme (import monopolies), and certain items were banned as exports (e.g. logs and rattan) to encourage domestic processing and value-added.

In short, the capital accumulation regime was one of classical developmentalism in terms of the central role of the state, the protection of domestic capital, and the regulation of international competition. It was similar to Malaysia and Thailand in this sense.

The welfare of the IG component of the period was substantial and productionist-orientated. Booth (2016) notes that between 1966 and 1969 there were various policies to help the poor, including agriculture support to smallholders of food and cash crops, subsidies and credit schemes, labour-intensive public works, and other poverty-related public expenditures. Robison (1986) argued that this ensured that growth did not undermine the social base of the New Order. Indeed, the extent of the IG regime in the 1970s is evident in the list of specific poverty-related policies, and the emphasis throughout the period on food, agriculture, and rural development. Suharto ensured rice policy entailed a modernization programme; investments in infrastructure and the green revolution package. BULOG, the rice agency, stabilized rice prices. This ensured not only poverty reduction but that rural income inequality was addressed because rice production was based on smallholdings and there was low direct taxation on rice.

Mishra (2009, pp. 59–64) notes the following examples of the focus on agriculture and rural development during the period: the credit to farmers programme (1966–8), the establishment of a state agency (BULOG) to manage rice markets (1968), a focus on food production in Repelita Plan I (1969/70–73/4), the rice intensification programme (1969), the public works programme (1969/70), the irrigation development scheme (from 1969), and the introduction of direct grants to regions for reducing inequality and increasing human development. Mishra further points to the emphasis on employment and inequality in Repelita II (1974/5–78/9), the development of a health posts network to improve public health services (in the 1970s), the INPRES primary school programme (1974), the focus on agriculture and food self-sufficiency in Repelita III, IV, and V (1979/80–93/4), the income-generation programme for farmers (1979), the rural women's programme for agriculture technology training, and an SME development support programme (in the 1980s).

In short, agriculture was consistently a central focus of the New Order development strategy. Dramatic success in rice production, due to the introduction of green technology in large-input subsidies (fertilizer, pesticides, irrigation), was evident, though non-food agriculture was far less impressive. Hill links poverty reduction to such rural policies (2002, pp. 201–3), the favourable initial conditions (a low level of inequality and nationalized landholdings), and the success of the rice sector, which comprised predominantly smallholders. Kian Wie (2012) concurs that the steady reduction of poverty was due to stable food prices, especially for rice.

In sum, the welfare component of the period was substantial and productionist-orientated. State investments in rural areas and in agriculture kept staple food prices low, and this likely had the biggest impact on material standards of living.

4.4.4 *Thailand*

In Thailand, as in Malaysia and Indonesia, classical developmentalism emerged strongly in the period, though with a longer lead-in from the 1950s.[20] The social structure of capital accumulation was, like Malaysia and Indonesia, based on a state–capital pact for national development that was broad-based, again within the context of elite concerns of the spread of domestic communism. Domestic capital was to be protected and strengthened as in Malaysia and Indonesia.

[20] Background sources for this section and parallel sections in Chapters 5 and 6 are: Amsden (2001), Dixon (1999), Doner (2009), Hewison (1989), Khan (2010), Raquiza (2012), Ricklefs et al. (2010), Rigg (2015), Robison (2012), Rock (2017), Sen and Tyce (2017), Siriprachai (1997), Warr (1994, 2004), Warr and Nidhiprabha (1996).

In the late 1960s and early 1970s, social tensions led to a decade of political evolution. Elections were held. Mass protests followed. A communist rural insurgency emerged. All of which weakened the military government and a transition began with new elections in 1975 which no party won. These were followed by a coup in 1976. A new constitution was established in 1978, which entrenched the role of the military in Thai politics. Khan (2010) argues that what was happening was that the pre-1969 dominance of bureaucrats and lawyers was gradually being replaced with business interests as money was becoming increasingly important to winning elections.

In Thailand, land was relatively equally distributed to ensure that the monarchy was not threatened by the rise of a landlord class. As a result, Thailand's economy was largely based on smallholder agriculture and exports of rice and rubber. In the 1960s, new lands were opened to cultivation and major land reforms were enacted following the 1975 Agricultural Land Reform Act. However, it is unclear if either these initiatives benefited the poorer parts of society.

State agencies were critical to economic development in Thailand. Raquiza (2012) argues that, because Thailand was not colonized like Malaysia and Indonesia, the Thai monarchy strengthened and modernized the state in colonial encounters to ensure its legitimacy and longevity. The Thai monarchy built national state institutions including the military and bureaucracy, leading to an elite of state and military bureaucrats. If individuals used their position within the state for rent-seeking in Thailand such behaviour was favourable to building domestic companies as state and military bureaucrats either owned companies, were board members, or had other joint interests.

From the 1970s onwards, the state and military bureaucrats pursued industrial development in a relatively insulated technocracy. Domestic firms were given tax breaks and protection by the state. Import substitution strengthened financial and industrial elites and was pursued alongside export-orientated industrialization. A close association between the ethnic-Chinese and an insulated, technocratic state apparatus evolved in the key agencies of the developmental state—the National Economic and Social Development Board, the BOI, the Central Bank, and the Ministry of Finance—providing a set of similarities with Indonesia, but differences with Malaysia, in terms of the relationship with ethnic-Chinese capital.

In terms of the relationship with international capital, the Thai bureaucratic elite were arbiters between foreign and domestic business, and the military was the final arbiter of any power struggle. Import substitution was promoted under the first two state plans (1961–6 and 1967–71). In this period, the BOI had substantial powers to grant incentives to firms such as guarantees of protection from competition, tax holidays, and the ability to impose protectionist tariffs.

Additionally, there was substantial infrastructure investment in and around Bangkok. In the 1970s, restrictive FDI laws in Thailand, as in Indonesia and Malaysia, reserved certain sectors. In the early 1970s, the third plan (1971–6) placed an emphasis on export-orientated industrialization and industrial promotion incentives were expanded to exports and the ISI sector at the same time. Monetary and fiscal policy became more conservative to fund subsidies. Dixon (1999) argues that up to the 1980s, agriculture and natural resources drove growth and were the main source of state revenues for development.

In short, the regime in Thailand was, as per Malaysia and Indonesia, one of classical developmentalism in terms of intra-elite cohesiveness, state-led economic development, and state support to and protection of domestic capital.

The need for a more significant IG regime became increasingly evident over time. The Rice Office kept rice prices stable and low through quantitative controls, and an export tax. The government helped smallholders to develop alternatives in cassava, chicken, and fruit and vegetables. In Malaysia and Indonesia similar efforts went into palm oil. Thailand also had the Tambon rural development programme which was in some ways the equivalent of Indonesia's INPRES programme for rural infrastructure.

Although rice prices were kept low, spatial and income inequality as well as weak employment growth emerged as issues which were subsequently emphasized in the third development plan (1971–6). These issues led to challenges to political power from various groups such as the middle class, farmers, trade unions, and others. At the same time, and somewhat similar to Malaysia, Thailand sought agricultural diversification and opened new land in the 1975 Agricultural Land Reform Act. However, the result was not particularly redistributive.

Thailand's third, fourth, and fifth plans (1971–6, 1977–81, and 1982–6) extended beyond growth to focus on the reduction of inequalities, and there were substantial funds for developmental infrastructure (water, roads, electricity), and credit, a wider-ranging land reform programme, free health care, and the expansion of education. However, Dixon (1999) notes that, although national development plans made commitments to reduce income inequality and eliminate poverty, in practice there were few specific policies and those policies that were introduced were underfunded. Furthermore, the period throughout the 1970s culminated in a crisis in 1979–80 following the global oil price hike, which led to an austerity and liberalization programme under the guise of the World Bank and widespread public protests resulted. In short, the welfare components of the period in Thailand were, as per Malaysia and Indonesia, agricultural and rural in focus and based on ensuring cheap staple foodstuffs.

To sum up, the period of classical developmentalism in South East Asia can be characterized as follows: a politically cohesive elite with a shared goal of the national development project, including the building and strengthening of a domestic capital class whilst ensuring the benefits of growth were broad-based.

4.5 Conclusion

The purpose of this chapter was to revisit the era of classical developmentalism in South East Asia to consider the social structure of capital accumulation and the variety of developmentalism. We have thus discussed the debate on developmentalism in East Asia, as well as the capital accumulation and welfare regimes in Malaysia, Indonesia, and Thailand in the period.

The period of classical developmentalism was successful in improving outcomes of ST and IG. Employment, output, and exports moved away from agriculture towards manufacturing as a Lewis-type transition began in earnest, whilst labour productivity was traded for employment growth, also in keeping with Lewis. This sat alongside substantial rural investment and the expansion of education, ensuring that the Kuznetsian upswing of inequality unleashed by ST was generally kept in check. Key contributory factors to these achievements were that the state acted as the handmaiden or conductor with specific agencies; and that agriculture was not neglected in industrialization and thus the state was able to ensure cheap and stable food prices. This reinforced the translation of productivity gains into employment growth as per Lewis's thinking rather than wage rises in real terms. The focus on agriculture, education expansion, and employment led to redistributive state capitalism that neutralized the forces Kuznets pointed towards. Indeed, income inequalities did not increase dramatically which, in turn, maintained the social structure of capital accumulation until changes in the global economy ended the wave of ST and capital accumulation as the oil boom ended.

In short, ST and IG were impressive under classical developmentalism. Furthermore, the developer's dilemma—the tension between ST and IG—and the Kuznetsian upswing ST unleashes was addressed by public policy interventions to ensure, counter-intuitively that agriculture and the rural sector thrived; that education expansion ensured that the skilled-unskilled workers did not diverge in income as much as they might have; and that employment growth ensured that the productivity gains were shared widely. All of which sustained the social structure of capital accumulation until changes in the global economy—specifically oil prices rising then falling, triggered crises in MIT.

In Chapter 5, we argue that the decline of classical developmentalism in MIT was not due to its exhaustion (though growth rates did show a downward trend over time, they were still strong), nor was it due directly to excessive debt (though external debts were reaching substantial levels towards the end of the period), nor to a dependency on manufactured imports (though despite a change in export structure, unambiguous and sustained trade surpluses remained elusive). It was, we argue due to the global oil price shocks which triggered the demise of the wave of capital accumulation and which led to a reincarnation of a new variety of developmentalism.

5

Pseudo-Miracles

Two-Tier Developmentalism in South East Asia

5.1 Introduction

In Chapter 4 we considered the first wave of structural transformation (ST) and capital accumulation in South East Asia. We labelled it as the first era of developmentalism, given the role of the state as Polanyi's handmaiden. It was the period in which the Lewis-type transition of labour, output, and exports away from low productivity agriculture began in earnest. It was accompanied for the most part by state intervention to ensure that the Kuznets upswing of inequality was largely neutralized. The focus of Chapter 4 is the second wave of ST and capital accumulation in a period of what we can label as 'two-tier developmentalism' because of the differential position of the state vis-à-vis national capital (protective) and international capital (selectively liberal). It is the period often associated with the label 'the East Asian miracle'. Indeed, Malaysia, Indonesia, and Thailand were three of the eight countries identified in the World Bank's (1993) oft-cited 'miracle' report.

The second era of capitalist developmentalism was—without a doubt—a very rapid acceleration of the Lewis shift away from low productivity agriculture and towards the higher productivity manufacturing sector. This is evident in sectoral shares of labour, output, and exports. At the same time in South East Asia a process of financialization is evident—meaning the expansion of finance and related services such as real estate and insurance—and influence on policy vis-à-vis financial and capital account liberalization.

This book argues that the idea that the wave of ST and capital accumulation in this period constitutes a 'miracle' is difficult to sustain, though it is likely the World Bank (1993) did not intend the label to be taken literally, of course. A miracle is typically thought to refer to a supernatural phenomenon that cannot be explained by science. It is due to factors beyond scientific or natural laws. The World Bank (1993) argued that the miracle in North East Asia was exceptional and attributed to culture (Confucianism) and the Cold War context, and, it was argued, it could not be replicated. In contrast, the World Bank (1993) posited that the miracle of South East Asia, notably Malaysia, Indonesia, and Thailand (MIT), was not exceptional and could be emulated in terms of the economic liberalization of the early to mid 1980s onwards and state intervention to address market failure.

In this chapter, we consider the miracle in its heyday of exceptionally fast growth rates and ST from the mid 1980s to the eve of the Asian financial crisis in the mid to late 1990s. We argue for a simpler explanation of rapid growth and ST in this period in South East Asia. That is, that changes in international prices—the global oil price shock—induced a crisis. Then a new form of developmentalism evolved which opportunistically took advantage of another change in international prices—national exchange rates vis-à-vis the US dollar and the yen, and international versus national interest rate differentials—to trigger, respectively, large inflows of foreign direct investment (FDI) and finance capital. These inflows were attracted by what the first era of developmentalism had built in infrastructure, financial systems, and human capital—in short, Myrdal's and Kaldor's circular causation or cumulative-causation thesis, that social processes tend to be cumulative and gather pace over time.[1] These inflows drove growth and employment until the exchange rate advantage diminished. National currencies appreciated due to the very inflows that drove ST, export growth declined, and the Asian financial crisis ensued. That, in due course, led to the regeneration of developmentalism in a third era (the subject of Chapter 6).

Here in Chapter 5, discussions once again are built on those in the first half of this book in the sense that those chapters have laid out the concepts and referenced theory. Once again, and in comparison to the first era of classical developmentalism, we consider state-orchestrated development and the management of the Lewis–Kuznets tension between structural change and

[1] As Myrdal (1957, pp. 12–13) put it: 'The notion of stable equilibrium is normally a false analogy to choose when constructing a theory to explain the changes in a social system. What is wrong with the stable equilibrium assumption as applied to social reality is the very idea that a social process follows a direction—though it might move towards it in a circuitous way—towards a position which in some sense or other can be described as a state of equilibrium between forces. Behind this idea is another and still more basic assumption, namely that a change will regularly call forth a reaction in the system in the form of changes which, on the whole, go in the opposite direction to the first change. The idea I want to expound... is that, on the contrary, in the normal case there is no such tendency towards automatic self-stabilization in the social system. The system is by itself not moving towards any sort of balance between forces, but is constantly on the move away from such a situation. In the normal case a change does not call forth countervailing changes but, instead, supporting changes, which move the system in the same direction as the first change but much further. Circular causation tends to become cumulative and thus often gathers speed.'

inclusive growth in MIT. We refer to the era as two-tier developmentalism, in the sense that the regimes of capital accumulation in MIT were selectively liberal in terms of international capital in the real sector, less selective liberalization in finance, and statist in relation to domestic capital. Again, in keeping with the discussion of the social structure of capital accumulation, this era of developmentalism holds within itself the seeds of its demise and its reinvention in a third era of developmentalism or 'new developmentalism' with a new social structure of capital accumulation, which, as noted, is the subject of Chapter 6.

This current chapter sits alongside Chapters 4 and 6 in terms of structure. It covers the period of the early to mid 1980s following the global oil shocks, through to the mid 1990s and the eve of the Asian financial crisis of the late 1990s. The decade or so between the two shocks was one of an unambiguous boom fuelled by substantial, exchange rate-induced inflows of FDI, and large, interest rate differential-induced inflows of short-term financial capital and overseas borrowing.

The purpose of this chapter is to revisit the second era of two-tier developmentalism in South East Asia from the early to mid 1980s to the mid 1990s. The chapter argues the following: (i) in keeping with the discussion of Lewis and Kuznets, the outcomes of ST and IG in the period were, like the first wave in South East Asia, impressive, though vulnerable to a reversal in exchange rate movements and market sentiments; (ii) in keeping with much heterodox theory and Polanyi, the key drivers of ST and IG were as before: a handmaiden or conductor role of the state and its core agencies; and an attempt to neutralize the Kuznetsian upswing with public policy or a Polanyi counter-movement through the attention to inclusive growth in poverty reduction, opportunity equalization (expansion of primary and secondary education), and employment creation. All sought to address the Kuznetsian forces that ST unleashes; (iii) in keeping with the heterodox theory discussed in Chapter 3 and notably structuralism, it is argued that the era of two-tier developmentalism was built on changes in global capital accumulation, notably changes in international prices—in the form of exchange rate movements and interest rate differentials—and the consequential relocation of large amounts of international capital. Again in keeping with much heterodox thinking, the end of two-tier developmentalism in South East Asia was due to changes in global capital accumulation and those exchange rate movements and interest rate differentials. It is argued that new iterations of old dependencies and subordination emerged, as they do during each period, albeit at higher levels of per capita income and more advanced economic development.

In sum, in the second wave of ST and capital accumulation, the drivers, orchestration, and social base for ST were, respectively, the change in global capital accumulation (exchange rates and interest rate differentials), two-tier developmentalism, and rapid employment growth in manufacturing in particular.

This chapter follows a similar format to Chapter 4: Section 5.2 characterizes two-tier developmentalism. Section 5.3 then discusses the empirical experience of South East Asia in the period. Section 5.4 analyses the social structure of capital accumulation, and Section 5.5 concludes.

5.2 Reinventing Developmentalism

In the preceding introduction, we refer to a form of developmentalism that we have labelled 'two-tier' as a distinct variety of developmentalism in the region of South East Asia in the period. One could view this as one handmaiden to domestic capital and one regulator to international capital. The purpose of this section is to characterize the era of two-tier developmentalism in South East Asia, how it emerged, and how it differed from the earlier era of developmentalism. This section argues that the regimes of MIT were neither entirely statist nor entirely liberal but selectively liberal to international capital and in contrast, more statist to domestic capital. More than anything, this variety of developmentalism was largely about countries in South East Asia taking advantage of a fortuitous set of historical/temporal and geographical factors in order to deal with the crisis of the first era of developmentalism generated by oil price changes. This section discusses the neo-liberal resurgence that framed the 1980s and onwards and the selective use of liberalisation in South East Asia with regard to international capital alongside statist support to domestic capital.

In the early 1980s, the debt crisis in the developing world had triggered, or was used ideologically to trigger, a sense that developmentalism and statism had failed and simply created highly indebted developing countries. Much heterodox theory was dismissed on this basis and orthodox theory resurged. Towards the end of the 1980s and in the early 1990s, this gave way to that triumphalism in the idea that liberal capitalism had won the Cold War. Accordingly, orthodoxy theory was packaged into what became known as the 'Washington Consensus', consisting of liberalization, privatization, and deregulation largely promoted across the developing world via the International Monetary Fund and the World Bank.

In response to the perceived failure of the state, a radical new or anti-state strategy grew out of an interpretation of the 'Washington Consensus' (WC), which was, as Williamson, its originator, put it, 'the conventional wisdom... among the economically influential parts of Washington, meaning the US government and the international financial institutions' (1993, 1329). The WC had a set of components (Williamson 1990): fiscal discipline (the avoidance of large and sustained fiscal deficits); public expenditure prioritization (reducing and eliminating subsidies and redirecting spending to education, health, and infrastructure development); tax reform (broadening the tax base and 'moderate' marginal tax rates); financial liberalization (interest rates to be determined by domestic finance markets); exchange rate liberalization (the adoption of competitive exchange rates, trade liberalization, and minimizing of tariffs); foreign direct investment liberalization (to encourage FDI entry); privatization of state-owned enterprises (SOEs); deregulation of the economy; and the enforcement of property rights (through the rule of law).

One might be surprised to see progressive taxation, the expansion of spending on public goods (albeit non-deficit financed), and institutional reform in Williamson's original list. However, the WC, as practised by the international financial institutions, became the wholesale dismantling of the developmental state, without such nuances (Kanbur 1999; Stiglitz 2002). The practice of the WC was largely wrapped up in stabilization and structural adjustment programmes. These were programmes which, critics argued, were imposed on developing countries to ensure that debts were serviced. Policy typically consisted of programmes that were under the remit of the IMF and addressed the short-run concerns of stabilization of inflation and the balance of payments (with an emphasis on restraining demand and consumption). Policies included the devaluation of currency, a high rate of interest, and cuts in public expenditures. Programmes also dealt with the medium term, generally under the remit of the World Bank, emphasizing expanding supply and production via establishing the conditions for export-led growth via privatization, trade liberalization, FDI liberalization, and financial market liberalization.

In South East Asia, the period of the early to mid 1980s began with a set of crises caused by changes in the global economy, notably the dramatic rise of oil prices in the late 1970s and the equally dramatic fall in oil prices in the early to mid 1980s. The rise in oil prices in the late 1970s, building on early oil price rises, triggered a crisis in Thailand as a net oil importer. The crisis, in short, was an over-dependency on imported oil for industrialization. In Malaysia and Indonesia, it was the collapse of oil prices in the early to mid 1980s that triggered crises. For them, the crises were an over-dependency on oil for export earnings and development finance. These crises in South East Asia led to a new search for drivers of national economic development, and developmentalism reinvented itself from classical developmentalism to a two-tier variety of developmentalism.

In South East Asia, the early 1980s marked a period of liberalization with respect to FDI and international financial capital. In the case of Thailand it was associated with a World Bank programme. In the case of Malaysia and Indonesia it was a 'voluntary' adjustment in the sense that it was a 'voluntary' domestic decision rather than one imposed by the World Bank or the

IMF. However, the regimes pursued were not those of the WC as the original iteration, nor that as practised by the IMF and World Bank, but highly selective liberalization to international capital in certain sectors. This selective liberalization was done to take advantage of fortuitous exchange rate movements vis-à-vis the US dollar and Japanese yen, and it led to the relocation of regional FDI.[2] MIT also took advantage of interest rate differentials and enacted further financial and capital account liberalization to attract international financial capital. In short, MIT took advantage of changing global prices in terms of exchange rate movements and interest rate differentials. That said, the liberalization of entry for international capital was coupled with the strengthening and expansion of protection for domestic capital, which was inherited from the first era of developmentalism.

There were evidently some differences across MIT. For example, only in Malaysia was there a substantial privatization programme, which transferred state assets to domestic capitalists by design rather than through open competition. Malaysia also engineered a shift in emphasis in its central developmentalist plank of the New Economic Plan (NEP) in the sense that the NEP sought to strengthen the indigenous capitalist class rather than have the state lead redistributive development per se. In Thailand, as noted, the period is initially shaped by a severe and non-voluntary structural adjustment programme following the oil price shocks. In Malaysia and Indonesia, the period is one of adjustment to declining oil prices. What is common across the three countries is a process of liberalization or opening to international capital, which differentiates it from the era of classical developmentalism discussed in Chapter 4. This is a process that, together with exchange rate movements, led to a large movement of capital—FDI, commercial loans, and portfolio capital—into South East Asia.

As noted in Chapter 4, strategies for ST and, implicitly, IG from the 1950s/1960s to the early 1980s were, to a considerable extent, driven by a strong developmental state. This is not a contentious argument. Similar arguments in some ways hold for the boom decade of the mid 1980s to the mid 1990s in MIT. It is not contested that the liberalization of finance and FDI triggered large capital inflows (and trade liberalization yet further added to the attractiveness to international capital). The state rolled back its remit in terms of international capital to drive capital accumulation or came to a new accommodation to allow international capital inflows whilst not removing protection for domestic capital. The timing was fortuitous in the sense that exchange rate movements and interest rate differentials vis-à-vis the global economy drove a boom.

[2] This is that which has been referred to Asia's 'flying geese paradigm/model' as regional capital relocates and countries gradually move up the value chain.

In a sense, rather than getting prices 'wrong' or 'right', it was more a case of MIT being in the right geographical *place* to allow relocation of international capital at the right *time* in history, following the G5 agreement in September 1985 (known as the Plaza II Accord), to manufacture a depreciation of the US dollar against the Japanese yen and German Deutschemark (DM) to correct trade imbalances. Consequentially, the yen and DM increased in value relative to the dollar and at the same time South East Asia, having already built infrastructure, human capital, and a financial system in the first era of developmentalism, became an attractive place for FDI to relocate to. Indonesia had major devaluations in 1983 and 1986 and Thailand too in 1984 and 1985. The Malaysian ringgit also depreciated substantially. The depreciations were against the dollar and yen in particular but also against the Korean, Taiwanese, and Singapore currencies. All of which lowered the cost of production in MIT for relocating FDI relative to other sites. Furthermore, the withdrawal of privileges to the North East Asian economies in 1988 under the General System of Preferences induced with further force the relocation of capital from North East Asia to South East Asia.

In short, within a framework best described as two-tier developmentalism, MIT pursued economic development from the early to mid 1980s to the mid 1990s via an accommodation with, or opening to, international capital to address an immediate crisis whilst, at the same time, keeping much of classical developmentalism or Polanyi's handmaiden with regards to domestic capital. It also represents Polanyi's double movement—the expansion of the market society and in due course the counter-movement. As it had done under classical developmentalism, the state played a protectionist–developmentalist role to indigenous capital but sought to be selectively liberal to international capital in the real sector, and less selectively liberal to finance capital.

The exchange rate movements suddenly made MIT highly attractive to relocating regional capital and MIT opened up FDI in specific sectors, notably textiles/apparel and electronics, to export-orientated FDI. Financial and capital account liberalization led to large financial capital inflows and a process of financialization gained speed. As Palley (2007, pp. 1–3) notes, financialization is a process of financial markets, institutions, and elites gaining greater political and policy influence.[3] The excessive expansion of the financial sector relative to the needs of the real sector for finance can lead to the dramatic

[3] Epstein (2001, p. 1) defines financialization thus: 'Financialization refers to the increasing importance of financial markets, financial motives, financial institutions, and financial elites in the operation of the economy and its governing institutions, both at the national and international level'. The measurement of financialization of a given economy is typically the share of GDP in Finance, Insurance and Real Estate (FIRE). However, an underdeveloped financial system can hinder growth. Additionally, in order to analyse how dependent the 'economy' is on the domestic financial sector, indicators such as domestic credit by financial sector (% of GDP) and stock market capitalization of listed domestic companies (% of GDP) could be analysed.

Table 5.1 GDP share accounted for by finance, insurance, real estate and business services (valued-added 2005 constant prices, 2005 US$)

	1970	1975	1980	1985	1990	1995	1996	1997
Malaysia	2.5	4.5	5.1	6.1	6.9	8.9	9.4	10.4
Indonesia	1.3	1.2	2.0	4.0	5.5	6.9	6.8	7.0
Thailand	1.2	1.3	1.6	1.8	4.6	7.2	6.9	6.2

Source: Author's calculation based on Timmer et al. (2015). Note: Data is for FIRE + renting + business activities (i.e. ISIC Version 3.1 Code J + K) in aggregate. Timmer et al. (2015) do not have separate data for finance and insurance (code J), Real estate and renting+business activities (code K).

expansion of debt, crises, and recession, and prolonged slower growth. Such a process of financialization is evident in the late 1980s and early 1990s in MIT towards the end of the heady second wave of ST and capital accumulation (see Table 5.1). Malaysia's FIRE ratio jumped from 5.1 per cent in 1980 to 10.4 per cent in 1997; Indonesia's ratio rose form 2.0 per cent in 1980 to 7.0 per cent in 1997 and Thailand's from 1.6 per cent in 1980 to 6.2 per cent in 1997.

The hyperactive orchestra conductor of classical developmentalism became a dual conductor of one kind to domestic capital and a conductor of another kind to international capital. In addition to the opening of certain production sectors, there were widespread financial and capital account liberalization measures. The loss of the conductor's control over international finance capital would become a major Achilles heel as the inflow of short-term capital grew. This reached a crescendo in the mid 1990s prior to the Asian financial crisis of the late 1990s, which demonstrated the limits of this variety of developmentalism, as its ST was ultimately based on exchange rate movements and market sentiments, both of which could change.

Those exchange rates and sentiments shifted quite suddenly in the mid 1990s in response to slowing export growth. This was partly as a result of appreciating real exchange rates in MIT due to financial capital inflows themselves, and of MIT becoming less competitive vis-à-vis the newly emerging low-cost producers, such as China and Vietnam, who had entered the very same global value chains of apparel/textiles and electronics assembly in the early to mid 1990s that MIT had entered in the 1980s. The crisis and outflow of capital was merely a surface-level reaction to underlying structural underdevelopment inherent in FDI-led growth, which emerged from two-tier developmentalism. This structural underdevelopment included poor domestic company linkages to FDI and thus FDI enclave economies, and a 'stickiness' in terms of MIT's entry point into global value chains due to FDI-dominated production (FDI was playing to the tune of a different conductor—their own management and board).

MIT had different starting points for the period, but the core elements of two-tier developmentalism were present. There was a redirection of the development project by the state towards international capital in response to the economic crisis that oil price changes caused. This was, in part, due to the strengthened hand of neoclassical economic technocrats who used the economic crisis to push, as far as was politically feasible, economic liberalization. This led to domestic capital protection remaining as a political response to the economy opening up to international capital. However, the state's role was not, as in other countries, to withdraw, privatize, fully liberalize, and deregulate. Rather, the state's role simply became strategic with regard to an accommodation with international capital.

Only in Malaysia were SOEs actually privatized and even then, that process was in no way a competitive tender but a sell-off to indigenous capitalists. Across MIT state-planning agencies, national development plans continued unabated. The banking sectors continued to be state-owned credit directors, protection of domestic capital continued alongside the liberalization of specific sectors to international capital, stock markets were launched and opened to international capital, and commercial lending overseas was substantially liberalized as crisis-hit countries sought new sources of development finance.

The protective state vis-à-vis domestic capital continued but took new forms. For example, as tariff barriers were lowered, non-tariff barriers to trade (e.g. safety requirements) rose to have the same effect, and although some sectors were open to international capital, monopolies, licences and so forth remained very much within state control and allocation, and were reserved for domestic capitalists where deemed appropriate.

In sum, capitalist developmentalism took the form of a two-tier variety across MIT due to changes in global capital accumulation which were to trigger a rapid acceleration of the Lewis transition and one in which the Kuznetsian upswing unleashed by ST had to be counterbalanced with public policy. In Section 5.3, we discuss the empirical experience of MIT in this period.

5.3 Two-tier Developmentalism in South East Asia: The Empirical Experience

The purpose of this section is to assess ST and IG during two-tier developmentalism in MIT. We revisit the period in terms of the same set of indicators discussed in Chapter 4. This section argues that the outcomes of ST and IG in MIT under two-tier developmentalism were spectacular though ultimately unsustainable. With reference to the Lewisian transition, we note again dramatic rises in manufacturing shares of employment and value-added. In contrast, service sector shares were largely static across the period. In short, a shift from agriculture directly to manufacturing was unambiguous. There were once again rapid rises in manufacturing productivity and these also extended to service sector productivity (as Kaldor predicted). Overall, growth was driven by physical capital inputs. With reference to Kuznets, it is evident that the attempts to address the forces of inequality that ST unleashed in the Lewisian transition were successful in the sense that, strikingly, the shares of gross national income (GNI) to the top and poorest half of society were surprisingly flat. Poverty also declined. However, at the same time the population in the insecure group ($2.50–$10) expanded as people moved out of poverty. Primary education completion became virtually universal, and attention shifted to lower secondary as the scope to address the skilled/unskilled wages divergence through expanding primary schooling was exhausted. Further, there was inclusive growth in terms of employment growth in manufacturing and services across MIT. Agriculture, too, in Indonesia continued to be inclusive in that sense. In contrast, Thailand and Malaysia agriculture did not. With reference to heterodox theory and structuralism in particular, we see ST, which continues to be shaped by large rises in manufacturing exports and, importantly, a decline in fuel and ore/metal exports. That said, ST remained financed to some extent by natural resource rents in Malaysia and Indonesia, FDI in Malaysia, and by external debt in both Indonesia and Thailand.

In this section we (i) consider ST in terms of sectoral ST, factoral ST, and integrative ST; (ii) consider IG in terms of changes in consumption (poverty and inequality) and capabilities (education levels and employment growth).

First, let us consider the experience of MIT in the period in terms of sectoral ST. If one takes the data in the Groningen Growth and Development Centre (GGDC) dataset in the period of the mid 1980s to the mid 1990s, like the classical developmentalism period preceding it, one sees that this was a period of rapid growth. The overall gross domestic product (GDP) growth rates during this period were phenomenal. This is all the more startling as growth rates were low at the beginning of the period. Aggregate growth rates were typically in the order of 6–10 per cent per annum and per capita growth rates in the region of 4–6 per cent (a notably higher rate than the preceding period). However, even before the Asian financial crisis, growth was unequivocally weakening in both Indonesia and Thailand. Sectoral growth rates (see Figure 5.1) were similarly phenomenal in manufacturing and services. In both, growth rates were around 10 per cent or more per annum for much of the decade. Agricultural sector growth was more robust in the earlier part of the period, though volatile. In the later part of the period, growth in agriculture was, in general, weaker, and even contracting in some years in Thailand and Malaysia. Fortunately, the movement of the labour force away from agriculture had begun in earnest.

The differing performances of each sector generated a period of unequivocal structural change. Figure 5.2 shows the increases in GDP shares to manufacturing and increases in shares of employment as well. Not surprisingly, value-added and employment shares diminished in agriculture accordingly. It is fair to say that there were no visible signs of the plateau in manufacturing shares

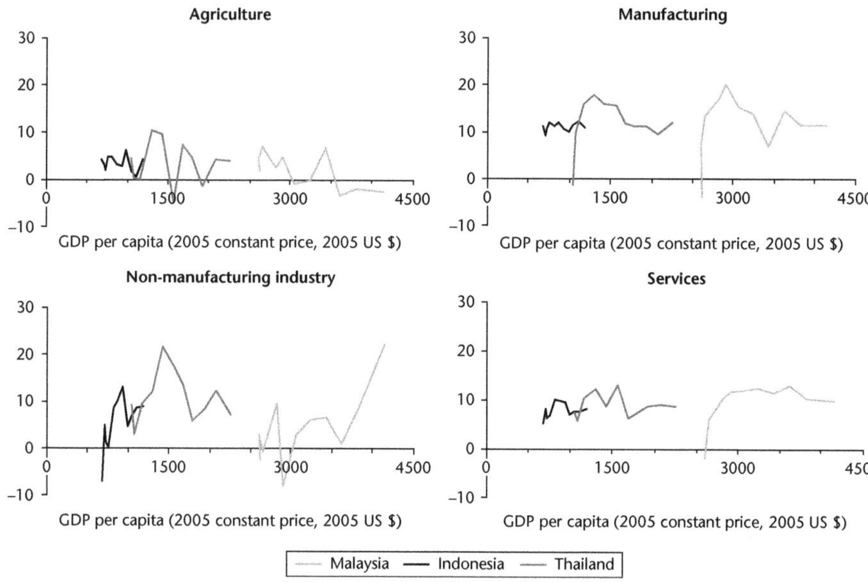

Figure 5.1 Sectoral growth rates (five-year moving average), 1985–1995 (or available years)

Source: Author's calculation based on Timmer et al. (2015).

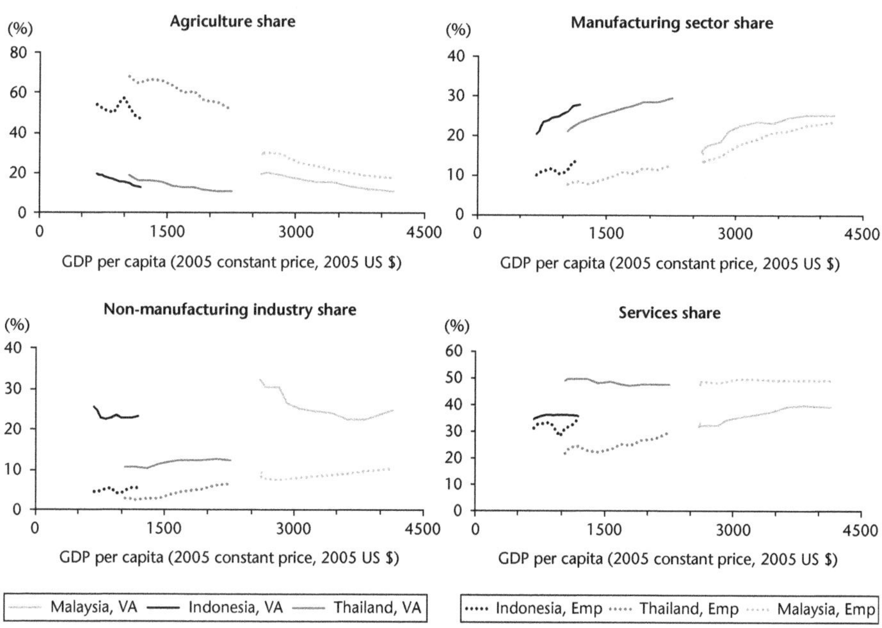

Figure 5.2 GDP and employment shares, 1985–1995 (or available years)

Source: Author's calculation based on Timmer et al. (2015).

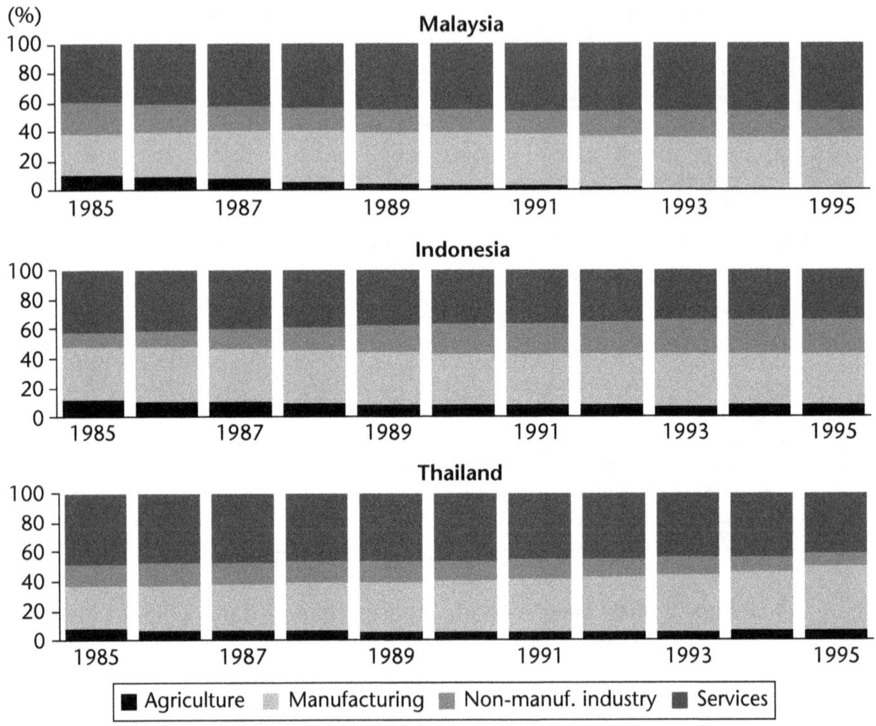

Figure 5.3 Growth decomposition by sector, 1985–1995 (or available years) (change in growth = 100.0)

Source: Author's calculation based on Timmer et al. (2015).

in MIT during the period that was to later emerge in the 2000s. The experience of services was more mixed. Value-added shares in services only increased in Malaysia (despite the high growth rates noted previously). However, employment shares in services increased notably in Thailand and Indonesia in the latter part of the period.

Figure 5.3 shows the decomposition of growth by sector. The total change in growth equals 100 per cent. The figure shows the importance of manufacturing and services in driving growth. Each country's growth has a substantial contribution from these two sectors, together accounting for 70–80 per cent of growth every year. Agriculture became almost irrelevant.

Next, let us consider factoral ST. If we consider, as in Chapter 4, demographic change, we find that in the 1985 to 1995 period the dependency ratio continued to fall (see Figure 5.4). This was rapid in Thailand (63 per cent to 48 per cent), though less so in Indonesia (74 per cent to 61 per cent), and

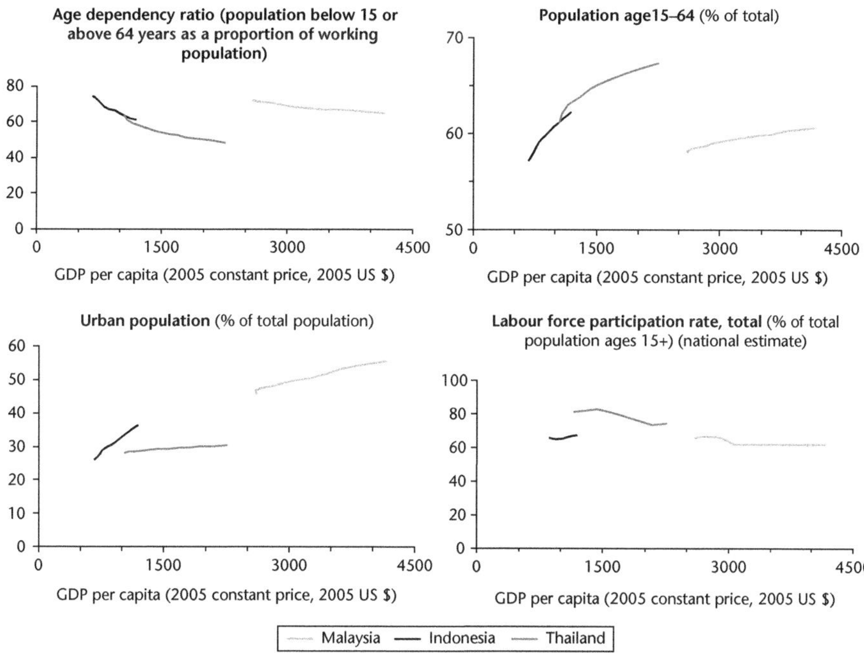

Figure 5.4 Demographic and urbanization trends, 1985–1995 (or available years)
Source: Author's calculation based on World Bank (2017).

Malaysia (72 per cent to 65 per cent) and was driven by declines in mortality rates and increases in working age population. The rate of urbanization was much less striking than the previous period, especially in Thailand where there was little growth in the urban proportion of the population. In Malaysia, the urban proportion rose a further ten percentage points, and in Indonesia it rose from a quarter to a third of the population.

What happened in terms of labour productivity? Figure 5.5 shows labour productivity by sector. The figure shows, as with the preceding time period, large increases in labour productivity in manufacturing and in services in this period. In contrast, and also in keeping with the preceding time period, labour productivity in agriculture barely grew with the exception of a large increase in Malaysia. Figure 5.6 decomposes growth by factor (change in growth = 100). The growth decomposition by factors shows overwhelmingly that the main factor in this period driving growth was physical capital accumulation. Labour inputs and total factor productivity (TFP) were important in Malaysia but still very much secondary to capital accumulation.

Finally, we consider integrative ST. Figures 5.7 and 5.8 show a dramatic shift in the trade structure. There were large increases in the share of manufactures in exports. In Indonesia, the manufacturing share amounted to more than

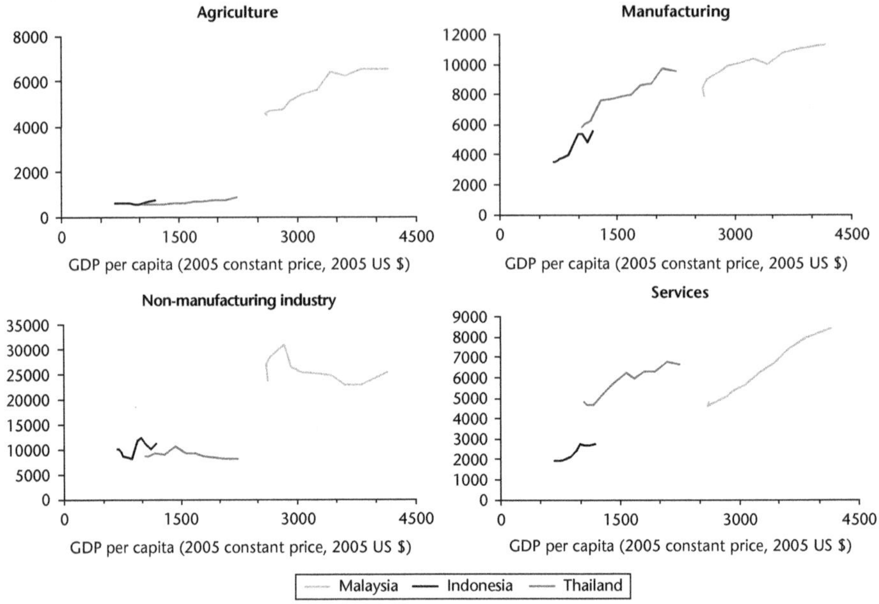

Figure 5.5 Labour productivity, 1985–1995 (or available years)

Source: Author's calculation based on Timmer et al. (2015).

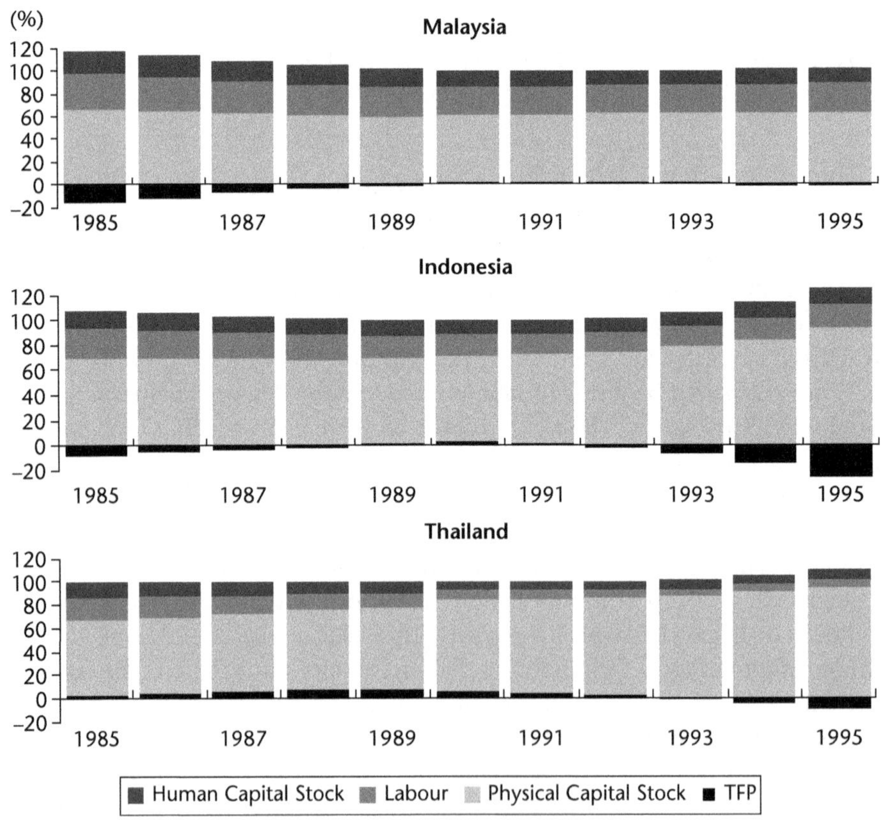

Figure 5.6 Growth decomposition by factor, 1985–1995 (or available years) (change in growth = 100.0)

Source: Author's calculation based on Timmer et al. (2015).

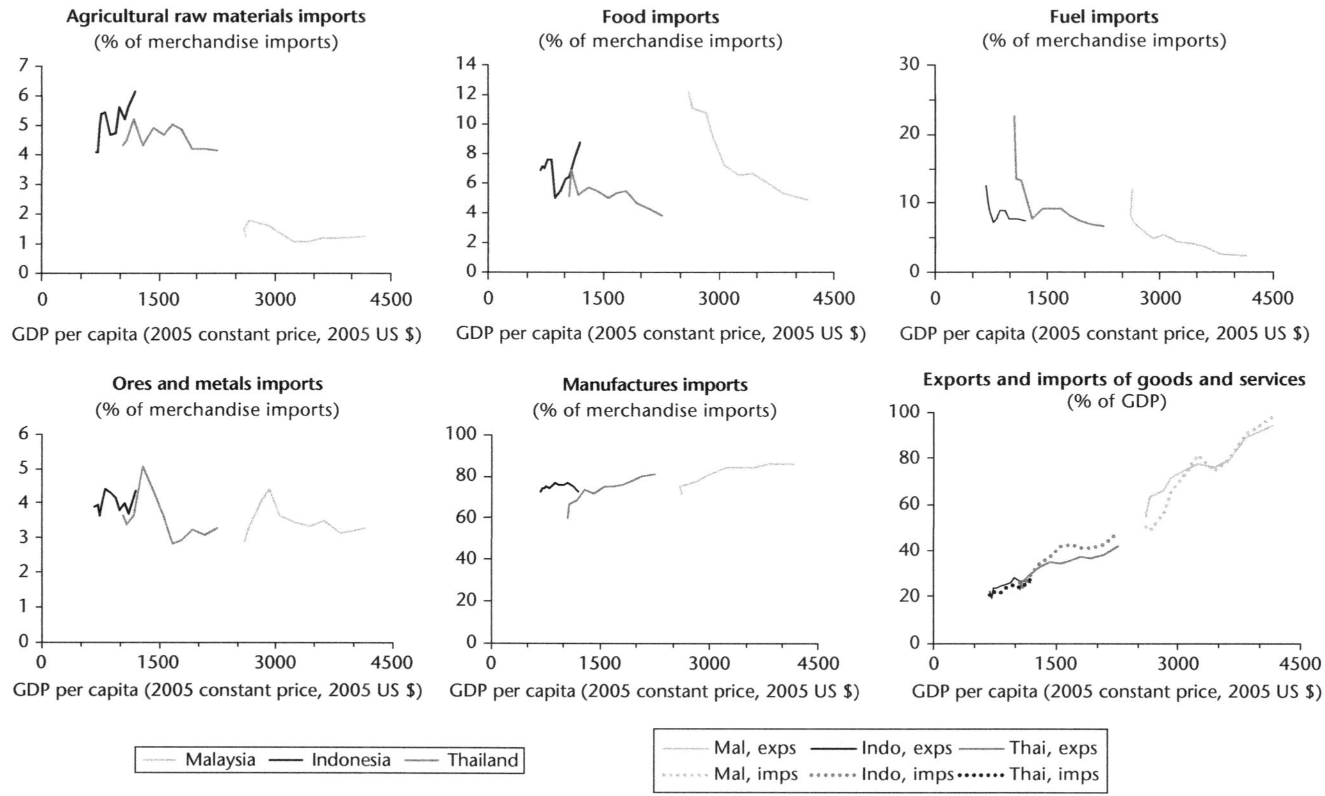

Figure 5.7 Composition of imports, 1985–1995 (or available years)

Source: Author's calculation based on Timmer et al. (2015).

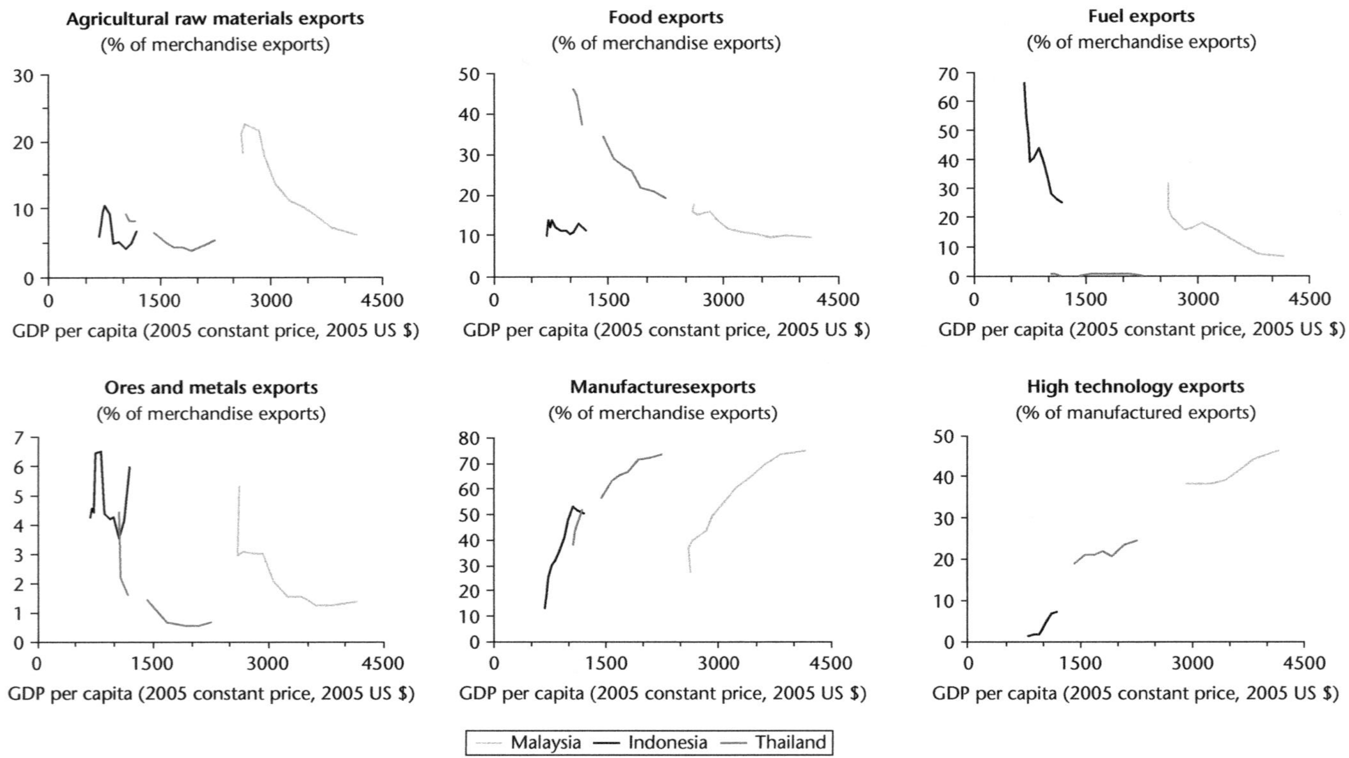

Figure 5.8 Composition of exports, 1985–1995 (or available years)

Source: Author's calculation based on Timmer et al. (2015).

half of exports, and in Thailand and Malaysia it reached close to three-quarters of exports. The proportion of high-tech in those manufacture exports also increased, though from a low base in Indonesia. In Thailand, a quarter of the manufacturing exports were high-tech exports. In Malaysia, almost half of the manufacturing exports were high-tech exports. Export shares of agriculture, food, fuel, ore, and metals exports all fell consequentially.

Import shares also shifted. Shares of fuel fell substantially, and food imports fell in Malaysia and Thailand. However, the share of manufactures in imports rose to around three-quarters or more of imports, suggesting that MIT were importing and assembling manufactured goods for export. The overall trade position corroborates this as, although Malaysia and Indonesia ran a trade surplus for much of the period, Thailand ran a trade deficit for the period and by the end of the period all three countries had a trade deficit. In short, the benefits of export growth were diminished by import growth. Although in Indonesia in 1995 the emerging trade deficit was relatively small (about 1.3 per cent of GDP), it followed a long period of trade surpluses. And in Malaysia and Thailand the size of the deficit was substantial (respectively 4 per cent and 7 per cent of GDP) and this was growing as a share of GDP over time.

It is important to note that though export growth is important, it does not, by itself, explain East Asia's rapid growth. Rodrik (1999) argues that it is the large increase in the investment-to-GDP ratio that explains export booms, suggesting that investment in the classical developmentalist period is in fact a causal factor in the subsequent export boom. This sustains the thesis of cumulative causation noted in the introduction.

Storm and Naastepad (2005) propose a formulation of East Asian growth in terms of such a cumulative-causation growth model in the Myrdal and Kaldor tradition. They argue that East Asia is a model of the Kaldorian 'virtuous cycle' of public-led investment (under import-substitution industrialization) which drove growth and productivity (with increased returns to scale), which then drove exports (with lower production costs that would have been the case) and this drove demand, output, and profits (which were further boosted by real-wage growth below labour productivity growth) which in turn produced a full 'virtuous cycle', back to new investment, new productivity gains, new growth, and so on. In short, demand growth promotes productivity growth as per Kaldor's thinking. Industrialization becomes cumulative as productivity growth increases demand, not via wages but via state management of aggregate demand and labour institutions, which lead productivity gains which promote investment (as it reduces the labour shares), leading to new employment creation because real-wage rises do not match productivity gains.

Figure 5.9 outlines sources of development finance. If we consider the sources of financing for development in the period of the mid 1980s to the mid 1990s we find some notable shifts. Natural resource rents (important for

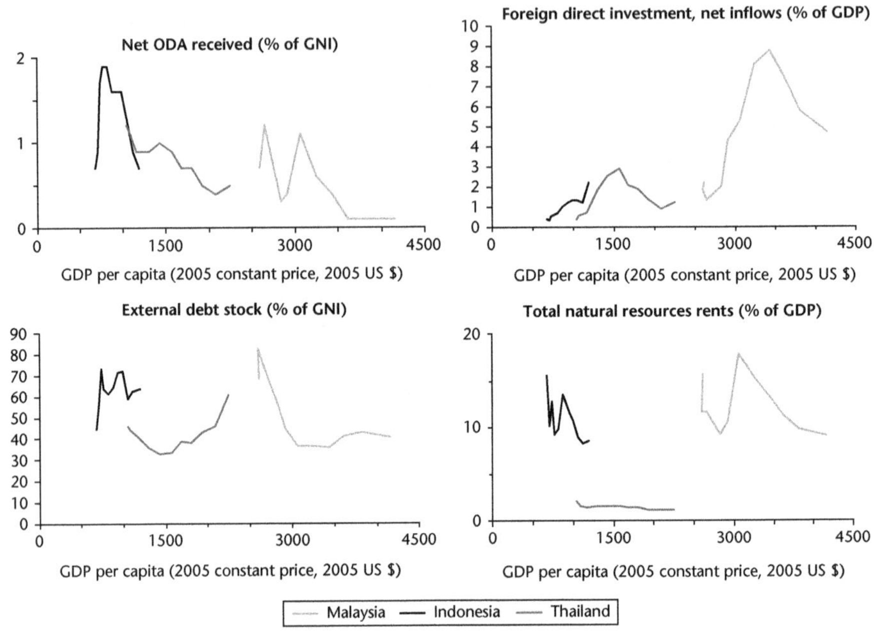

Figure 5.9 Sources of development financing, 1985–1995 (or available years)
Source: Author's calculation based on World Bank (2017).

Indonesia and Malaysia in the previous period) became less important given the decline of global commodity prices, most notably oil prices. Official development assistance (ODA) remained of limited relevance to both Malaysia and Thailand. However, as with the earlier period, ODA in Indonesia was of some significance rising to close to 2 per cent of GDP from 1987 to 1992, following oil prices changes. The more significant changes in this period, relative to the previous, were a notable increase—following the selective liberalization of trade and investment, and the Plaza Accord and its impact on exchange rates—in FDI to Malaysia, Indonesia, and Thailand. The rises in Malaysia were striking. The rises in in Indonesia and Thailand were less striking, though they were effectively a shift from very low levels to about 2 per cent of GDP in Indonesia by the mid 1990s, and 3 per cent of GDP in Thailand. Furthermore, towards the end of the period, Malaysia actually became a substantial source of outward FDI (rising to 3 per cent of GDP). This is in part explained by the encouragement and facilitation of outward Malaysian FDI through the Malaysian South-South Corporation Berhad, which provided export credit and insurance. International capital in the form of foreign borrowing also grew dramatically in terms of the total debt stock (as a per cent of GNI) for Indonesia and for Thailand. In both countries, it grew to 60 per cent of GNI. In contrast, after having reached very high proportions of GNI in the mid 1980s, the external debt stock actually fell in Malaysia.

Next, we turn to the distributional aspects and to IG (see Figures 5.10 to 5.12). We consider changes in income/consumption and capabilities. Figure 5.10 presents the data for poverty rates at the lower poverty line of $2.50 per day (2011 PPP). Poverty at this level fell across MIT. The falls in Indonesia and Thailand were noteable. Rates at the $10 poverty line were much more 'sticky' through the late 1980s though they fell in the early 1990s. At the end of the period, poverty at $10 per day still affected almost all Indonesians other than the top 1 per cent, three-quarters of the population in Thailand, and half of the population in Malaysia. Figure 5.10 also shows inequality of opportunity via the proxy of the expansion of primary and lower secondary education. In terms of capabilities and equalizing opportunities, primary school completion rose to very high levels in Malaysia and Indonesia and lower secondary completion rose in Indonesia. For Thailand and Malaysia there was too little data to assess trends in the period.

Figure 5.11 shows inequality of outcome and fiscal redistribution. Net income shares to the richest one per cent were steady in Malaysia but declined in Thailand notably. Indonesia only had one data point in the period. Inequality measured by the net Gini was steady in Malaysia and Thailand and rose slightly in Indonesia. Fiscal systems showed little sign of redistribution

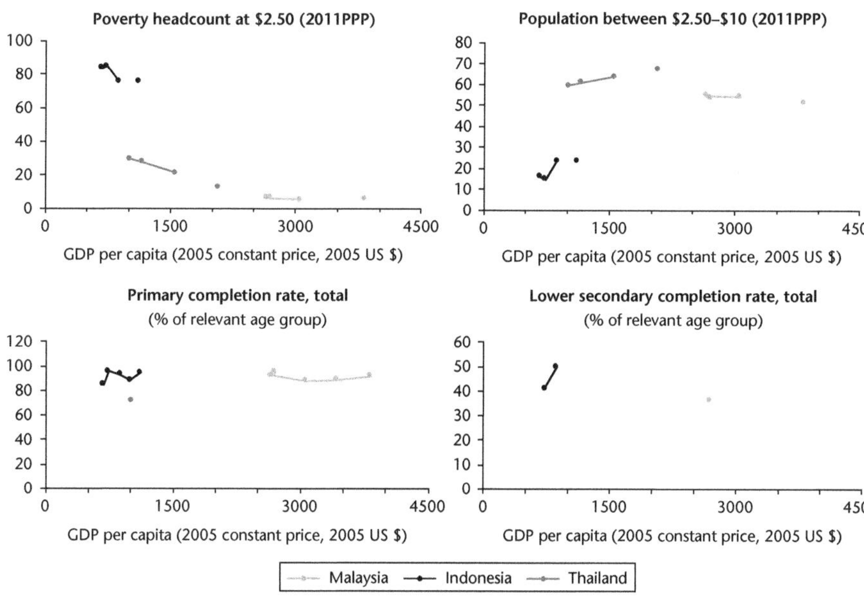

Figure 5.10 Poverty, insecurity, and inequality of opportunity, 1985–1995 (or available years)

Source: Edward and Sumner (2016) and World Bank (2017).

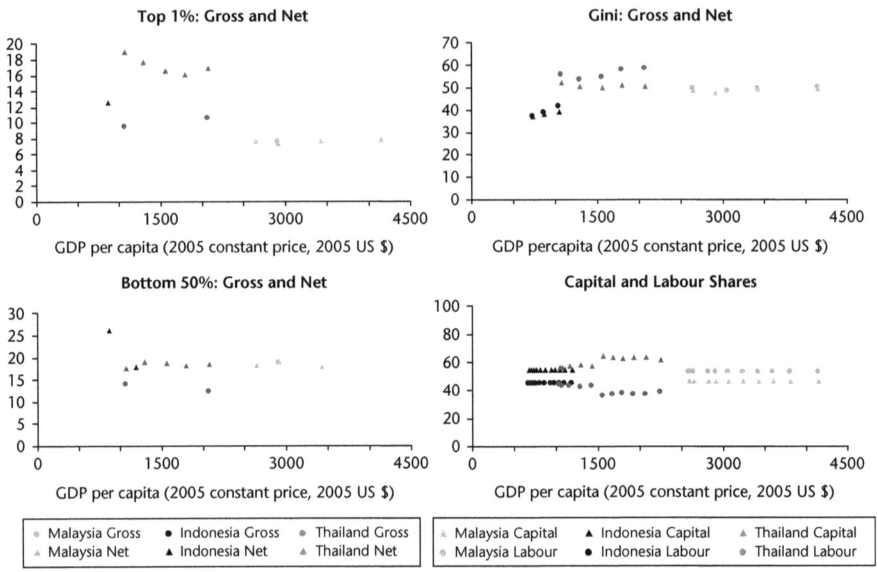

Figure 5.11 Inequality of outcome and fiscal redistribution, 1985–1995 (or available years)

Note: Inklaar and Timmer (2013) assume labour shares remained constant or if missing years linearly interpolation and a set of rules are used (see pp. 20–21).

Sources: Inklaar and Timmer (2013); UNU-WIDER (forthcoming).

in Malaysia and Indonesia. This can be seen in differences between gross and net Ginis in Malaysia and Indonesia. In Thailand, though, gross and net Ginis diverged, showing redistribution more clearly. Shares of income to capital and labour were steady with the exception of Thailand where the labour share rose slightly.

Finally, we consider employment growth. The GGDC dataset shows that much of the job creation in the period in Malaysia was in manufacturing and services, whilst job creation in agriculture in Malaysia was negative. In Thailand, job creation was most substantial in services and to a much lesser extent manufacturing, whilst, again, job creation in agriculture was also negative. Job creation in Indonesia was much more mixed. In the late 1980s, agriculture was still a major supplier of new jobs but the service sector was the most important job creator in that period. In the early 1990s, when manufacturing job creation became more notable, agricultural job creation became negative.

Figure 5.12 explores the relationship connecting ST and IG. This is the relationship between employment growth and value-added growth at the sectoral level. Figure 5.12 shows, as with the preceding period, agriculture in Indonesia and Thailand to be on the employment rich side of the dotted line, though in Thailand the curve is flattish, showing that in that sector more

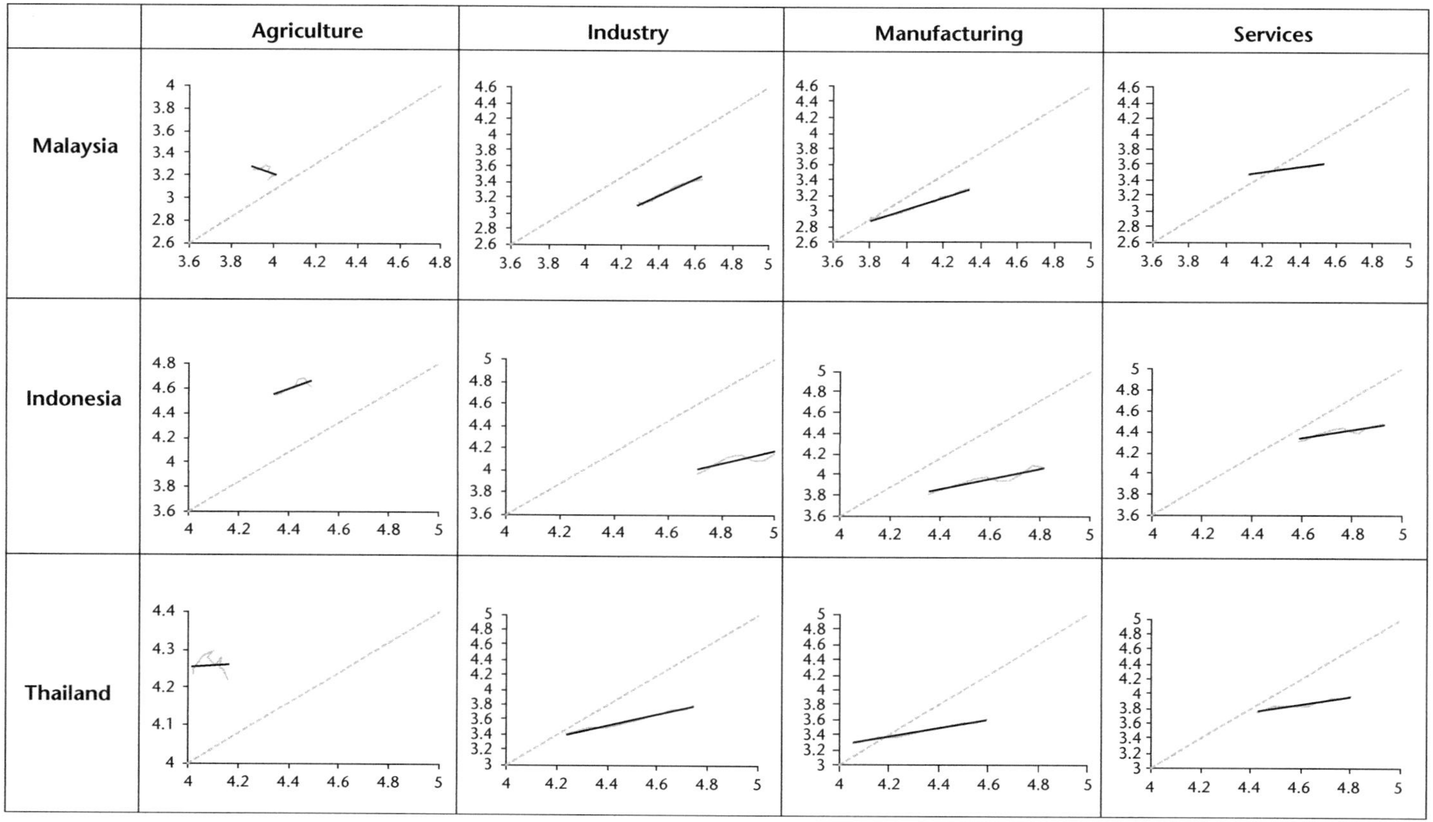

Figure 5.12 Value-added versus employment growth by sector, 1985–1995 (or available years)

Source: Author's calculation based on Timmer et al. (2015).

value-added was not creating a proportional amount of employment. In the other sectors, the plots are very much on the other side of the dotted line across MIT. Most notably, in manufacturing and services. The plots, in general, are diverging from the one-to-one line, and flatish suggesting that over time fewer jobs are being created per unit of value-added.

In sum, structural change and inclusive growth in South East Asia in the period of two-tier developmentalism was impressive and achieved without dramatic increases in inequality. In Section 5.4, we discuss the period's social structure of capital accumulation.

5.4 Two-tier Developmentalism in South East Asia: The Social Structure of Capital Accumulation

5.4.1 *Overview and Context*

In this section we are concerned with two questions: what was the social structure of capital accumulation from the early to mid 1980s to the mid 1990s and how did that differ across MIT? Of course, the timelines should not be taken as hard cut-offs; some liberalization began in MIT before the mid 1980s and the crisis really took hold in 1997–8. Thus, such temporal cuts-offs should not be taken as absolutes.

We are interested once more in the variety of developmentalism, the role of the state in the ownership or regulation of capital, and the modalities of global incorporation. Whereas the previous era (1960–85) was classical—meaning highly statist—developmentalism, the period of the early to mid 1980s to the mid 1990s was one of two-tier developmentalism. This meant, not that the state stepped away, but that economies were selectively opened and that rapid incorporation into the global economy in production and finance ensued, to an extent that had not previously been the case.

The argument of this section, with reference to the varieties of developmentalism, is that the era was one of a two-tier developmentalism. MIT achieved substantial ST and IG, though in a way that was unsustainable. The previous era's variety of developmentalism laid the foundations by its public investments for productive forces, such as SOEs, infrastructure, and primary education expansion. These ISI foundations made export-led growth possible. In contrast to the earlier period, MIT pursued a two-tier developmentalism that entailed the protection of domestic capital and accommodation of international capital in specific sectors for FDI-led exports and finance capital inflows. This does not mean that MIT embraced laissez-faire capitalism or the Washington Consensus, rather that some real sectors were open to international capital (e.g. textiles/apparel and electric/electronics) but with the capacity to ensure continued regulation. The opening to financial capital inflows was much less selective. Further, other than in Malaysia where it was a transfer of state assets to the indigenous Malay capitalist class, SOEs barely saw any privatization. In terms of IG, poverty fell at the lower line of $2.50 though was still high at the $10 line; inequality was—in general—steady and capabilities were attended to in terms of educational attainment and employment growth.

5.4.2 *Malaysia*

In the early 1980s, the new Malaysian prime minister, Mahathir Mohamad, led what was in some ways continuity—in the sense that the core political concerns were economic nationalism and a continuing state–domestic capital alliance—and in other ways a redirection, initiating a heavy industrialization programme and a reorientation of the New Economic Policy as well as austerity, financial liberalization, and privatization.[4]

In the mid 1980s, the terms of trade fell sharply, leading to a period of crisis. GDP and manufacturing exports declined, and unemployment rose to 8 per cent. A large capital outflow led to a sharp fall in the value of the currency and a consequential large increase in overseas-denominated debt. The real effective exchange rate fell by about 20 per cent. This lowered production costs and, accompanied by relaxation of various rules related to FDI, made Malaysia attractive to FDI, leading to a surge in FDI inflows in export-orientated manufacturing. As a result, by the end of the decade, almost a fifth of the labour force was employed in manufacturing.

Mahathir Mohamad shifted the developmentalism of the NEP from inter-ethnic inequality to building a domestic capitalist class, and a wide-ranging privatization programme was enacted. Tan (2013) argues that the emergence of a much stronger Malay business and middle class redirected the United Malays National Organization (UMNO). The shift from the NEP to the more liberal 1990 New Development Policy demonstrated a change in strategy. The liberal stance included the partial privatization of subsidiaries of Petronas (Petronas Dagangan and Petronas Gas), the national energy company, and a large sell-off of state-owned assets to a politically connected indigenous elite.

Mahathir Mohamad also put in place a 'Look East policy', which sought to emulate heavy industries in Japan, South Korea, and Taiwan. Managed by the state agency, the Heavy Industries Corporation of Malaysia, this policy included iron, steel, petro-chemicals, ship-building/repairs, petroleum refining, cement plants, small engine factories, and a national car project. Heavy protection to

[4] Sources for this section are the same as the equivalent section in Chapter 4. Additional sources are Johnston et al. (1997), Schneider (2001).

maintain viability and massive borrowings from overseas to fund projects were necessary.

Tan (2014) identifies the period of 1980 to 1997 as one of an emerging industrial dualism evident between an FDI-dominated, non-resource-based, industrial high-tech, competitive, dynamic export sector situated in free-trade zones (FTZs) based on electronics and electrical components, and which accounted for half of total exports, and a domestic sector of small- and medium-sized enterprises (SMEs) in assembly, sub-contracting, and with few linkages to the former or high-tech industries or heavy industry. In short, there was a failure of domestic capitalists despite the NEP in the sense that high levels of protection and support had not led to a dynamic, domestic capitalist sector. There followed a set of policies and programmes to address the problems in the First Industrial Master Plan, and other plans and programmes introduced in the 1980s, and the fifth and sixth Malaysia National Plans (from the mid 1980s to the mid 1990s).

Alavi (1996) refers to the early 1980s as a period of ISI and domestic market-orientated heavy industry promotion in consumer durables, as well as intermediate and capital goods. In the mid 1980s, this gave way to an export-orientated industrialization strategy in the Industrial Master Plan and Promotion of Investment Act. In the late 1980s, FDI inflows expanded further, following the 1986 Investment Promotion Act (which gave ten-year tax holidays and relaxed domestic ownership restrictions in priority sectors). The appreciation of the yen and US dollar against the Malaysian ringgit after the 1985 Plaza Accord was instrumental in the relocation of FDI to Malaysia. There was a dramatic growth in the electrical/electronic components sector. Consequentially, employment in export manufacturing increased dramatically, especially so in Malaysia's FTZs. However, real wages were low and labour unions repressed.

In short, whereas the drivers of economic development up to the mid 1980s were SOEs and domestic conglomerates, in the late 1980s and 1990s the drivers of economic development became FDI and privatized entities, as well as the remaining major conglomerates. Boo Teik (2010) argues that the multiple roles of the state evident in the NEP years led to a rupture between state, domestic, and foreign capital as the state expanded. Most significantly, Mahathir's privatization programme established a new state–capital pact and transferred assets to Malay entrepreneurs, and domestic capitalists were favoured in the award of contracts for large projects or the establishment of new services.

In each of MIT, financial and capital account liberalization were widespread from the mid 1980s onwards, and financial and capital account liberalization were much less selective than the liberalization of the real sector. In Malaysia, in the early 1990s, there were very large non-FDI private capital inflows, due as with Indonesia and Thailand, to differences between domestic and international interest rates. The Kuala Lumpur Stock Exchange boomed due to privatization, and the liberalization of entry and exit requirements.

Malaysia had accepted IMF Article VIII (the liberalization of foreign exchange movements) much earlier (1968) than its neighbours and has had a fairly open capital account since. Portfolio inflows and foreign borrowing by banks were unhindered from the mid 1980s. In the late 1980s, financial liberalization was pursued and an offshore financial centre was established in the Labuan International Offshore Financial Centre in 1993. Substantial current account deficits were financed with short-term capital inflows.

The capital account was further liberalized for portfolio investment inflows, and regulations on foreign borrowings were relaxed. The private sector's medium- and long-term external debt mushroomed from RM5billion in the late 1980s to more than RM60bn in the mid 1990s. In the same time, short-term debt rose from RM7bn to RM43bn, and the share of stock market capitalization in foreign equity rose from 25 to 40 per cent. In 1994, controls on capital inflows had to be introduced to manage foreign borrowing by banks.

In terms of inclusive growth, though contingent on low wages to be competitive internationally, export-orientated industrialization was labour-intensive and employment-creating. Malaysia, despite austerity, enacted a set of poverty programmes during this period. Notably, a comprehensive programme focused on the poorest villages.

In short, the period was one of a social structure of capital accumulation based on an accord between state and private capitalists, which shifted the emphasis on state-led capital accumulation to private sector-led developmentalism. The social base was employment growth in manufacturing in particular, which reduced poverty, and together with education expansion and rural investments prevented inequality from rising.

5.4.3 *Indonesia*

In Indonesia, the period was also one of two-tier developmentalism.[5] Van Zanden and Marks (2013) refer to the period as one of 'reorientation'. Similar to Malaysia, the period of the mid 1980s was one of crisis triggered by the fall in oil prices, which strengthened the role of technocrats. As a result, liberalization and deregulation ensued, though this was not extended to any major privatizations of SOEs. When oil prices fell, the government responded with tight monetary and fiscal policy and large currency devaluations. As

[5] See Chapter 4 for background sources for this section and additionally: Lindblad (2015), Pangestu et al. (2015), Johnston et al. (1997), Schneider (2001).

with Malaysia, in light of exchange rate movements, a large amount of FDI relocated from the North East Asian countries and Japan.

The period from the mid 1980s onwards was one of liberalization and deregulation, including the reduction of numerous trade tariffs, the end of import monopolies for steel and plastic, the opening of new sectors to FDI, the removal of the need for local shareholders, the relaxation of divestment regulations, and the removal of local content requirements in some sectors. SOEs survived any major attempt at privatization as, following the economic domination of foreign enterprise under colonialism, they are institutionalized in the constitution and because vested groups had influential connections.

Although substantial in Malaysia, foreign investment in Indonesia was small in the early 1980s. The major effect of the reforms was a reduction in state shares in economic output and a shrinking oil and gas sector in relative terms (though constant in absolute output). Inflows of FDI induced a boom in labour-intensive manufacturing exports (albeit many of which are import-intensive) such as textiles, footwear, electronics, furniture, toys, and sports goods.

Financial liberalization was also evident in Indonesia. Financial sector reform began with interest rate reform in the early 1980s and in the late 1980s Article VIII of the IMF obligations was accepted. Banking reforms in 1983 and 1988 removed entry barriers and most credit subsidies. However, some controls remained on FDI inflows (domestic ownership requirements), portfolio inflows (equity ownership was not allowed by foreigners), and external bank borrowing. In the early 1990s, commercial bank borrowing grew substantially which led to the reintroduction of quantitative controls on external borrowing. In the crisis, short-term dollar debt was way in excess of Forex reserves because Indonesian companies had taken advantage of the differences between domestic and international interest rates between 1995 and 1997.

In terms of inclusive growth, the FDI-led growth generated substantial employment. Kian Wie (2012) argues that this employment growth was central to poverty reduction accompanied as it was by the stabilization of rice prices. There was also expansion of social programmes in the 1990s. Mishra (2009, pp. 59–64) notes, for example, Repelita V (1989/90–93/4), which had a strong focus on agriculture, maintaining food self-sufficiency, and the promotion of employment opportunities. Furthermore, the backward villages (Inpres Desa Tertinggal) programme was launched in 1993 for the poorest villages as well as the establishment of a credit programme and a school-feeding programme.

In short, the period was one of a social structure of capital accumulation based on a continued state–domestic capital pact led by the state but extended to international capital. The social base, like Malaysia, was largely based on manufacturing employment growth and education expansion with its implied redistribution of future chances.

5.4.4 *Thailand*

In Thailand, the crisis came earlier on.[6] As an oil importer, Thailand was more sensitive to price rises in oil than were Malaysia and Indonesia, who were oil exporters. The oil price shocks of the mid and late 1970s became more significant by the early 1980s because natural gas endowments had been exhausted. Thailand dealt with the oil shocks, which cause a deterioration in the terms of trade, by overseas borrowing, and as interest rates rose in the early 1980s, a crisis ensued leading to the debt-burden-induced adjustment. The major crisis led to a five-year structural adjustment programme with the World Bank, which included austerity, and aimed to fully open Thailand to international capital and the global economy. Consequently, the fifth (1982–6) and sixth (1987–91) development plans shifted emphasis from classical developmentalism to deregulation and private sector-led growth.

As in Malaysia and Indonesia, the late 1980s to the mid 1990s saw a period of large FDI inflows and an FDI-led export boom. The currency was devalued and FDI-attracting incentives were introduced. In 1985, several export and import taxes were abolished and the tax system was reformed. In Thailand, in the 1980s net inflows of FDI rose from an annual average of 6bn baht in the early 1980s to approaching 50bn baht annually in the late 1980s and through until the mid 1990s. Fiscal deficits turned to surpluses as growth boomed.

In 1979, selected by the winning political party, General Prem had become prime minister.[7] Under Prem, the Board of Investment was reorientated to support export industries, export processing zones were established with relaxed labour laws, tax incentives were applied, and infrastructure rolled out. Prem stepped down in the late 1980s. A coup in the early 1990s led to military rule and a new constitution. Unrest ensued and a period of instability led to a series of governments.

Sino-Thai capitalists dominated the contracts, licences, and investment incentives from the Board of Investment, whilst technocrats dominated the Central Bank and Ministry of Finance. Politicians and bureaucrats joined the boards of companies. As with Indonesia, there was little in the way of privatization of SOEs. A privatization programme was initiated in the early to mid

[6] See Chapter 4 for background sources for this section in equivalent section. Additional sources: Johnston et al. (1997), Schneider (2001).

[7] In 1978, a constitutional modification allowed the military to sit in parliament and the cabinet, and allowed a military officer to serve as prime minister.

1980s but only 13 SOEs (which accounted for just 2 per cent of SOE assets) were fully privatized. Instead, SOEs were forced to franchise and grant contracts/licences/concessions to private companies.

In Thailand, large capital inflows started in the early 1990s due to an open capital account, the financial liberalization of inflows in the mid 1980s and early 1990s, and the acceptance of IMF Article VIII in 1990. Capital outflows were liberalized more gradually in the early to mid 1990s. As with Indonesia and Malaysia, there were large interest rate differences between domestic and international interest rates. A series of financial sector reforms was enacted, including the opening of the Bangkok International Banking Facility, which stimulated the capital market and supported Thai firms to borrow overseas. Thai firms borrowed heavily especially short-term, unhedged, and unregulated, and large capital inflows ensued. This led to stock market and real estate bubbles and a currency appreciation. In 1995, and when the crisis hit harder in mid 1997, Thailand made use of capital controls.

In terms of inclusive growth, FDI generated substantial employment in manufacturing as in Indonesia and Malaysia. However, unlike Indonesia and Malaysia there was a much less meaningful expansion of the welfare regime in terms of poverty programmes in Thailand.

In sum, in Thailand, like Malaysia and Indonesia, an economic crisis ensued in the early 1980s and the state's response was to continue protection of domestic capital but to open up some sectors to international capital to drive capital accumulation and employment growth as a social base for capital accumulation. In each of MIT, there was liberalization of international capital.

5.5 Conclusion

This chapter has argued the following thesis: the era of the early to mid 1980s to the mid to late 1990s was one of a two-tier variety of developmentalism. This was a variety of developmentalism that broke with the earlier era of classical developmentalism in the sense that it opened selectively to international capital. Two-tier developmentalism was neither entirely statist nor entirely liberal but a selective mix or two-tier system: statist for domestic capital whilst selectively liberal for international capital in the real sector, though less selective in terms of financial liberalization and international financial capital inflows. The ST and IG that ensued were triggered by two price differentials between national and global prices. First, relative exchange rates made MIT attractive to relocating FDI. Second, interest rate differentials made MIT attractive to financial capital.

As before, this era of developmentalism holds within itself the seeds of its decline and its reinvention in a third era of developmentalism or neo- or new developmentalism, which is the subject of Chapter 6. The outcomes of ST and IG were, though not sustained, striking. The decline of the variety of developmentalism was due to changes in global capital accumulation and underlying structural dependencies and subordination, which remained. Exchange rates and market sentiments shifted and a spectacular crisis engulfed the region. New iterations of dependency and subordination had emerged.

As with the earlier era of classical developmentalism, the Polanyi handmaiden or hyperactive conductor role of the state was core and exemplified in its agencies. In Indonesia and Thailand, these agencies remained almost entirely in state hands whilst in Malaysia they were passed to private indigenous capitalists, though that transfer was to prove to be temporary, as we shall see in Chapter 6.

What the period does demonstrate is that the developer's dilemma—the tension at the heart of economic development between ST and IG—can be addressed with policies seeking to neutralize the Kuznetsian upswing in inequality that the Lewisian transition and ST unleashes. Specifically, continuing major agriculture and rural public investments and food price management ensure the urban–rural divergence did not expand as much as it might have otherwise; the continuing expansion of education ensured that the skilled–unskilled wage divergence was not as great as it might otherwise have been, and finally, the focus on employment growth spread the benefits of ST much more widely than if real wages had risen accordingly with productivity growth. In fact over the period the distribution of consumption/income barely changed. All of which ensured the social structure of capital accumulation was stable until global prices shifted upon which the wave of capital accumulation was driven.

In Chapter 6, we discuss how that fragility of the 'miracle' or pseudo-miracle became apparent and developmentalism was—in due course—reincarnated into its next iteration or variety. Furthermore, the Lewisian transition abruptly stalled and Kuznetsian forces moved in different directions across MIT—rising in Indonesia, more or less steady or falling slightly in Malaysia and falling in Thailand.

6

Arrested Development?

The Rise of New Developmentalism in South East Asia

6.1 Introduction

In the previous chapters, we considered the debate on the East Asian 'miracle' and, in particular, the first and second eras of developmentalism in South East Asia and, respectively, classical developmentalism and two-tier developmentalism. The former was very much an unleashing of the Lewisian transition of structural transformation (ST), though one in which the forces of the Kuznetsian upswing were neutralized. The latter was one of a rapid acceleration of the Lewisian transition of ST and again one in which the Kuznetsian upswing was counterbalanced.

In this chapter, we discuss the third wave of developmentalism in South East Asia, which is a post-Lewisian transition or a deindustrialization. There has been a divergence across Malaysia, Indonesia, and Thailand (MIT) in terms of managing Kuznetsian forces. The period begins with the crisis of the second wave of ST and capital accumulation in the late 1990s. We identify the next incarnation of developmentalism in a nascent, new developmentalism and the ascendancy of Polanyi's regulator or handmaiden, in the form of state intervention in the economy and a less liberal approach to international capital.

The purpose of this chapter is thus to consider the emergence of a nascent or third era of 'new developmentalism' in South East Asia from the mid to late 1990s to the present day, a period which has been one of crisis, recovery, and 'plateauing' in terms of the Lewisian transition of ST and an emerging post-Lewisian deindustrialization. The period has also been one of emerging democratic and popular political forces.

In anthropology and psychology, 'arrested development' refers to the idea that a plateau (of development) has been attained. It is often used in relation to the state of productive processes at a group or individual level, and the limitations that have set in on expanding those processes. For example, theories of skill acquisition note that the skills plateau is the point at which a human being can do something automatically, after which repeating leads to little progress or improvement due to 'arrested development'. In this chapter, we consider the emergence of arrested development or what could be called the 'middle-income development plateau' in MIT in the period from the mid to late 1990s to the present day. This is a period where industrialization has peaked in terms of a peak in manufacturing shares of GDP, employment, and exports. Furthermore, although the crisis of the late 1990s curtailed temporarily the expansion of finance and related services such as real estate and insurance, the continued process of financialization—the expansion of the financial sector in terms of GDP shares and influence on policy—became more evident in Malaysia, whilst in Indonesia it was not curtailed to any significant extent. Only in Thailand was it pushed back (see Table 6.1). In Malaysia, the FIRE ratio jumped from 10.4 per cent in 1997 to 15.2 per cent in 2011. Over the same time Indonesia's ratio declined slightly from 7.0 per cent in 1997 to 6.2 per cent in 2011, and Thailand's from 6.2 per cent in 1997 to 3.7 per cent in 2011.

This was also a period of considerable political turbulence, pointing towards changes in the social structure of capital accumulation, including the emergence of democratization in Indonesia, a reform movement supressed in Malaysia, and the rise of, and later backlash to, populism in Thailand.

The Asian financial crisis and its aftermath opened up questions of the potential for democratic developmental states rather than autocratic developmental states. In Indonesia a vibrant democracy emerged. However, in Malaysia a similar reform movement was repressed. Thailand shifted from periods of democracy to periods of military rule and back to democracy and military rule again.

Rock (2017) argues that elites hijacked democratic processes in their own interest. He noted that Indonesia has turned to democracy though it has led to the oligarchs of the New Order embedding themselves in political parties and

Table 6.1. GDP share accounted for by finance, insurance, real estate, and business services (valued-added 2005 constant prices, 2005 US$)

	1997	1998	1999	2000	2005	2010	2011
Malaysia	10.4	10.8	10.8	10.7	12.6	15.0	15.2
Indonesia	7.0	5.7	5.2	5.2	5.9	6.1	6.2
Thailand	6.2	4.6	2.7	2.4	2.9	3.4	3.7

Note: Data is for FIRE+renting+business activities (i.e. ISIC Version 3.1 Code J + K) in aggregate. Timmer et al. (2015) do not have separate data for finance and insurance (code J), Real estate and renting+business activities (code K).
Source: Timmer et al. (2015).

new institutions of democracy by reaffirming the 1945 constitution, a unitary state, and presidential government as well as adopting proportional representation and electoral rules that limited party competition to three major parties and pulled politics towards the centre. Big bang decentralization in 2001 ensured greater autonomy whilst maintaining a unitary state. A further mechanism is highlighted by Martinez-Bravo et al. (forthcoming). They note that mayors appointed by Suharto were allowed to finish their five-year terms rather than be replaced immediately. This gave them an opportunity to build new networks, buy votes, or strike deals.

Rock (2017) notes that Malaysia met the emerging reform movement with full force repression despite elections. The reform movement was led by imprisoned opposition leader, Anwar Ibrahim's wife, Wan Azizah Wan Ismail. However, the reformasi—the reform movement—failed in Malaysia according to Rock because of a lack of elite support, as well as internal ideological differences within the coalition.

Thailand turned towards democracy initially when a populist politician—Thaksin Shinawatra—sought to take on the traditional elite leading to conflict, a coup, and elections which his sister—Yingluck Shinawatra—won. A further coup occurred in 2014.

Early on in the period in Thailand a new constitution emerged, in 1998, with a focus on more stable accountable government following political instability. Electoral change was made to bring about two large parties who would compete. In subsequent elections in 2001 and 2005 the Thai Rak Thai party of Thaksin Shinawatra emerged as the winner. Thaksin ran on a populist platform of redistribution, including health insurance coverage, a village grant programme, and a three-year debt moratorium on farmers' debts. The Democrat Party's programme was, in contrast, in keeping with the International Monetary Fund (IMF) and a neo-liberal programme.

Thaksin, though, antagonized the traditional elite by strengthening his supporters in the military and police via patronage, reorganizing the bureaucracy and appointing business associates. He also sought to control state media criticism and led extra-judicial killings as a law enforcement model. In 2006, elites and the middle classes mobilized and a coup led to a new constitution in 2007 and then a return to democracy. Thaksin's political party was replaced with the Pheu Thai Party led by Yingluck Shinawatra, who won a majority in 2011. In 2014 there was a further coup.

In short, the period between the mid to late 1990s and the present has been one where democratic and populist forces have emerged. Since the Asian financial crisis (AFC), growth rates have generally been weaker (relative to the pre-crisis period), poverty reduction slower, and ST has plateaued or even gone into reverse. It is not surprising then that the crisis and its aftermath has led to the emergence of a 'new developmentalism', which was still nascent in the early 2000s but has emerged more visibly since the 2007/8 global financial crash. This is in light of the US's own response to the 2007/8 crisis of state protection and state financial support for US companies, which had relegitimized state action after the ideological onslaught of the Washington Consensus years. State capitalism, also propelled by the Chinese example, has taken a firmer root in a new developmentalism, albeit within the constraints of global and regional trade and investment agreements, which set the boundaries for any variety of developmentalism.

In the two-tier developmentalism period, selective liberalization led to a foreign direct investment and debt-fuelled boom, which was instrumental in making possible ST and economic growth. Structurally, what caused the decade-long boom—exchange rate movements and interest rate differentials, as well as the enormous capital inflows and overseas borrowing they triggered—also caused the crash by appreciating the exchange rate and slowing export growth. In the early to mid 1990s, Malaysia, Indonesia, and Thailand had current account deficits as much of manufacturing exports were based on large imports of manufactures for assembly and export. The deficits were financed via short-term capital inflows (necessitating a higher rate of interest to attract capital) and thus MIT were vulnerable to their withdrawal.

Whilst movements—appreciations—in the exchange rates for MIT ultimately undermined competitiveness and were the primary cause of the crisis, it was the change in market sentiments—triggered by perceptions of higher than publicly declared indebtedness, particularly in Thailand—that played a role in generating a sense of panic in financial markets. This panic was further fed by the actions of the IMF in calling for major reforms of East Asian economies, pointing towards fundamental economic problems.

We discuss the period via the lens of varieties of developmentalism and the quiet resurgence of what could be called a nascent, 'new developmentalism' consisting of: the revival of state-owned enterprises (SOEs) or state support of various kinds to indigenously-owned private conglomerates in Malaysia; state-directed or managed credit and other subsidies to SOEs and the domestic private sector; and performance requirements on FDI traded for market access to a newly emerging consumer market. This 'new developmentalism' of the late 1990s to the present sits in contrast to the two-tier developmentalism of the earlier period in the sense that it is increasingly less liberal and more regulatory, especially so of international capital. What is common across the three countries is the uneven expansion of welfare regimes, which are, in part, a response to distributive pressures. This is just one difference between classical and new developmentalism. Another difference is that the types of policy are subtler than crude import-substitution industrialization-type policies, for example, tariff versus non-tariff protectionist measures.

The thesis of this chapter is that: (i) in keeping with the heterodox theory, it is argued that the era of two-tier developmentalism ended due to changes in global capital accumulation; in the contemporary period, the emergence of direct competition from China and other countries such as Vietnam in similar export sectors to MIT (i.e. in textiles, due in part to the end of the World Trade Organization (WTO) Multifibre Arrangement for textiles and clothing); China's WTO entry leading to the reconfiguration of regional global value chains towards China, diminishing the role of MIT in those same chains;[1] and the commodity boom in the 2000s to some extent encouraging the deindustrialization process; (ii) that the outcomes of structural transformation and inclusive growth might have puzzled Lewis and Kuznets in that the period since the late 1990s because it has been marked by a stalled ST and even premature deindustrialization, and despite the emergence of more visible welfare regimes, weaker outcomes in terms of IG due to the exhaustion of primary and lower secondary education expansion and weak employment growth; furthermore, that the end of absolute poverty in Thailand and Malaysia has led to a burgeoning of a group of the population above the poverty line but still economically insecure, and although Kuznetsian forces were curtailed in Thailand with redistribution to rural areas in particular and a new healthcare coverage programme that was instrumental in this redistribution, there was a substantial rise in inequality in Indonesia; inequality in Malaysia fell slightly; and that, in keeping with heterodox theory, the state re-emerged to seek to drive ST via the renationalization of assets in Malaysia, and recapitalization of assets that were never privatized in Indonesia and Thailand.

This chapter follows a similar format to Chapters 4 and 5: Section 6.2 sets out the characteristics of a nascent, new developmentalism, Section 6.3 then considers the empirical experience of South East Asia and Section 6.4 discusses the social structure of capital accumulation during the period, with Section 6.5 concluding.

6.2 New Developmentalism

In the preceding introduction, we referred to a form of developmentalism, which we have labelled as a nascent, new developmentalism. The purpose of this section is to characterize the era of new developmentalism in South East

[1] As noted in, for example, Gereffi (1994, 2005) production has become increasingly fragmented and various components of a final good may be located in a number of countries. In short, production takes place not within a country but within a global value chain (GVC). In the mid 1980s, MIT entered these value chains via the expansion of FDI. At that time, there were very few countries in the region in GVCs (Singapore and Japan notably). Then in the mid to late 1990s and culminating in entry to the WTO in 2001, China entered these GVCs.

Asia, and to describe how it emerged and how it differs from the earlier varieties of developmentalism. There is much in this debate that structuralists and other proponents of heterodox theory from the 1960s, 1970s, and beyond would recognize. The argument of this section is as follows: the capital accumulation regimes of MIT have swung back to statism but in new ways. Though remaining open and generally liberal to trade and international capital, they are more suspicious and more likely to introduce measures that continue to favour domestic capital. Many of the measures are subtler measures than crude ISI. The measures utilized in this period include, but are not limited to: awarding government contracts and directing government (concessional) credit to SOEs and domestic companies; the proliferation of non-tariff barriers to insulate domestic capital from international competitive pressures; and—most notably—the resurgence of classical developmentalism restrictions and requirements on FDI such as local sourcing.

This is not a debate solely specific to South East Asia. Since the global crash and even in the late 1990s, discussions of this new developmentalism have emerged globally. New developmentalism has two iterations. One largely focused on ST or catch-up strategies (see Ban 2013; Bresser-Pereira et al. 2011; Frenkel 2006; Fritz et al. 2016). The second is a social developmentalism, which is concerned with domestic demand generation through income redistribution and wage rises, and combining growth with redistribution (see Amado and Mollo 2015; Bastos 2012; Carneiro 2012). Concurrently, a body of thought labelled as 'neo-structuralism' evolved from the United Nations Economic Commission for Latin America and the Caribbean (UN ECLAC or CEPAL) on new forms of state intervention in the contemporary global economy that integrate growth, employment, and equity. Such debates have responded to two major middle-income country problems according to Fritz et al. (2016, p. 5):

> [T]he tendency of wages to increase below the productivity rate, due to the availability of an unlimited supply of labor; and the tendency towards the overvaluation of the exchange rate, which is derived from two structural factors: (i) the problem of 'Dutch disease' in commodity exporters countries, which generates an appreciation trend of the domestic currency in the long run that is consistent with the balance in the current account but renders economically not viable other tradable industries; (ii) an additional currency appreciation caused by net flows of foreign capital, stimulated by the policy of growth-cum-foreign savings.

In light of these middle-income problems, new developmentalist strategies are to keep wages growing in line with productivity and exchange rate management to avoid overvaluation. In this approach export-led growth drives ST, and a trade surplus is a central objective. In contrast, social developmentalism is more in keeping with Kuznets and the focus is on redistribution and employment policies to expand the domestic market and minimum wage increases, social spending expansion and cheap credit, and public investment in economic and social infrastructure.

Aggarwal and Evenett (2010) empirically assess the post-global crash shift in government intervention.[2] They argue that Asia-Pacific governments in particular have substantially reinvigorated industrial policy in a protectionist manner in general and especially so in growth sectors.

In this section we discuss the concept of a post, or augmented, Washington Consensus in the early 2000s and the resurgence of nascent, new developmentalism, and the selective use of illiberal interventions in South East Asia.

The Asian financial crisis and its aftermath in the late 1990s led to much discussion throughout the early 2000s on the concept of a 'post-Washington Consensus' (see in particular, Stiglitz 1998a, 1998b). The post-WC was primarily a critique of the WC as practised by the IMF and the World Bank in the 1980s and early 1990s rather than a new conceptualization. Stiglitz (1998a, p. 34) argued that the WC was 'incomplete' and 'misleading', that there was a lack of understanding of economic structures (ontological assumptions that were too unrealistic), a narrow set of objectives (too economic), and a narrow set of policy instruments (too limited). However, many have argued that the difference between the post-WC and WC is relatively small. The post-WC in Stiglitz's iteration only repudiates fiscal discipline, liberalization of the capital account and tight monetary policy. Elsewhere there is only caution or sequencing rather than opposition to trade and FDI liberalization and privatization (Perraton 2004, p. 897). Rodrik (2002, p. 1) instead conceptualized an 'augmented WC', arguing that the WC describes the desirable features of development but not how to get them, and added ten policies to Williamson's original list to form an 'augmented WC'.[3]

The Asian financial crisis (and the earlier Latin American crash) shook faith in open markets to a considerable extent, though this was typically about faith in the liberalization of finance and the capital account initially and this spread

[2] Aggarwal and Evenett (2010) construct a new dataset called the 'Global Trade Alert' which records the number of measures announced and number of measures implemented in terms of 'protectionist' or 'liberalizing' from 2007–present based on the following list: bail-out/state aid measure; competitive devaluation; consumption subsidy; export incentive; export taxes or restriction; import ban; import quota; import subsidy; import tariff; intellectual property protection; investment measure; localization requirement; migration measure; non-tariff barrier (not otherwise specified); other service-sector measure; public procurement; public procurement localization; public procurement preference; sanitary and phytosanitary measure; state trading enterprise; state-controlled company; sub-national government measure; technical barrier to trade; trade defence measure; and trade finance.

[3] These set of ten were: corporate governance measures, anti-corruption measures, flexible labour markets, signing of WTO agreements, financial codes and standards, 'prudent' capital account liberalization, non-intermediate exchange rate regimes, independence for central banks and inflation targeting, social safety nets, and targeted poverty reduction.

in due course to other policy areas. In the late 2000s, it was the global financial crash and the rapid growth in China that triggered more statism. The first characteristic of this was the resurgence of the utilization of SOEs in national economic development. Although some SOEs had been privatized in the developing world many had only been part-privatized and governments had retained some form of ownership or control in key industries.

Musacchio and Lazzarini (2014), as noted in Chapter 3, emphasize that the resilience of state capitalism is startling given the extensive privatization programmes that were implemented in developing countries: in many developing countries, the ratio of SOE output to GDP has barely changed since the end of the Cold War. Even when ownership of SOEs was minority ownership rather than majority ownership, it was of a sufficient magnitude to ensure that the state remained the largest single investor and thus shaped the direction of the enterprise. In short, the Washington Consensus resulted in a partial privatization in many countries with governments retaining ownership or 'golden shares' in part-privatized SOEs.[4]

A second characteristic of a nascent, new developmentalism is the re-emergence of substantial domestic protectionism, subtle in its statism. Kim et al. (2017) notes three particular areas of emerging protectionism since the global crash: 'buy national' measures, stronger technical barriers, and safety regulations and controls on foreign investment. They note that the resurgence of a set of policies to encourage domestic production by state or the private sector, and incentives or requirements on foreign investors to source inputs locally have been put in place in the US and several large emerging economies.[5] This signals the 'acceptability' or normalization of such policies to other countries around the world. Of course, one could add that far fewer countries are aid-dependent than during the 1980s and 1990s, so a broader set of nationally determined policies is likely to emerge.

Furthermore, non-tariff barriers such as technical barriers and sanitary and phytosanitary regulations have been expanded. Kim et al., note that the total number of non-tariff barrier notifications almost doubled from 506 in 2007 to 968 in 2011 in developing countries. For example, imported capital equipment has been required to meet national standards.

Finally, controls on FDI, in terms of foreign share of ownership in natural resource sectors of energy and raw metals, have been rising. The opening of sectors to FDI has been halted in other countries, such as retail in India.

[4] A 'golden share' is a technical term for a share that gives the government a majority (or decisive) voting share. In many cases the governments of developing countries have simply retained significant ownership without creating golden shares.

[5] In the US, the 2009 American Recovery and Reinvestment Act had a provision to 'buy American' which required federally funded construction projects to buy US steel and iron. The same year China followed suit for government procurement. Brazil and India followed.

This pattern is in keeping with the global data on policy changes in developing countries within which there is a trend towards less favourable policies to foreign investors compared to domestic investors even before the global crash.

The 'new' or 'neo-developmentalism' was baptized with ten propositions at the Sao Paulo School of Economics in 2010 and signed by a number of heterodox economists including Alice Amsden and Robert Wade. The ten propositions (Amsden et al. 2012, pp. 336–8) are outlined in the following lengthy citation:

> Development is a structural process of utilizing all available domestic resources... the state has a strategic role in providing the appropriate institutional frameworks to support this structural process...The demand side is where major growth bottlenecks unfold...The tendency of wages to increase more slowly than productivity growth is due to the existence of an abundant supply of labour and the political economy of labour markets...A legal minimum wage, cash transfers to the poor, and principally a government guarantee to provide employment at a living wage could be used to neutralize this tendency to underpay labour. The alternative—chronic overvaluation of the national currency that increases purchasing power—is not a sustainable strategy...The tendency to cyclical overvaluation of the exchange rate in developing countries has been due to both the excessive reliance on external savings in the form of foreign capital flows and the Dutch disease in the context of excessively open capital markets and lack of appropriate regulation...Economic development should be financed essentially with domestic savings. In order to achieve this goal, the creation of public financial institutions to ensure full utilization of domestic resources, in particular labour, finance innovation and support investment is required.

In short, the new developmentalism sought to recognize the failure of neo-liberal policies but also the limitations of the state and classical developmentalism.[6] Bresser-Pereira (2013) argues that what distinguishes the new developmentalism or what he calls the 'new national developmentalism' is not only the role of the state and industrial policy, but a growth model based on domestic, not foreign, savings, and macroeconomic policy based on moderate interest rates and competitive exchange rates rather than high interest rates (to attract foreign capital), and an over-valued currencies.

The new developmentalism resonates with Gore's (2000) account, written a decade earlier, on the 'latent southern consensus' which was a synthesis of East Asian developmentalism (which Gore characterized as state-facilitated

[6] Relatedly, there was discussion of a 'Beijing Consensus' following the global crash. The Beijing Consensus has had various attempted definitions but typically is taken to mean state-orchestrated capitalism as per the Chinese economic development (Dirlik 2006; Ramo 2004; Rebol 2010). Williamson (2012) described the Beijing Consensus in contrast to his Washington Consensus as one of incremental reforms, innovation, experimentation, export-led growth, state capitalism, and authoritarianism.

private sector-led development) and Latin American neo-structuralism (which Gore framed as a concern with centre-periphery relations in delivering the conditions for national development).[7]

At the same time a more significant intellectual revival in structuralism is identified by Storm (2015), drawing inspiration from historical figures such as Kaldor (1967) and also Gerschenkron (1962), and more contemporary writing including Thirlwall's Keynesian growth law and the balance of payment constraint (see Thirlwall 1979, 2011), Pasinetti's (1983, 1991) demand-driven approach, Taylor's (1983, 1991, 2004) structuralist macroeconomics, Reinert's (2007) historical school approach, Cimoli and Porcile's (2014) synthesis of structuralism with Kaldor and Pasinetti's structural dynamics, and others writing in the structuralist tradition.

In sum, a ferment of new developmentalism is evident. It is, on the one hand, partly a revival of older ideas within structuralism and more broadly, heterodox theory. On the other hand, it is 'new' in the sense that inclusive growth is an important part as it addresses demand-side policies, minimum wages, social transfers, and full employment. It advocates development via domestic savings. The aim is capitalist development (it is not revolutionary in terms of a socialist society), but with full employment and financial stability. It is similar to classical developmentalism in the sense that it sees development as ST and the structure of the global economy as a constraint to that process. It is different in that it advocates an open economy. However, as infant industry is already built, it states that industrial policy should support firms to compete internationally via state-supported upgrading. It also places importance on price and financial stability. It is a new iteration of developmentalism, or an attempt by developing countries to achieve national economic development.

In South East Asia, the Asian financial crisis of the late 1990s induced, as with crises in the late 1960s and early to mid 1980s, a reincarnation or morphing of developmentalism into a new developmentalism. In this new developmentalism the state is central. That said, new developmentalism is often subtler than the historically cruder forms of 'old' developmentalism. It is also useful to distinguish the direction and the level of protectionism/liberalization. The key difference between two-tier and new developmentalism is the

[7] Gore (2000, p. 796) identifies five groups of policies: (i) the strategic integration of the national and international economy rather than rapid liberalization (i.e. gradual import liberalization, promotion of exports, and promotion of FDI with local linkages); (ii) growth and structural change by 'productive development policy' (controlling inflation, fiscal discipline, but also full employment and state facilitation of this through, for example, human resource development); (iii) a developmental state linking government and business cooperation where the private sector leads but the government sets the framework (i.e. overcoming technology imperfections); (iv) the 'managing' of distribution and growth to ensure productive employment (i.e. agrarian reform); and (v) regional integration and cooperation.

changes in the direction of economic policy: during the former period the direction shifted from protectionism to liberalization and during the latter period the direction shifted from liberalization to protectionism. A difference between 'new' developmentalism and two-tier and classical developmentalism has been the emergent forces of democratization and populist politics of different kinds in MIT. Whilst the stability of democratic institutions is questionable, there is no doubt that forces advocating democracy have been spreading. This new 'democratic developmental state' has been the subject of discussion in terms of its welfare policies (see, for example, White 1995, 1998) though less so to date in Southeast Asia given the relative recent spread of democracy in Southeast Asia (though there is some discussion on Indonesia in Rock (2017)).

The extent of the rise of populist and democratic forces is clear in MIT. In Malaysia, the Asian financial crisis was least severe in immediate economic terms due to the unorthodox response that was pursued. Nevertheless, the crisis brought to the fore an intra-elite structural conflict within the Barisan Nasional, the coalition that has been a dominant force in Malay politics. That conflict was between those such as Deputy Prime Minister Anwar Ibrahim, who favoured a market-based response to the crisis and Prime Minister Mahathir who wished to bail out indigenous private conglomerates. Ibrahim was subsequently imprisoned and this became a central issue in Malaysian politics. Malaysia has, over time, become more authoritarian in its political context. The 1999 election was won by a new coalition or 'alternative front' led by Ibrahim's wife but political repression expanded. Abdullah Badawi succeeded Mahathir (who retired) but pursued a Mahathirist path. When Najib Razak replaced Abdullah the repression and the imprisonment of Anwar continued. Not only was the imprisonment of Anwar of political consequence, but it was also economic in that Anwar was economically liberal in outlook and those opposing him were not so.

In Indonesia, the Asian financial crisis was severe and removed Suharto and the New Order, ushering in a new period of democratization. Indonesia's transition to democracy has been reasonably smooth. It was not given, though, that Jokowi would win the presidency. Indeed, the election was close at times in the opinion polls and his opponent was very much a Suharto-era figure with a very different and conservative platform. That said, Jokowi's election, and political appointments since, suggest an accommodation has been met with various factions of the Suharto era. The most important process within democratization has been an extensive decentralization programme that has been put in place. At the same time, a new business class has emerged and the military have stepped back from politics. Poczter and Pepinksy (2016) argue that there has been a simultaneous (at least at the national level) rise of the private sector and decline of the military as avenues to political influence, and this pre-dates democratization. At a sub-national level, however, Buehler (2016) discusses political dynasties with an emphasis on former New Order bureaucrats becoming elected politicians.

In Thailand, the Asian financial crisis was also severe and the political landscape shifted radically after the crisis towards populism under Thaksin's leadership, and a major redistribution. This was followed by a political backlash to control the extent of the redistribution and the social forces of populism. Khan (2010) argues that many more senior political positions were filled by the business class during the 1990s and that the expansion of, in particular, rural business-led coalitions, undermined the formal technocratic institutions. What emerged was a period of populism until the late 2000s when there was a backlash of 'authoritarianism with a democratic face'. A Thaksin-associated party (though he was in exile) won the 2007 election but not with an absolute majority.[8] Chaotic scenes emerged in occupations by the yellow shirts (the royal colour) versus Thaksin-supporting red shirts and, in 2008, the Democratic Party, which represents the old oligarchy/business and middle classes, was elected. The political friction ahead is about reaching an accommodation between the groups Thaksin has mobilized, largely the rural poor, and the provincial elites.

In sum, across MIT the Asian financial crisis triggered or accelerated the expansion of business interests in politics, often at the expense of military interests and unleashed democratic or popular political forces. These were allowed to expand in Indonesia but were repressed in Malaysia. In Thailand the forces were allowed to expand and then were constrained, and then expanded and constrained again. In Indonesia it is thus possible to discuss a 'democratic developmental state'. The same is not the case in Malaysia and Thailand so far. White (1998) argues that the developmental state is based on autonomy (of state institutions and political elites which allows the strategic pursuit of development) and social embeddedness (the state is an alliance of social groups). These are not easy to sustain in a democratic polity, he argues.[9] So far Indonesia has had both democracy and a renaissance of the developmental state. A new state–capitalist pact was defined across MIT in terms of the social structure of capital accumulation, which was more statist (though often

[8] The backlash was driven by Thaksin's visible corruption in the allocation of resources. Although Thaksin won the election (boycotted by opposition), a parliament could not be established due to unfilled seats in the south of the country, and growing urban middle-class protests led to the coup in 2007.

[9] He argues such democratic developmental states are unlikely to emerge because they require a set of supporting factors such as higher-levels of socio-economic development and a lack of extreme inequalities, a well organized political party system not organized on sectional or personalistic lines, state institutions where executive authority is concentrated and the state is staffed by professional civil servants, and where national autonomy is not undermined by external political or economic dependence.

subtly so) than the period of the mid 1980s to the mid 1990s. At the same time, the expansion of welfare regimes has become increasingly important politically in terms of winning elections across MIT.

6.3 New Developmentalism in South East Asia: The Empirical Experience of South East Asia

It is too early to fully assess if nascent, new developmentalism is likely to achieve more than the earlier incarnations of developmentalism. What is evident so far is a stalling of the Lewisian transition in MIT. In this section, we consider what has happened so far in terms of ST and IG since the mid to late 1990s. The discussion of the data that follows argues that the crisis was a turning point in terms of ST and IG in MIT. As before, we discuss the dimensions of ST (sectoral, factoral, and integrative) and the dimensions of IG (changes in consumption and capabilities).

The argument of this section is that the outcomes of ST and IG in MIT in this period are much less impressive than previous periods. With reference to the Lewisian transition, we note stalled manufacturing expansion in employment, output, and export shares. There has been declining agriculture employment shares in Indonesia and Thailand accompanied by a large increase in the shares of service-sector employment. Economic growth has been driven by total factor productivity in contrast to earlier waves of ST and capital accumulation. We can see that absolute poverty has declined to very low levels in Malaysia and Thailand (but remains an issue for Indonesia). The decline in poverty has been accompanied by a rise in the share of population living in economic insecurity, who have simply crossed above the poverty line but remain a long distance from the $10-per-day security from poverty line.

At the same time, education completion at lower secondary level has become universal, suggesting an exhaustion of the potential to address skilled/unskilled labour income divergences without expansion at higher education completion levels. Overall, consumption/income inequality has followed diverging trends across South East Asia. Inequality has fallen in Thailand, risen substantially in Indonesia, and fallen slightly in Malaysia. We can say that growth has been exclusive in terms of employment growth in agriculture and in manufacturing, but more inclusive in services.

Finally, with reference to heterodox theory and structuralism in particular, we can see a wave of ST which entails a clear decline of exports in manufacturing and high-tech manufacturing, and a rise in fuel exports, and the peak and subsequent decline of natural resource rents in Malaysia and Indonesia with the commodity boom and its end; volatile FDI across MIT and declining external debt in Indonesia and Thailand sit alongside the rise of external debt in Malaysia.

First, let us consider the period in terms of sectoral ST. If we take the data on aggregate and per capita GDP growth rates in MIT for the period, the severity of the Asian financial crisis is immediately evident. Each of the countries posted economic contractions. In Indonesia, where the economic crash was most severe, the recovery was a return to approximately 6 per cent GDP growth rates on average per annum. In Thailand and Malaysia there is a second period of negative growth towards the end of the 2000s. Sectoral growth rates (Figure 6.1) show some sectoral growth was, for some periods, at respectable levels. However, only in Indonesia were the sectoral growth rates of agriculture, manufacturing, and services sustained over the period. Most notably, manufacturing and service-sector growth ended the period weakening in both Malaysia and Thailand.

Consequently, the period since 1995 has been one where ST has differed between countries (see Figure 6.2). Value-added in agriculture declined slightly across MIT, and employment shares in agriculture continued to fall, rapidly so in Indonesia and Thailand. Value-added shares in manufacturing fell in Indonesia whilst plateauing in Malaysia and Thailand. Employment shares in manufacturing were stagnant and even fell substantially in Malaysia. In contrast, employment and value-added shares rose in services across the

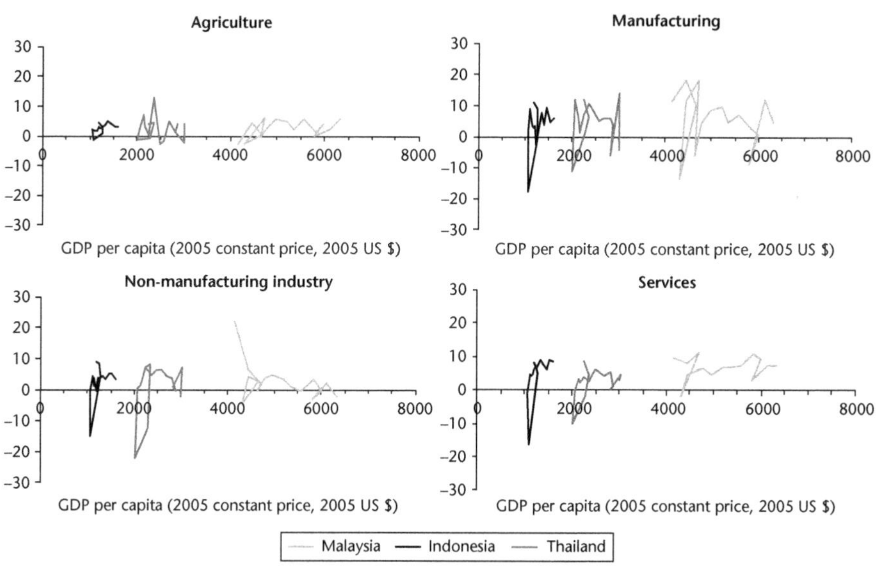

Figure 6.1 Sectoral growth rates (five-year moving average), 1995–2011 (or available years)

Source: Author's calculation based on Timmer et al. (2015).

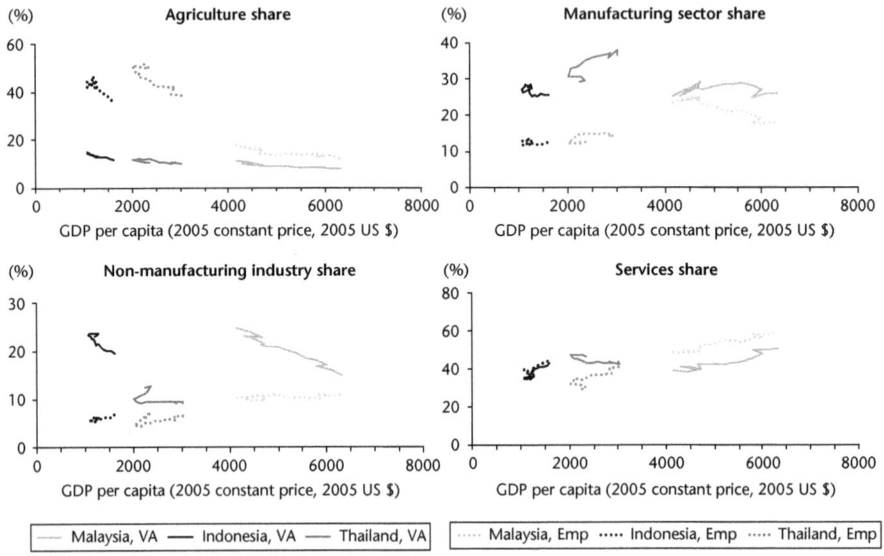

Figure 6.2 GDP and employment shares, 1995–2011 (or available years)
Source: Author's calculation based on Timmer et al. (2015).

three countries with the exception of a slight decline in value-added shares in services in Thailand.

What is surprising given the level of GDP per capita is the persistence of Lewisian dualism in that more than a third of the labour force remains in agriculture in Indonesia and Thailand, and even in Malaysia over a tenth of the labour force remains in agriculture. Informal employment, too, remains large. ILO (2017) data shows that—the majority—more than half of the Indonesian labour force (in 2009) remains in the informal sector (and the informal sector accounts for three-quarters of non-agriculture employment in Indonesia).[10] The World Bank (2010) argues that these workers are split evenly between agriculture and non-agriculture but are typically rural dwellers (70 per cent of total), and poor or near-poor resonating with a Lewisian characterization of a modern and a traditional sector. As well as conditions and social insurance there are large differences between median wages in formal and informal sectors. Informal sector wage rates are half those of formal sector permanent staff and informal sector workers are also trapped in the sense that there is very low mobility between the formal and informal sectors (World Bank 2010, p. 16). In comparison, the ILO (2017) estimates that two-thirds of total employment is accounted for by the informal sector in Thailand

[10] The ILO (2017) definition is consistent across MIT. Specifically, that informal employment includes persons who are informal employees, own-account workers, and family workers or producers of goods exclusively for own final use.

but non-agriculture is more formalized—approximately forty per cent of non-agriculture employment is informal (in 2011–2013). In Malaysia, only a tenth of non-agriculture employment is accounted for by the informal sector (2012 and 2013). One question to ask is how far the Lewis turning point (the exhaustion of surplus rural labour) is ahead. Indonesia and Thailand are unlikely to have got to this point, given that a third of the labour force remain in agriculture.[11]

A crude proxy might be taken to be trends in rural unemployment (with data drawn from ILO 2017; see Table 6.2). The ILO definition includes those without work (not in paid or self employment) and currently available and actively seeking work (have taken specific steps to seek paid or self employment in the period). The eradication of rural unemployment would suggest the Lewis turning point was reached. The data shows that rural unemployment was low in Malaysia (at about 100,000 in 2014) and Thailand (at about 180,000 in 2014) and substantial in Indonesia (3m in 2013). In each case, rural unemployment fluctuated in the late 2000s or early 2010s.

Manning and Purnagunawan (2017) discuss whether Indonesia has passed the Lewis turning point, when unskilled labour becomes scarce, wages rise, and capital deepening and technological progress occurs—and if it matters. They note the surge in formal sector employment since 2010, and look for three signs (2017, p. 14): a sharp fall in agricultural employment or increases in agricultural productivity and wages; narrowing of inter-sectoral differentials between agriculture and other sectors; and contraction in both size and growth of the informal sector relative to the formal sector in non-agriculture. Manning and Purnagunawan (2017) argue that with regard to all three criteria there is evidence of tightening labour markets in Indonesia during the periods of rapid economic growth pre-AFC, and in the mid 2000s to the present. However, low productivity agriculture is still a very large employer, as is the informal sector in Indonesia as noted. Wage differentials between agriculture and non-agriculture are still large, even if they are narrowing, and in absolute numbers of workers there has been hardly any change in agriculture from the mid 1980s to the present, and this is the case in Java and elsewhere. They conclude that labour markets in MIT are less integrated spatially, so the Lewis turning point in a land or resource-abundant country may be harder to identify—there may be regional transitions.

Figure 6.3 shows the decomposition of growth by sector. As before, the total change in growth equals 100 per cent. The figure shows that in Indonesia, Malaysia, and Thailand there was a shift towards services as a more significant

[11] Taking a Kuznetsian approach, Kanbur and Zhuang (2013, p. 142) put the turning point for national inequality (the sum of the components) at an urbanization rate of 85 per cent for Indonesia (currently it is 54 per cent).

Table 6.2. Unemployment, thousands (15 years of age and over)

	2005	2006	2007	2008	2009	2010	2011	2012	2013	2014	2015	2016
Malaysia												
National	368.1	353.5	351.4	368.5	418	395.8	391.9	395.5	424.5	399.4	450.3	–
Rural	132.3	123.4	123.0	131.5	139.2	136.8	136.2	129.5	127.2	105.2	108.1	–
Urban	235.8	230.1	228.4	237	278.7	259	254.8	266.7	297.6	294.3	342.2	–
Indonesia												
National	–	–	10011.1	9394.5	8962.6	8319.8	7700.1	7245	7410.9	–	7560.8	7031.8
Rural	–	–	4386.6	4206.9	3810.2	3662.8	2973.9	2881.3	3125.8	–	4679.2	2688.5
Urban	–	–	5624.5	5187.7	5152.4	4656.9	4726.2	4363.7	4285.1	–	2881.6	4343.3
Thailand												
National	–	–	–	–	572.3	402.2	262.4	230.8	305.6	326.6	–	362.5
Rural	–	–	–	–	392.8	265.3	154.8	139.1	187.7	179.9	–	170.5
Urban	–	–	–	–	179.5	136.9	107.6	91.7	117.9	146.8	–	192

Source: ILO (2017).

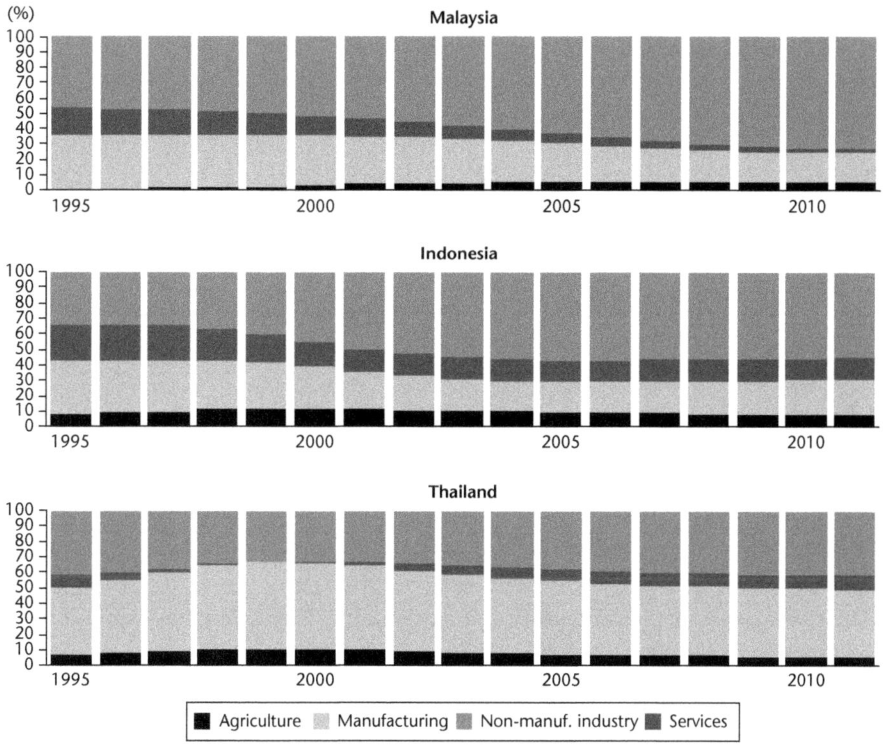

Figure 6.3 Growth decomposition by sector, 1995–2011 (or available years) (change in growth = 100.0)

Source: Author's calculation based on Timmer et al. (2015).

driver of growth, with manufacturing squeezed in importance in each country, though less so in Thailand where it remained important.

Next, let us consider factoral ST. If we consider demography, from the mid 1990s to the present day, Malaysia, Indonesia, and Thailand saw continued declines in the age dependency ratio (see Figure 6.4). In Malaysia, this was a fall from 65 per cent to 45 per cent, in Indonesia, a fall from 61 per cent to 50 per cent, and in Thailand, a fall from 48 per cent to 39 per cent.

Malaysia's population has continued to urbanize rapidly (from a half to three-quarters of the population) and Indonesia and Thailand have also experienced substantial urbanization from about a third of the population to about half of the population in the last few years.

Figure 6.5 shows labour productivity by sector. The figure shows that the period was an important one for labour productivity growth in manufacturing and services. Figure 6.6 decomposes growth by factor (change in growth = 100). The figure shows that growth continued to be driven by capital accumulation overall. That said, in each of MIT, to differing extents, total factor

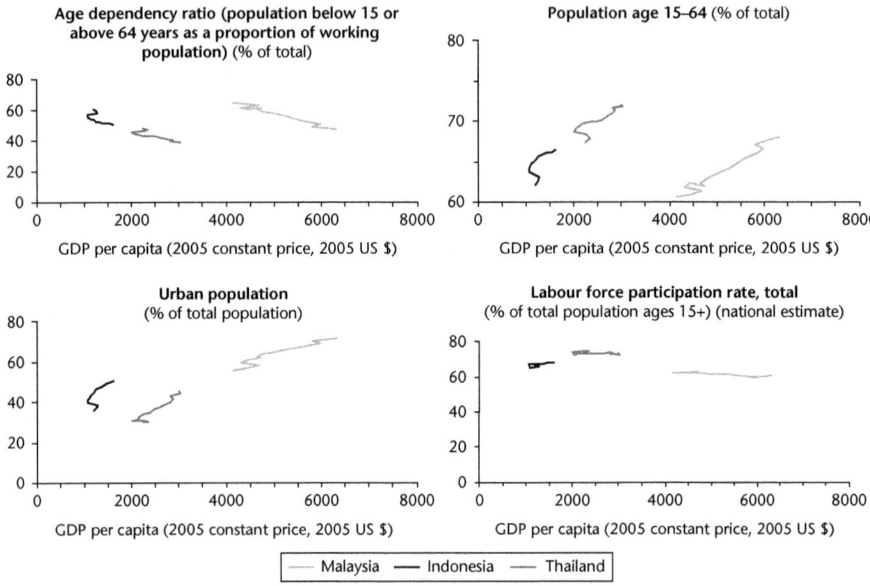

Figure 6.4 Demographic and urbanization trends, 1995–present (or available years)
Source: Author's calculation based on World Bank (2017).

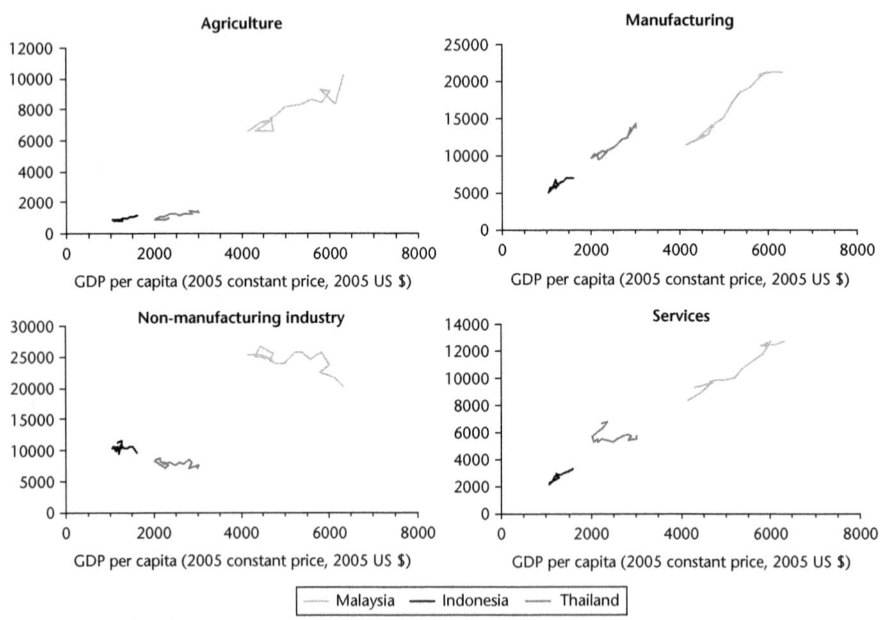

Figure 6.5 Labour productivity, 1995–2011 (or available years)
Source: Author's calculation based on Timmer et al. (2015).

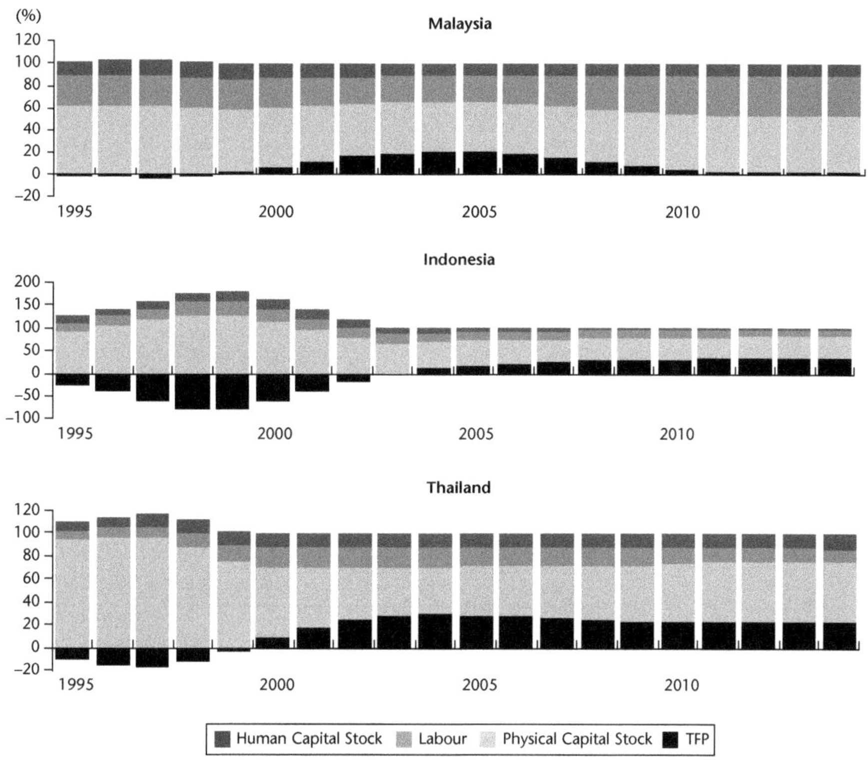

Figure 6.6 Growth decomposition by factor, 1995–2011 (or available years) (change in growth = 100.0)

Source: Author's calculation based on Timmer et al. (2015).

productivity became more important over time (though in Malaysia this was only during the middle of the period).

The period was a turning point for capital productivity (see Figure 6.7). In the classical developmentalism period the productivity of capital (the capital-output ratio or the amount of capital needed to produce one output unit) was declining quite notably. The productivity of capital stabilized in the early 1980s in Thailand and in the late 1980s in Malaysia and Indonesia. The current period of new developmentalism is one that is associated with a turning point in terms of the rising productivity of capital. This could be as a result of the Asian financial crisis, in that it was only the efficient firms that survived, not the inefficient ones. It is also associated with weaker employment growth, which has implications for IG and the stability of the social structure of capital accumulation.

Finally, we consider integrative ST. Figures 6.8 and 6.9 show an emerging shift in the trade structure. The composition of exports shifted substantially, though in differing directions in each of MIT. Shares in manufacturing exports

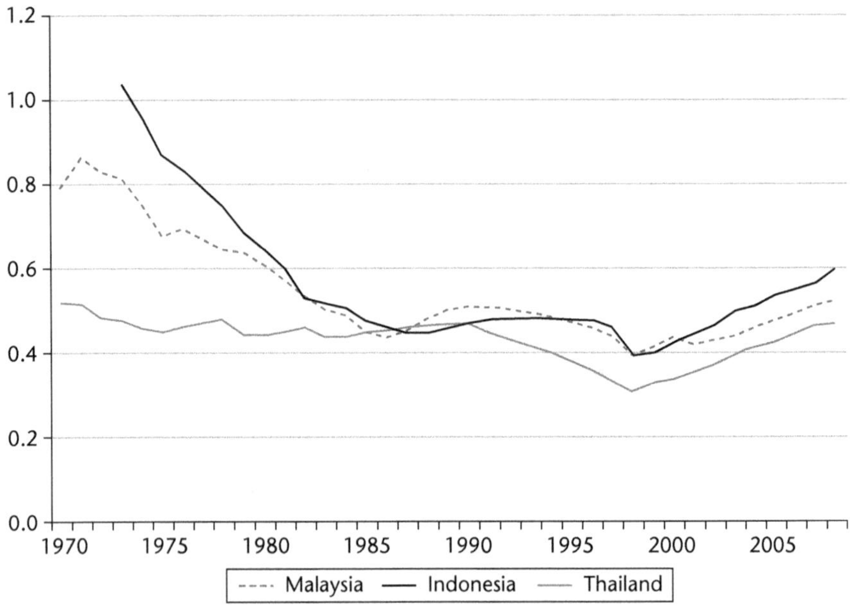

Figure 6.7 Productivity of capital (output-capital ratio), 1970–2010 (or available years)
Source: Based on data from Marquetti and Foley (2011).

fell notably, with large declines in Indonesia and Malaysia, though less so in Thailand. Furthermore, and alarmingly, the share of high-tech in those manufacturing exports fell substantially. At the same time, fuel exports and exports of ores and metals rose, reflecting the commodity boom of the 2000s. Import composition also shifted. Fuel imports and ores and metal imports increased. The net impact on trade balances was that, in general, each of MIT were in trade surplus, Malaysia substantially so, for much of the period.

Figure 6.10 shows sources of development finance for the period. The sources shifted somewhat. Although official development assistance (ODA) was important to Indonesia around the 1997/8 crisis, it declined to irrelevance shortly after, as was the case throughout Malaysia and Thailand. Natural resource rents in both Indonesia and Malaysia saw a resurgence in importance with the commodity boom in the 2000s. In the late 2000s, natural resource rents in Indonesia, at their peak, almost hit a fifth of GDP. Even in Thailand, where historically natural resource rents were less important, such rents rose from about 1 to 7 per cent of GDP.

To some extent, FDI inflows languished in Indonesia and Malaysia. In Indonesia, such flows were even negative for part of the period and became more important only in the late 2000s when the commodity boom ended. At this time, FDI quickly rose from relatively low levels to 3 per cent of GDP. In Malaysia, although FDI inflows remained important, they were highly

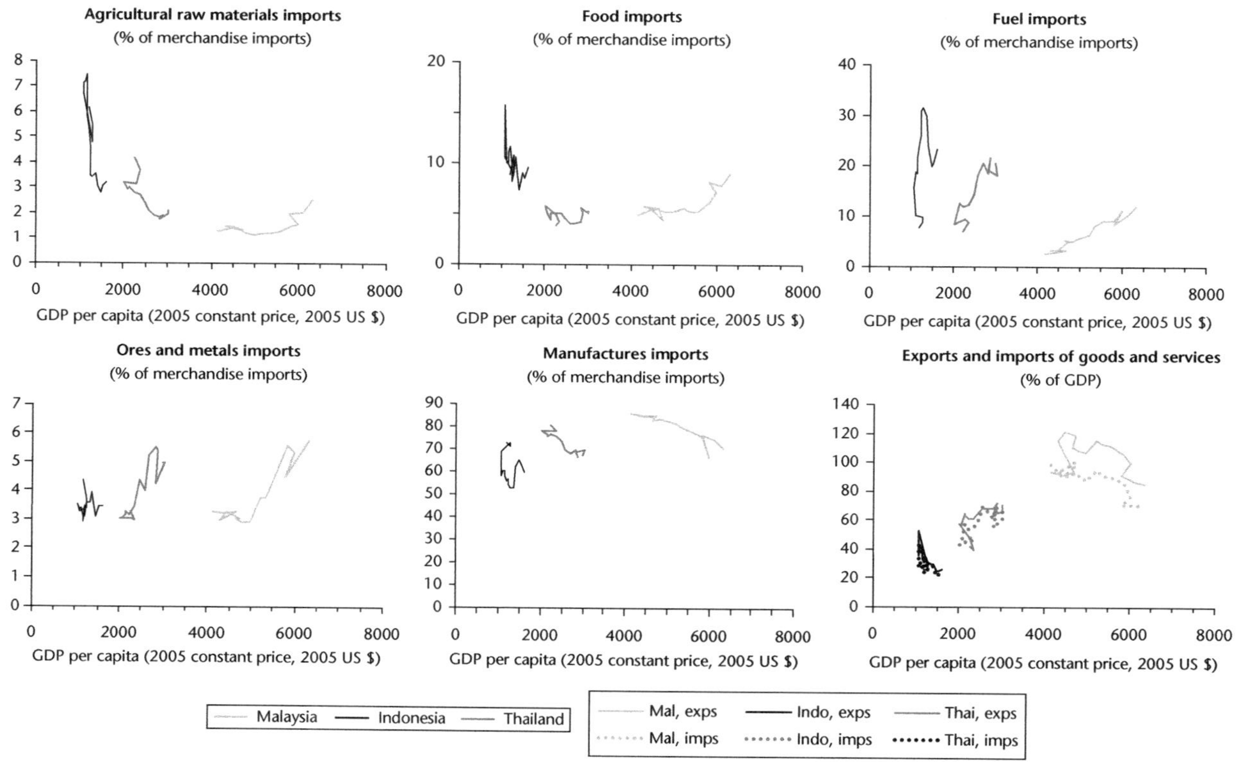

Figure 6.8 Composition of imports, 1995–2011 (or available years)

Source: Author's calculation based on Timmer et al. (2015).

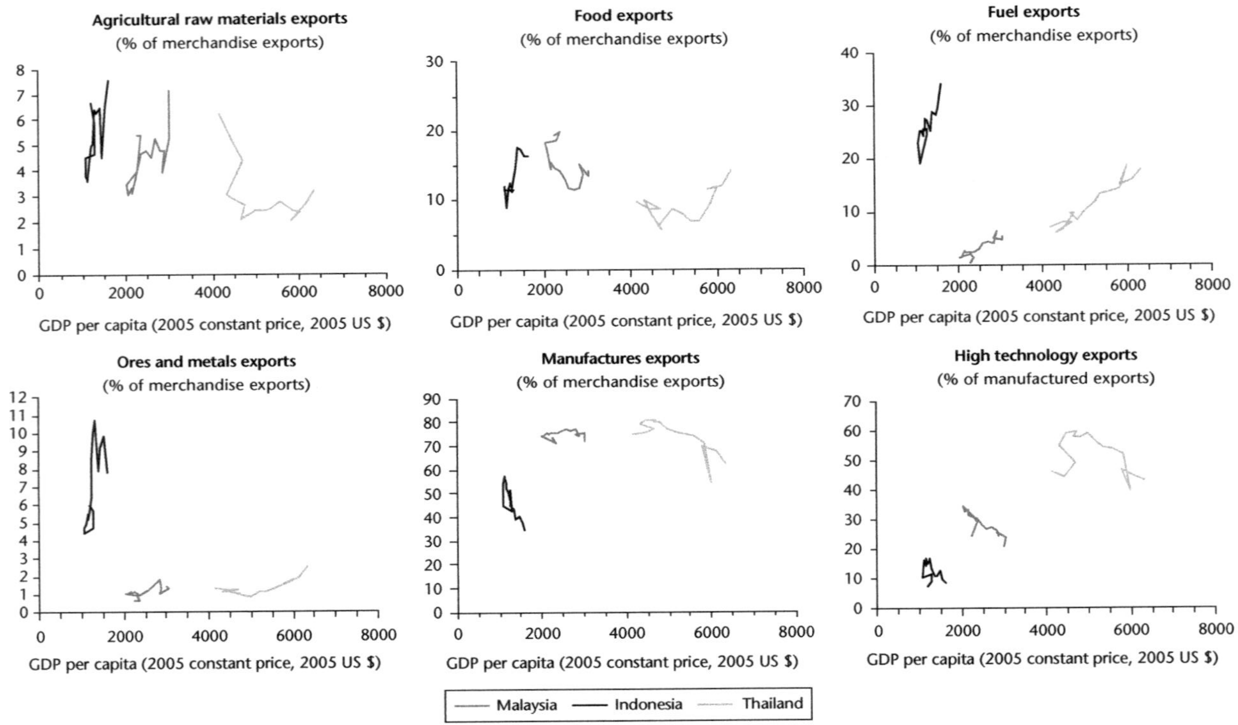

Figure 6.9 Composition of exports, 1995–2011 (or available years)

Source: Author's calculation based on Timmer et al. (2015).

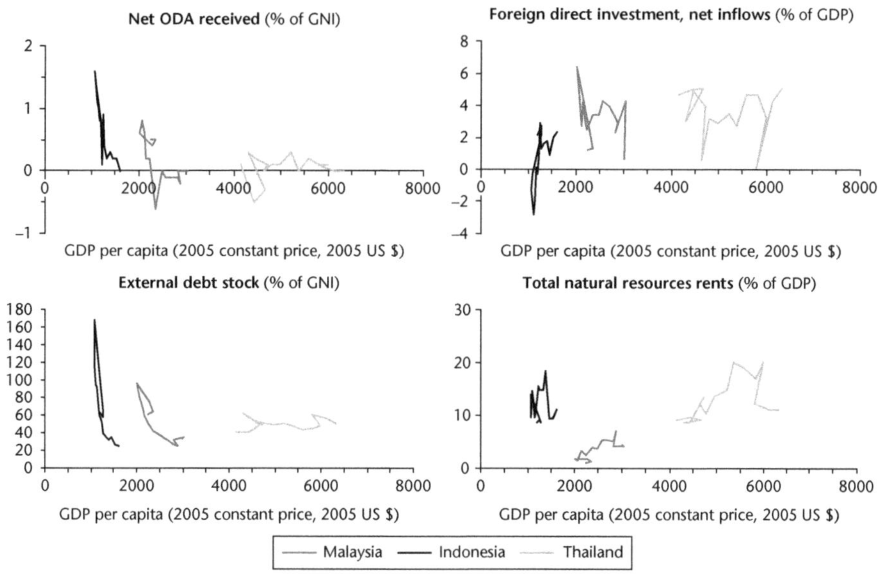

Figure 6.10 Sources of development financing, 1995–present (or available years)
Source: Author's calculation based on World Bank (2017).

volatile, and no higher at the end of the period than the start. Only in Thailand did FDI inflows expand over the commodity period, rising from around 1–3 per cent in the mid 1990s to peaks of 3–4 per cent, but with considerable volatility reflecting the political tensions in Thailand in the late 2000s. Outward FDI, particularly from Malaysia, grew to significant levels, doubling to around 5–6 per cent of GDP by the end of the period. Furthermore, Thailand and Indonesia also became sources of outward FDI. Though starting from a very low point, outward FDI rose to levels of 2–3 per cent by the end of the period (though with some volatility) in Thailand and at a lower, though significant level of 1 per cent of GDP or more in Indonesia.

External debt became much less important in Indonesia and Thailand, falling from peaks of 160 per cent of GDP in Indonesia to a fraction of that level. Conversely, in Malaysia the opposite happened with a rise in the external debt stock from the mid 1990s onwards, rising in the late 1990s, then falling, then rising again in the late 2000s at the end of the commodity boom.

Next, we turn to IG. Figure 6.11 shows how poverty rates at $2.50 per day fell across the countries to the point where absolute poverty has been virtually eradicated in Malaysia and Thailand. In Indonesia, absolute poverty still affects one in four of the population, but this fell from two-thirds of the population in the late 1990s. That said, poverty at the $10 per day level fell

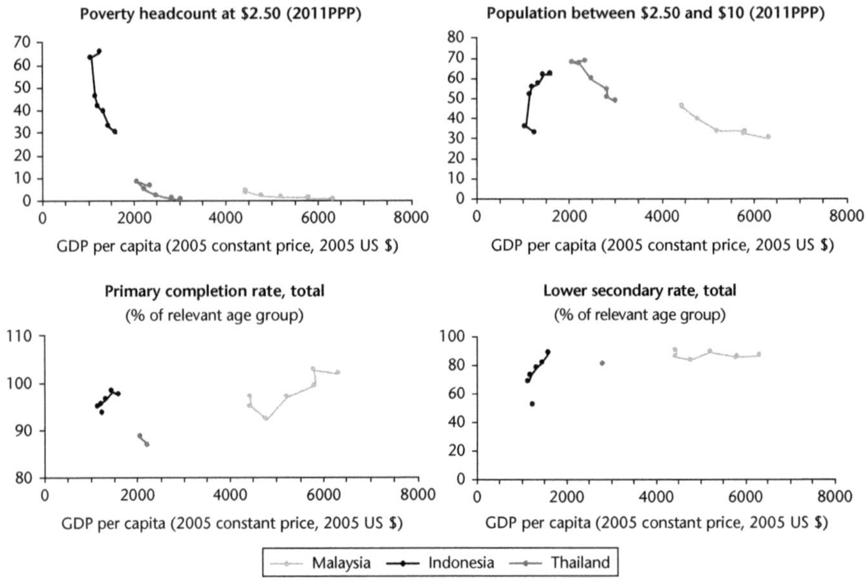

Figure 6.11 Poverty, insecurity, and inequality of opportunity, 1995–present (or available years)

Source: Edward and Sumner (2016) and World Bank (2017).

but still affected a quarter of all Malaysians, almost half of all Thais, and 90 per cent of Indonesians. In short, something approximating insecurity has replaced absolute poverty.

Figure 6.11 also shows the proxy for equalizing opportunities, primary school completion rates which were very high across MIT, and lower secondary completion rates which are 80–90 per cent of the relevant age group across MIT. The equalizing effect of education expansion is thus approaching a point of exhaustion at primary level and possibly at lower secondary in due course.

Figure 6.12 shows changes in inequality of outcome and fiscal redistribution. The share of the richest 1 per cent has fluctuated in Indonesia but fallen in Thailand. Malaysia only has one data point. The share to the poorer half of the population has unambiguously fallen in Indonesia and risen in Thailand. The net Gini has risen in Indonesia notably, fallen in Thailand dramatically, and has fallen just slightly in Malaysia. Labour and capital shares were more or less steady.

The Groningen Growth and Development Centre (GGDC) data show that job creation was largely service sector-led. In Malaysia, the service sector was the largest contributor of new jobs. In some years, manufacturing contributed

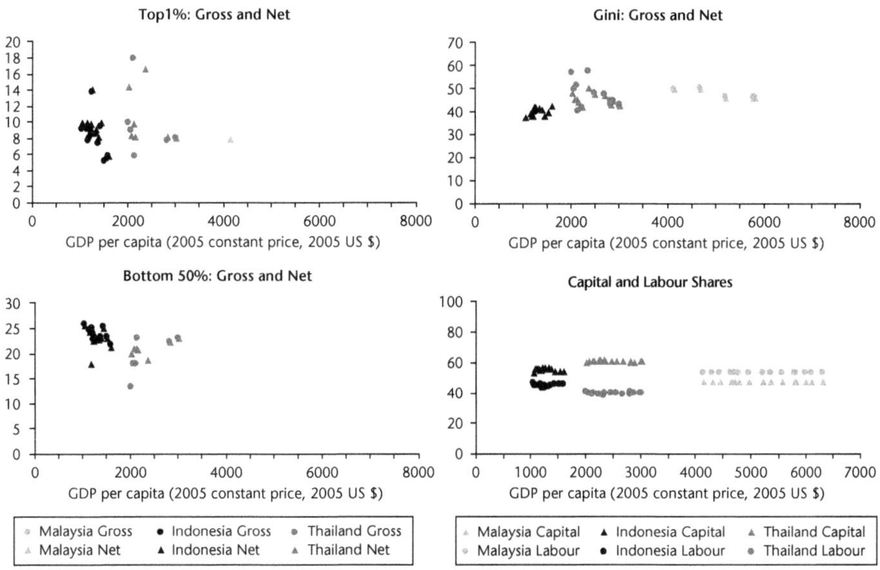

Figure 6.12 Inequality of outcome and fiscal redistribution, 1995–present (or available years)

Note: Inklaar and Timmer (2013) assume labour shares remained constant or if missing years linearly interpolation and a set of rules are used (see pp. 20–21).

Sources: Inklaar and Timmer (2013); UNU-WIDER (forthcoming).

to job growth though not on the same scale as earlier periods. A similar picture can be painted for Thailand and Indonesia where job creation was dominated by the service sector and was accompanied by negative job creation in agriculture. Figure 6.13 shows the sectoral perspective. The most notable change to the earlier period is that growth in agriculture in both Indonesia and Thailand moved over the dotted line. In other sectors, too, the plots are not only a considerable distance away from the one-to-one line and in the exclusive growth space, they also diverge further from that dotted line, suggesting that growth is becoming less inclusive over time in MIT. This is particularly the case in manufacturing.

In sum, structural change and inclusive growth in South East Asia in the period were uneven across Malaysia, Indonesia, and Thailand. The Lewisian transition weakened considerably and MIT experienced a middle-income plateau in terms of industrialization. Kuznetsian forces diverged across MIT. Poverty is being replaced by insecurity over time. In Section 6.4, we discuss the period's social structure of capital accumulation.

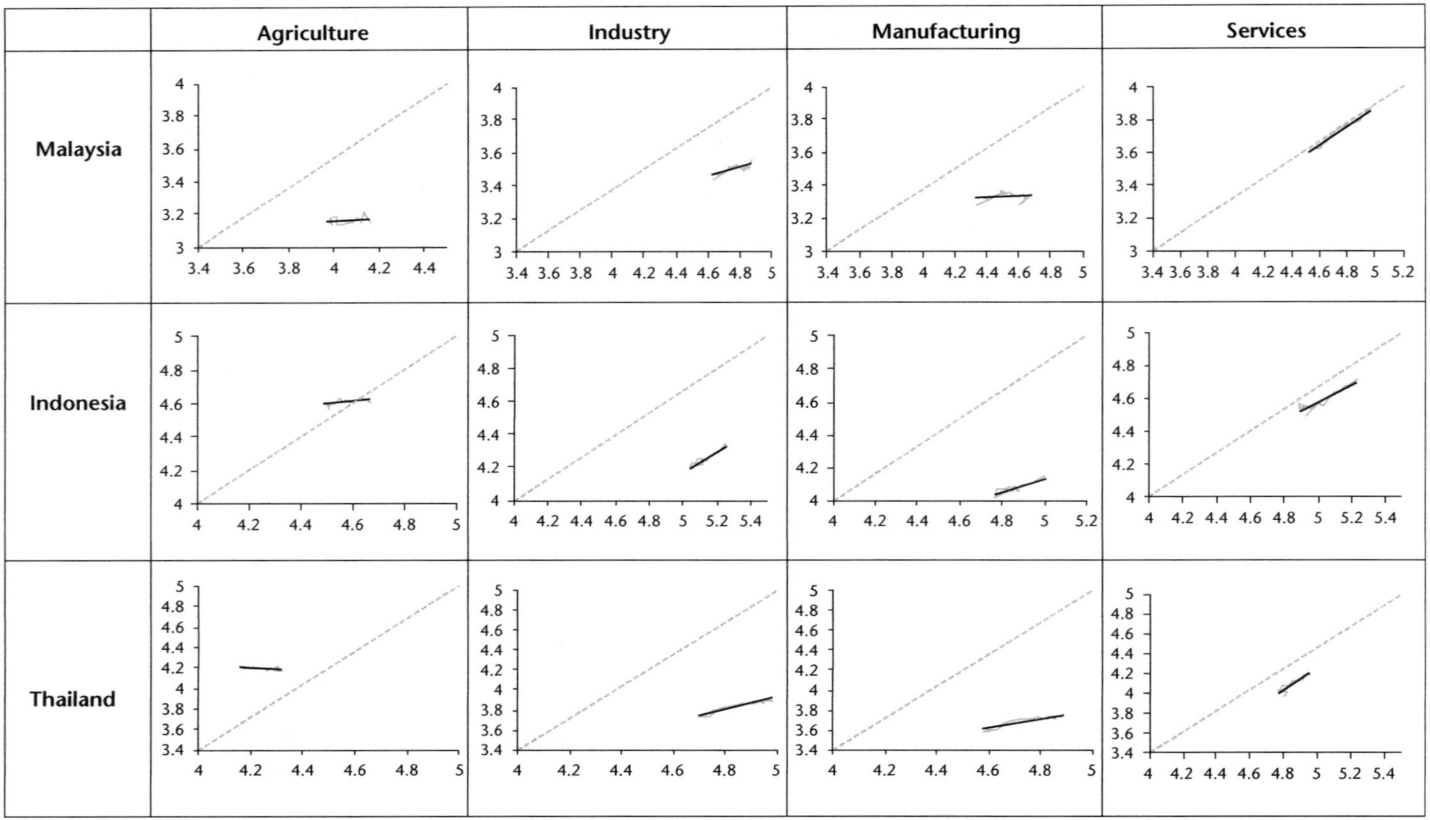

Figure 6.13 Value-added versus employment growth by sector, 1995–2011 (or available years)

Source: Author's calculation based on Timmer et al. (2015).

6.4 New Developmentalism in South East Asia: The Social Structure of Capital Accumulation

6.4.1 *Overview and Context*

The purpose of this section is to discuss the social structure of capital accumulation from the mid 1990s to the present day in MIT. We take the mid 1990s as the beginning of this period because it marks the eve of the Asian financial crisis. Although we date this era to the present, further important contextual factors were the commodity boom from the early 2000s to late 2000s; the 2007/8 global financial crisis, in the sense that the US response (state intervention) has, to some extent opened space for new developmentalism; the subsequent slow growth in OECD countries; and the entry of China and other countries such as Vietnam into the global economy in the 2000s, which have all had a substantial impact on MIT.

The argument of this section, with reference to the varieties of developmentalism, is that (i) the era was one of new or nascent revivalist developmentalism which has much in common with classical developmentalism in its suspicion of international capital, although it is open in many other aspects and is a subtler form of statism; (ii) that new manifestations of dependency and subordination emerged in the late 1990s, notably that MIT are potentially 'stuck' at a certain access point in global value chains. In short there is a lack of domestic firms that could achieve higher valued-added entry points in global value chains. The causes of this are the foreign ownership of MIT manufacturing which achieved so much in the previous era, but which had its own limitations as it ensured a semi-periphery maintenance by mediating against upgrading by domestic small- and medium-sized enterprises (SMEs).

In short, industrialization is possible via global integration (in contrast to the many heterodox theories discussed) but only to a point, after which new forms of dependency or subordination and industrial 'stickiness' emerge. The importing of foreign labour to keep real wage growth low, visible in MIT, and the need to maintain competitive advantage in manufacturing has made matters worse. It has 'locked in' the problem, in the sense that failure to create a tight labour market for lower-skilled jobs has resulted in MIT remaining somewhat competitive for a time, or at least slowing the decline but without upgrading to higher valued-added activities.

In this period, as noted previously, MIT could access resources for financing development from aid (during the Asian financial crisis) and then via the commodity boom up to the late 2000s. Consequently, international capital, notably, FDI became less important in relative terms. MIT pursued a nascent revivalist or new developmentalism, which has much in common with classical developmentalism and suggests that much of state or state-linked capital (especially so finance) and statist ideology survived the Washington Consensus years. The main difference is that revivalist developmentalism is a more open form of developmentalism in contrast to classical developmentalism, which was based on autarky to some degree, at least initially. This shift reflects or indeed frames the changing nature of industrialization. Industrialization under classical developmentalism entailed the building of new, domestically owned industries. Now industrialization is about accessing global value chains that are controlled by TNCs, and developing countries seek to move up the value-added chain by upgrading labour force skills, infrastructure, and domestic company capabilities as suppliers.

The Asian financial crisis led to a consolidation of indebted enterprises into state-holding agencies and the renaissance of SOEs in different ownership structures. The main instruments of new developmentalism are non-tariff barriers (rather than tariff barriers) to protect domestic capital, state-directed credit to SOEs and non-SOEs on a large scale, and local content requirements on FDI. In short, although strands of classical developmentalism may be discernible, the new variety of developmentalism is one of a strategically open economy.

If we use the global trade alert dataset (of Aggarwal and Evenett 2010), we find the new developmentalism. The dataset specifically records policy changes as liberal or protectionist using a traffic lights scheme, coding green as liberal and red as protectionist. Here we use the policy implementation data. Since the global financial crisis, which is when the recording of this dataset begins, all three countries, Malaysia, Indonesia, and Thailand, have pursued net protectionist positions virtually every year. Indonesia in particular has introduced many measures on the protectionist side. Figure 6.14 shows

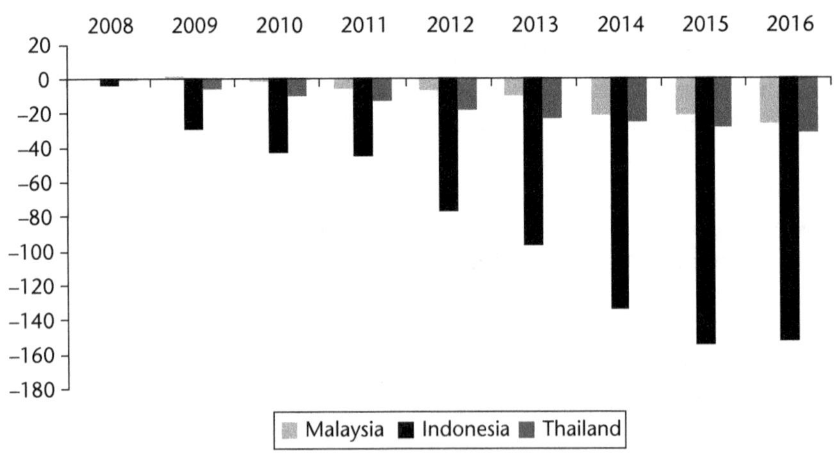

Figure 6.14 Cumulative net policy measures that are liberal (+ve) or protectionist (–ve), 2008–present (or available years)

Notes: Measures where coded green (liberal measure) = +1; orange = –0.5; and red (or protectionist measure) = –1.

Source: Global Trade Alert dataset.

the cumulative position which, for each country, and Indonesia in particular, illustrates a growing strength of the net protectionist position. If one drills down on the specific measures, in Malaysia, the dominant protectionist measures introduced are export taxes or restrictions, non-tariff barriers, and trade defence measures. In Indonesia, those three measures are also dominant protectionist measures, but additionally there are substantial numbers of import bans, quotas, tariffs, investment and localization measures, and state aid measures. In contrast, in Thailand the dominant measures of protectionism are state aid and trade defence measures.[12]

6.4.2 *Malaysia*

Malaysia has shifted considerably towards a new developmentalism.[13] The period started with the crisis, its management, and political disagreements on what approach to take to the crisis.

In late 1997, Malaysia introduced an IMF-type package itself, rather than through an IMF programme. There was an exchange rate devaluation, an austere budget, interest rates were raised, and credit growth limited. All of this did little to stem the volatility, leading instead to a contraction of output. In 1998, the free convertibility of the ringgit was ended and a currency peg adopted. Following this, capital controls were introduced that finally ended the exchange rate volatility. As the crisis hit, many Malaysian firms required the state to purchase bad loans, which was done by a set of new state agencies. Principal among these were the seven newly formed Government Linked Investment Companies, which were a new form of nationalization of corporate equity. These consisted of an asset management company, which acquired excessive non-performing loans from banks and financial institutions, a special vehicle to recapitalize the banking sector, and a corporate debt-restructuring committee. These agencies reduced non-performing loans, recapitalized the financial sector, and restructured corporate debt. They drew funding for this

[12] A further measure is that of the FDI Regulatory Restrictiveness Index (see OECD 2017) which provides indices from 1997–2016 for twenty-two economic sectors in selected economies which includes Malaysia and Indonesia (not Thailand). The FDI index is concerned with statutory restrictions on FDI though only when they are discriminatory against foreign investors. Thus state ownership and state monopolies are not part of the scoring unless they are discriminatory. The index for Malaysia has been static since the late 2000s. In contrast, Indonesia dropped significantly in the aftermath of the Asian financial crisis, but stayed high throughout the 2000s and even increased slightly in the first half of the 2010s. The index for Indonesia's mining and quarrying sector is particularly notable: after dropping from 0.16 in 1997 to 0.08 in 2003, it jumped during the 2000s and reached 0.60 in 2014, one of the highest levels in the countries in the dataset. As a result, one of the least protected sectors has become one of the most protected sectors in the country.

[13] See equivalent section in Chapter 4 for sources for this section.

from Petronas reserves, the Employees Provident Fund, and external loans and bonds issued by the government and Petronas.

The years following the Asian financial crisis were a period of renationalization and the retirement of Mahathir. Since 2003, a new emphasis on restructuring has emerged and petroleum and palm oil have boomed, reversing ST in the structure of output. Growth in manufacturing has been slow since 2000 in the sector of electronics and has contracted in the sector of textiles. There are few domestic suppliers as most domestic companies are in the highly-protected rentier sectors of extractives, finance, infrastructure, and property. The result is that Malaysia has been 'squeezed' by its lack of local linkage industries. Henderson and Phillips (2007) argue that industrialization stalled due to this problem of upgrading. Malaysia's domestic companies have been unable to shift from their current integration into global value chains. Malaysia's access to global value chains is mediated by foreign investors and supplier industries are dominated by SMEs in low value or lower tier assembly activity. In fact, Malaysia has been dependent on other East Asian countries for intermediate components in electronics.

Tan (2014) discusses the post-AFC in terms of renationalization and resurgence in state-led capital accumulation via government-linked corporations (GLCs). HICOM was also renationalized. The New Economic Model in 2010 emphasized dynamic industry clusters and greater private partnerships with GLCs, and a reduction in direct state intervention. WTO, ASEAN, and APEC rules pushed reduction in incentives and tariffs, but also pushed activity into rentier activities such as finance, insurance, construction, property/real estate, and stock markets.

In recent years, a scandal related to the Malaysia Development Berhad (the state investment fund) and missing funds had reshaped politics in Malaysia. The Prime Minister, Najib Razak, has been weakened. The Barisan Nasional which has dominated politics since independence lost its two-thirds parliamentary majority in 2008 for the first time since 1969 and lost the popular vote in 2013, though retained sixty per cent of seats in parliament. At the same time, a number of high-profile figures have left the governing United Malays National Organization (UMNO), forming a new nationalistic opposition party led by the former prime minister, Mahathir. Mahathir has re-emerged as a force in Malaysian politics but as an opposition leader together with his son.

Inclusive growth became somewhat secondary in the early 2000s as Malaysia prioritized growth. That said, data for public spending on education and health in Malaysia contrasts with Indonesia and Thailand. Figure 6.15 shows notable increases in public spending on education and on public health spending. For example, public education spending as a proportion of GDP increased accross MIT. However, Indonesia and Thailand, in 2014, still did not surpass

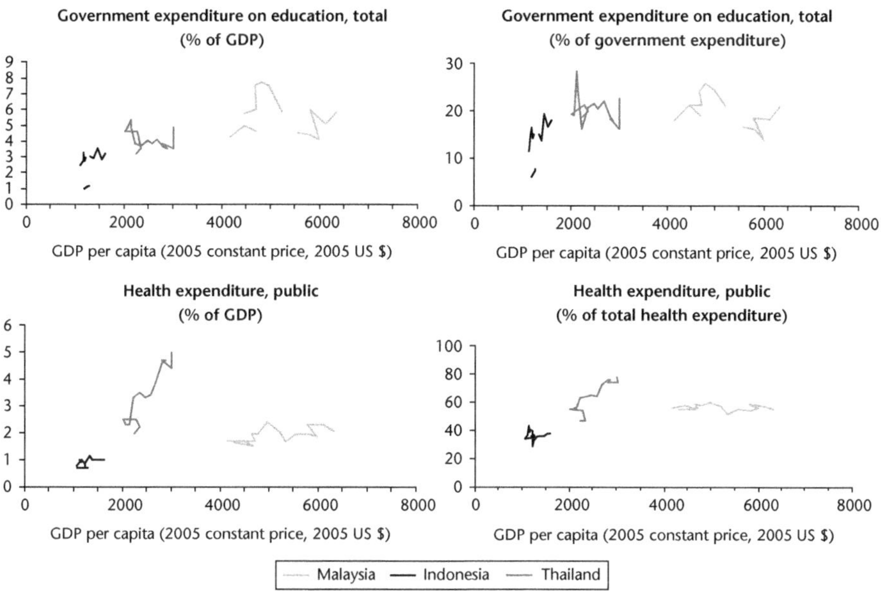

Figure 6.15 Government expenditure on education and health, 1995–present (or available years)
Source: World Bank (2017).

the levels of spending as a proportion of GDP of Malaysia in in the late 1990s. At the same time, public spending on health (as a % of GDP) also increased in Indonesia, but from a very low base. In Thailand, the increases were substantial in health (as a % of GDP). The data on the share of government spending on education and health too point towards increases in education though such increases in health are less clear other than in Thailand.

6.4.3 *Indonesia*

Indonesia has also shifted considerably towards a new developmentalism since the Asian financial crisis.[14] The Asian financial crisis was particularly severe in Indonesia. The rupiah fell from 2,500 to 17,000 to the US dollar in six months, GDP contracted by 13 per cent, and millions of people fell below the official poverty line due to inflation and job retrenchments, and sixteen banks were closed. Indonesia followed a very orthodox route through the crisis with IMF programmes which also sought to break up various monopolies of the Suharto family and associates.

[14] See equivalent section in Chapter 4 for sources for this section.

The economic crisis was accompanied by a political crisis, which further undermined confidence in the rupiah. After Suharto's resignation, three presidents followed in a period of five years (BJ Habibie, Abdurrahman Wahid, and Megawati Sukarnoputri). Habibie pursued tight monetary policy to control inflation and reduce capital flight. He also introduced a set of social programmes such as subsidized rice, school fees assistance, education, health, and rural development grants to sub-province governments. The presidencies of Abdurrahman Wahid and Megawati Sukarnoputri were relatively less significant in terms of policy changes (1999–2004) and rather more significant in the rollout of a massive political and fiscal decentralization programme.

The early part of the period—the late 1990s and early 2000s—were dominated by the IMF programme requirements. For example, all import monopolies other than in rice, sugar, and cloves were ended, as well as export bans, and tariff and export taxes were reduced. Further, all non-tariff barriers were removed and many sectors were opened up to FDI. However, the 2002–4 period saw the re-emergence of many of these import and export restrictions. At the same time, the end of the WTO Multifibre Arrangement for textiles and clothing (a quota system) led to increased competition from China, Vietnam, and Bangladesh.

Susilo Bambang Yudhoyono (known as SBY) was elected in 2004 and was president for two terms. His presidency was framed by a commodity boom to a considerable extent. However, oil was actually a burden to the budget in terms of large fuel subsidies and Indonesia became a net importer of oil. As a result of the commodity boom, non-commodity policies were somewhat under-emphasized and subject to change. Exporters of manufactures failed to upgrade and remained in low-skilled labour-intensive textiles and electronics. Policies towards international capital oscillated. For example, in 2007 FDI was liberalized to allow 100 per cent foreign ownership across the board. Then, some months later, a negative FDI investment list was published. Many trade restrictions were reduced in the 2000s but replaced with non-tariff barriers. As commodity prices fell, a trade deficit emerged and in response to this, many trade restrictions were reintroduced. BULOG, the state agency, was revived as the importer of rice, and as a buyer of sugar and cattle. Additionally, import licencing and monopolies were reintroduced in sugar, steel, and textiles. Towards the latter part of the Yudhoyono presidency, trade policy oscillated yet more. For example, import controls were introduced on agriculture products then removed; there was a ban on rattan exports and raw mineral exports in 2014. Then the 2014 trade law allowed temporary tariffs; and strengthened import and export regulations.

At the end of the SBY period, one notable piece of legislation was a new industrial bill because it gave the state powers to intervene in strategic industries, and created the scope for the state to financially support industries that suffer from changes in the global economy. It also allows the government to promote the use of domestically produced products in government procurement (where local content must be maximized) and even allows for import substitution. In parallel, a new trade bill with measures noted above gives a greater role to the state in restricting imports and exports to protect domestic companies, and in the limiting or halting of exports of strategic commodities to ensure the supply for domestic industry. Other signs of new developmentalism include tax incentives, fiscal incentives, and import duty exemptions to certain sectors. Furthermore, 'Made in Indonesia' policies have been introduced in several sectors, including automobiles, the construction sector, and smartphones/tablets. Furthermore, following a 2004 law on a National Social Security System the SBY administration issued a new law that set in motion key social welfare programmes. In health there was what is now known as the *Kartu Indonesia Sehat* and schemes were introduced in terms of pensions, old-age savings, disabilities, and death benefits. These were only effectively implemented in 2014 and 2015.

Jokowi Widodo (known as Jokowi) became president in 2014. Yusuf and Sumner (2016) discussed the extensive set of economic packages he set in motion in 2015/16. They included the ending of fuel subsidies and the relocation of spending towards social development and infrastructure, and major liberalization alongside major statist policies such as large capital injections into, and the strengthening of, SOEs. For example, the economic packages simplify the application process for investment and planning permits, land acquisitions, and procurement but also accelerate strategic state-led projects. On the one hand, they introduced tax holidays of up to twenty years, whilst, on the other, supporting the operational costs of domestic industries by reducing the prices of fuel, electricity, and gas. Furthermore, BAPPENAS, the state planning agency, which was weakened in the early 2000s, experienced a renaissance under Jokowi in budgetary terms and political status.

Other issues of note over the 2000s include the introduction of a new labour law in 2003 and the strengthening of labour institutions, evident, for example, in the growth in minimum wages. Dong and Manning (2017) show that minimum wages grew faster in the late SBY period—growing 20 per cent per year in Jakarta and other major industrial centres. Jokowi introduced new minimum wage legislation in 2015 with a new methodology—national economic growth plus national consumer price inflation. Perhaps this is a mute point given the persistence role of informal and agricultural labour. That said farm holdings may only provide a third of household income (Booth, 2016).

In sum, since the late 1990s, Indonesia's policy regime has oscillated between being more liberal and being protectionist, sometimes in relatively short periods of time. Indonesia reaped financial benefits from the commodity boom but experienced reverse ST in that the share of agricultural commodities and the share of mining and minerals increased substantially in exports.

Indeed, exports of raw commodities actually overtook manufactured products in the late 2000s as a share of exports.

In terms of IG in Indonesia, the period since the AFC has been one of rising inequality and weak employment growth. Furthermore, the employment elasticity of growth has been declining. There has, though, been expansion of social programmes. These have included expansion of the subsidized rice for the poor programme, cash transfer programmes, employment generation programmes, a new village fund, and expanded SME credit support schemes.[15]

In short, Indonesia has developed quite an extensive set of welfare policies, which are generally targeted but contain some universal aspects. Beyond those already mentioned, the welfare regime includes: funds for elementary and secondary schools as a part of the implementation of the nine years of compulsory education programme, educational grants for all children of school age (6–21 years of age) from poor families, health insurance for the poor and near-poor, and a set of poverty alleviation programmes that is managed by various ministries and institutions.

6.4.4 *Thailand*

Thailand has also shifted considerably towards a new developmentalism.[16] The Asian financial crisis hit hard in Thailand. The Thai baht lost almost half its value in a few months in 1996. A severe IMF austerity package commenced in 1997. The Asian financial crisis and the IMF's response eroded the confidence of the Thai elite in globalization and led to the re-emergence of economic nationalism, protectionist measures for domestic capital, and populism. The rise of populism in Thailand was, in part, a product of the strength of the IMF agreement conditions. Dithering within the ruling coalition on the IMF agreement led to stronger terms and triggered public anger, which resulted in the resignation of Prime Minister Chavalit Yongchaiyudh. This resignation then spurred an alliance of social forces, led by the middle classes, to push for a constitutional committee staffed by civil society. This committee wrote a radical new democratic constitution that controlled election spending and established an electoral commission, constitutional court, and corruption agency.

In 1998, Thaksin Shinawatra set up the Thai Rak Thai party with an economic nationalist programme, which resonated with the country following

[15] Jokowi's government has generally continued the social programmes that were in place during the SBY era but renamed them. For example, the Kartu Indonesia Pintar programme, which was central to Jokowi's presidential campaign was in fact the continuation of SBY's programme of Bantuan Siswa Miskin (BSM) (cash transfers for poor students) with only a small modification.

[16] See equivalent section in Chapter 4 for sources for this section.

the Asian financial crisis.[17] It had a focus on small entrepreneurs and farmers including a rural debt relief programme, spending programmes, and a health insurance coverage plan. Thaksin Sinawatra then led his party to victory in the 2001 election under the new constitution with an economic nationalist agenda and an anti-IMF platform. He enacted the Village and Community Fund, a rural uplift programme based on debt relief, spending programmes, and most significantly a universal health scheme, which together reached 52 million people of the then 64 million total population. The basis of funding in general taxation made it highly redistributive given out-of-pocket costs for much of the population for health care prior to its introduction.

Not surprisingly, Thaksin was very popular and won a landslide in 2001. Thaksin also sought to strengthen the developmentalist agencies of the Board of Investment (to focus on technology) and the National Economic and Social Development Board (NESDB). He introduced an industrial policy based on incentives (tax incentives linked to output targets and local content requirements) and cheap credit in a small set of strategic sectors (automobiles, computers, textiles, food, and tourism). A state agency, the Thailand Asset Management Corporation (TAMC), was established by Thaksin to assist recovery from the crisis by dealing with bad bank loans and lending to priority sectors.

Towards the end of his term, Thaksin reinvented his party for the 2005 election as the party of the poor. This led to a landslide victory but a resurgence of corruption and authoritarianism. In response, the middle classes mobilized and eroded through protests Thaksin's ability to govern. There was a coup in 2006 and following this, the constitution was rewritten. Concerns rose among the establishment that Thaksin would entrench a democracy that favoured his political party through patronage in rural areas. Thaksin was removed by a military coup, which eventually led to fresh elections and the election of Thaksin's sister, Yingluck Shinawatra (Prime Minister 2011–14) who continued the populist endeavour. Thaksin-linked parties were re-elected in 2007, 2011, and 2014 and in response anti-Thaksin protests grew after each election. In 2014, the Thai military led by General Prayuth Chan-o-cha took power from the Shinawatra government. A military-dominated committee rewrote the constitution and won a referendum on it, reducing the democratic aspects of previous constitutions.

In sum, the period in South East Asia can be characterized as follows: the severe crisis that ensued in MIT in the late 1990s was due to changes in relative exchange rates and market sentiments. The state response was to liberalize

[17] Khan (2010) argues that the crisis and constitution that it ushered in, though intended to spread democracy, had the opposite effect and Thaksin's dominant party coalition weakening the political power of capitalist institutions, as well as their connected political organizations.

initially and then to reintroduce a range of developmentalist measures to protect domestic capital and place limits on international capital. The decade or so that followed has been one of very limited, and in some cases reversed, ST and more mixed IG in terms of poverty reduction, inequality, and employment growth.

6.5 Conclusion

The purpose of this chapter was to consider a third wave of ST and capital accumulation in South East Asia. This chapter has argued the following thesis: the era of the late 1990s to the present has been one of nascent, revivalist, or new developmentalism in South East Asia. This is a new variety of developmentalism. It has aspects in common with two-tier developmentalism such as being generally open to international capital and protective of domestic capital. Yet in other ways, it has more in common with classical developmentalism as it is much more restrictive in the qualitative nature of its openness to international capital.

Each variety of new developmentalism has within it new forms of dependency and subordination. The stalling of the Lewisian transition is evident across MIT. As, too, is the weakening of employment growth to manage the tension between ST and IG. These relate—via upgrading—to a situation whereby local production capabilities will only move up global value chains if FDI moves up in local production. However, FDI will only move up if domestic producers fill the gaps left behind. The result is a 'stickiness' of production at value chain points and the observed outcome of stalled ST or even premature deindustrialization as competitiveness is not sustainable as other countries enter the same industries.

What the future holds is of course never certain. The new developmentalism may face a crisis in the sense that there are in-built limitations to ST and capital accumulation under it. The discussion thus far suggests some instability in the social structure, and that there are signs that ST has halted, plateaued, or even reversed. Furthermore, a weakening of IG in the form of employment growth is evident.

In sum, ST and IG have stalled in MIT. This does not diminish the distributional tension of the developer's dilemma—that tension between structural change and inclusive growth—but rather brings it to the fore in the sense that both are required to ensure a stable social structure. The stability of the social structure is weakened by insufficient rural and agricultural development, which remains home to a surprising proportion of the labour force, as well as the exhaustion of education investment as an avenue to address skilled–unskilled workers' income divergence and the resurgence of capital productivity, which has been associated with weak employment growth.

7

Conclusion

7.1 Introduction

This book has sought to contribute a fresh perspective on the contemporary economic history of South East Asia by taking the Lewisian transition and Kuznetsian distribution dynamics, and combining these with recent debates on inclusive growth (IG), together with heterodox theory on developmentalism, to generate a narrative to explain the experience of Malaysia, Indonesia, and Thailand (MIT).

The central idea of this book is that governments can intervene and shape distribution; and that the forces of structural transformation (ST) may unleash divergences between sectors or groups, but it is not inevitable that those forces need shape the 'developer's dilemma' because governments can provide countervailing forces.

To recap, developing countries are seeking the Lewisian transition of economic development which requires structural transformation and productivity growth via intra and inter-sectoral reallocation of economic activity, notably labour, and which tends to push up inequality, as Kuznets argued, and has been empirically demonstrated by Sumner (2016a, 2016b) and Baymul and Sen (2017). At the same time, developing countries are also seeking some form of broad-based or 'inclusive growth' which can be defined in various ways; typically as, who benefits from growth, in what way, and by how much. Inclusive growth is best achieved, or the inclusivity of growth maximized, with steady or even falling inequality, and certainly not with dramatically rising inequality. In short, the 'developer's dilemma' is a distribution dilemma or tension at the heart of economic development. One region of the world, South East Asia, did achieve both substantial structural transformation as well as broad-based inclusive growth.

The core arguments of this book are as follows. First, that the experience of South East Asia validates the view that ST and capital accumulation in the developing world can be state-directed to a greater or lesser extent, but that the parameters and timings are framed (as outlined by heterodox theorists, notably the structuralists) by global incorporation and the global economy at that point in time and history; and that ST and capital accumulation occur in waves and capitalism reincarnates following a crisis when the previous social structure of capital accumulation reaches its demise.

Second, that whilst both ST and capital accumulation tend to generate distribution tensions, these can be managed in each period to some considerable extent by a focus on expanding public policy intervention, on specifically, urban–rural income divergence; the skilled–unskilled worker wage divergence; and the capture of productivity gains vis-à-vis capital and labour shares and the within-labour shares, and the extent to which productivity growth is translated into wage growth or employment growth or captured by capital as Lewis envisaged. Thus, ST requires—counter-intuitively—highly activist rural and agricultural policy and public investments to constrain the urban–rural income divergence; large investments in public education to constrain the skilled–unskilled worker wage divergence; and state–capital–labour pacts to ensure substantial employment growth is the consequence of productivity growth.

In this concluding chapter, we draw together the book's discussion. This chapter is structured as follows: Section 7.2 provides a retrospective of the book and the main arguments. Section 7.3 responds to three core questions outlined in the introduction. To recap these were: How deep and of what nature was the structural transformation and inclusive growth in Malaysia, Indonesia, and Thailand? How did Malaysia, Indonesia, and Thailand deal with the distributional tensions that rapid change often entails? And how did Malaysia, Indonesia, and Thailand achieve such rapid economic and social transformation in a relatively short space of time? In other words, what does the experience of those countries imply for theories of economic and social transformation? Section 7.4 then concludes.

7.2 Retrospective

In this book, we have made a number of arguments, which we review here. In Chapters 2 and 3 we discussed concepts and theory. In Chapter 2, we laid out the key concepts related to the 'developer's dilemma', specifically, the meaning and assessment of structural transformation and inclusive growth, and how the concepts are situated in a model of economic development. The discussion drew from the works of pioneering development economists of the 1950s; notably, Arthur Lewis and the Lewis model of the labour transition, and Simon Kuznets on inequality dynamics during the transition.

The thesis of Chapter 2 was that both ST and IG have tended to be defined in a reductionist sense, and in a way that disconnects the two concepts analytically (and that the former has been neglected relative to the attention given to the latter). This is significant because the connection and tension between the two concepts is important for understanding the developer's dilemma, and the Kuznetsian forces of upward inequality unleashed by ST and how those are addressed to maintain the social structure of capital accumulation of that particular wave of capital accumulation. We considered the Lewis model as a point of departure within which to situate ST and IG.

In Chapter 3, we reviewed the elaborate theories of the drivers and impediments to the Lewisian transition and linked them to questions of distribution and IG. There was discussion of orthodox theory and then heterodox theory as a reaction to orthodoxy with an emphasis on developmentalism. We took developmentalism to mean the state orchestrated attempt at national economic development. We argued that both orthodox and heterodox theories tend to see capitalism as one core unified mode of economic development, even if the latter, heterodox theorists conceptualize a core and a periphery capitaism within a global system. Contemporary debates in comparative capitalism-studies have argued for an analysis of the heterogeneity of capitalisms.

It was argued that neither orthodox nor heterodox theories of industrialization adequately explain the experience of late development because of that heterogeneity of late capitalisms. That said, heterodox theories, which coalesce in the nature of the incorporation of developing countries into the global economy, do retain conceptual usefulness and their focal point, developmentalism, can provide a set of 'varieties of developmentalism' as a reference point, much in the way that neoclassical economics uses the abstract perfectly competitive market as its reference point (see discussion of Fischer 2014).

In the second half of the book (Chapters 4–6) we then explored the issues raised by the developer's dilemma, within the varieties of developmentalism pursued in South East Asia, using a detailed, empirical, comparative, country case study approach to three distinct waves of capital accumulation separated by major crises. We argued that ST and IG are evident in each period to some extent, though weaker in the post-Asian financial crisis period, but at the same time new forms of dependency or subordination in the global economy evolve, meaning developing countries never escape the limitations set on their development by both the historic and contemporary global economy.

In Chapter 4, we considered the first wave of capital accumulation in South East Asia from the late 1960s to the early to mid 1980s. We characterized this period as one of 'classical developmentalism', which we argued was the import-substitution, industrialization-led model. This was founded on a state–capitalist pact that ensured an elite without intra-group structural conflict, and ideologically coherent in terms of the shared goal of broad-based national development in the face of the internal threat of communist movements, and protective of domestic capital vis-à-vis foreign dominance. In this period ST and IG were impressive. The 'conductor' role or directional thrust of the state and its core developmentalist agencies was central to economic development. Further, the focus on agriculture and rural development ensured that a social basis for the social structure of capital accumulation would remain generally stable and compensate for the lack of meaningful democracy by ensuring cheap and stable food prices, which meant that the large labour productivity gains were translated into rapid capital accumulation.

In Chapter 5, we considered the next wave of capital accumulation in South East Asia, dating from the early to mid 1980s to the mid 1990s. This was the period between the crisis of the early 1980s and the crisis of the late 1990s. We characterized this period in South East Asia as one of 'two-tier developmentalism' which was a variety of developmentalism built on the protection of domestic capital but with selective openness to international capital, and opportunism built on global economic changes. In other words, ST and IG were opportunistically built on changes in international prices—in the form of exchange rate movements and interest rate differentials—and subsequent relocation of large amounts of international capital. In this period, ST and IG were again dramatic, and the conductor role of the state and its key agencies was again clear.

In Chapter 6, we focused on the Asian financial crisis period and beyond, up to the present day. We argued that there is a nascent, 'new developmentalism' emerging. This is evident in the resurgence of the importance of, and financing for, state-owned enterprises (SOEs) and state agencies of economic development that survived the Washington Consensus more or less intact, or were recreated following the crisis in the guise of new state agencies to deal with managing indebtedness. However, the contemporary period has been one of stalled and possibly reversed ST, even premature deindustrialization, and a weakening of IG. New developmentalism is a response to this malaise. In Indonesia, a new social structure of capital accumulation post-Asian financial crisis brought with it democratization which has been accompanied by a dramatic rise in inequality. And although this is not the case in Malaysia and Thailand, indeed inequality has fallen in the latter, severe political turbulence has risen to the fore in those countries, suggesting that the social structure of capital accumulation is unstable.

7.3 Three Core Questions

As noted in the introduction to this book and recapped in the introduction to this chapter, we have sought to address three core questions. Each of those questions is now considered in turn.

7.3.1 *How Deep and of what Nature was the Structural Transformation and Inclusive Growth in Malaysia, Indonesia, and Thailand?*

The thesis of this book has been that ST and IG in Malaysia, Indonesia, and Thailand have, in general, been dramatic and impressive. However, at other levels it has not been as 'deep' as it may first seem and structural barriers remain on the journey from low- to high-income country status. It is true to say that labour, gross domestic product (GDP), and exports transited out of low productivity agriculture and absolute poverty fell dramatically. Despite this, deeper questions remain, given that production and exports in high value-added sectors of manufacturing are dominated by foreign investments, and thus upgrading to higher value-added points in global value chains remains challenging. Further, although absolute poverty fell to very low levels, poverty at higher lines associated with a permanent escape from absolute poverty, such as $10 per day, remains substantial and the employment intensity of growth has weakened, adding to social pressures. Furthermore, dualism remains in employment to a considerable extent in Indonesia and Thailand. A third of the labour force in both Indonesia and Thailand remains in agriculture and over a tenth in even higher income per capita Malaysia. Informal employment in non-agriculture too remains large—three-quarters of non-agriculture employment in Indonesia, more than forty per cent in Thailand, and a tenth of non-agriculture employment is accounted for by the informal sector in Malaysia.

What would Lewis have said if he were alive today? He might have been surprised by the persistence of dualism. He might have argued that surplus labour remains in the subsistence sectors and the turning point has yet to be reached. Lewis would also have likely noted that underlying the empirical experiences of developing countries is heterogeneity in forms of structural transformation. He might have been surprised that the very notion of industrialization has shifted from infant industry-building to global value chain access via foreign direct investment or domestic suppliers and he might highlight the consequences of international ownership or control. He might have noted how the assumption of labour transfer from traditional or rural sectors to modern or urban sectors was just one route for ST. In fact, it is one of ten potentially progressive modes of sectoral ST (each of which can reverse, making twenty modes of sectoral ST), one or more of which may be the dominant driver of productivity gains, and each with specific distribution dynamics of the labour transition. He would have probably been surprised that developing countries such as MIT could go from agrarian/rural in the 1970s to industrial in the 1990s and begin to deindustrialize in the 2000s, all in the space of thirty to forty or so years.

One substantial surprise to Lewis would be the emergence of premature deindustrialization. The idea that the process of ST could go into reverse at a lower level of development than previously observed would have no doubt raised an eyebrow. Lewis did not discuss in depth nor anticipate premature deindustrialization per se, though he did envisage that the dependency on a handful of agricultural or primary exports, whose value fell relative to what is needed to be imported, could become a new dependency. This would be where a handful of manufacturing exports, which are falling in value relative to what countries need to import, take the place of primary exports; in short, the replacement of primary commodity dependency related to a small number of commodities with manufacturing dependency based on a small number of manufactures and a difficulty in upgrading.

7.3.2 *How did those Countries Deal with the Distributional Tensions that Rapid Change Often Entails?*

The thesis of this book has been that Malaysia, Indonesia, and Thailand achieved ST with IG in various senses—with the exception of rising inequality in Indonesia over the last decade—through a determined set of interventions to counterbalance the forces that Lewis, Kuznets, and others identified that ST was to unleash. In fact, three interlinked factors can explain how the distributional tensions that rapid change entails were dealt with in Malaysia, Indonesia, and Thailand.

First, and counter-intuitively, there was a focus not solely on urban or manufacturing—most likely the Lewis modern or capitalist sector—but on rural and agriculture development—most likely the Lewis subsistence or traditional or non-capitalist sector, where much of the population resided in the 1960s and 1970s. Even today, as noted above and after more than forty years of economic development, a quarter of Malaysians, a half of Thais, and half of Indonesians live in rural areas. This was done through extensive and substantial public investments in rural infrastructure, rural employment creation, and rural development, which ensured cheap and stable availability of basic foodstuffs. The privileging of the rural and agricultural sector in this way thus provided a counterbalance to the pressure on inequality induced by structural transformation towards higher productivity manufacturing. This strong focus on rural development through rural public investment thus constrained the disparities of income between rural and urban workers and thus counterbalanced the likely impact of ST in bringing relatively more benefits to the urban sector than the rural sector, in line with Lewis's thinking on the relationship between the two sectors and how the more modern or capitalist sector can benefit the more traditional or non-capitalist sector.

Second, and once again counter-intuitively, there was little in the way of immediate redistributive programmes such as transfers, but a large focus on redistributing the future (rather than the present) via large public investments and the consequential mass expansion of primary and lower secondary education to completion. This had an equalizing effect on future incomes to some extent and again, addressed the distributive pressures that structural transformation may bring, given that the benefits of structural transformation likley disproportionately help more skilled labour, by constraining the skills premium between skilled and unskilled workers. The mass expansion of education, especially at primary but also at lower secondary level, constrained the divergence of income between skilled and unskilled labour to less than it would have been otherwise.

Third, and again counter-intuitively, there was a focus not on the growth of real wages but a focus on widespread employment growth. This means the gains of productivity growth, and the translation of productivity growth into employment growth, become the dominant force rather than the translation of productivity growth into growth in real wages and thus its capture by smaller groups of those employed only. Employment growth thus spread the benefits of growth around more than they would otherwise be if captured in rises in real wages.

The growth of real wages was less than might have been expected partly because food prices were kept low and employment growth was substantial. This was done implicitly and explicitly through repressive labour institutions. That said, the provision of cheap and stable prices of food and its wide availability weakened the pressures for rises in real wages. At the same time, employment-intensive growth ensured that many people benefited from growth in the most tangible way possible—direct participation in employment.

The disparities in income that structural transformation bought were, to some extent, constrained as rather than wages rising for some and creating disparities, employment growth ensured that productivity gains were spread widely within the labour share of income.

In short, a set of three interlinked factors explains how MIT managed to keep inequality more or less steady over time (not perfectly so but without large rises in inequality) by counterbalancing the forces unleashed by ST with activist public policy to ensure that disparities between rural and urban incomes; skilled and unskilled wages; and employed and unemployed workers did not increase as much as they would have otherwise.

What would Kuznets have said if he were alive today? Kuznets might be pleased to see that his 'statistical pipedream' was nearer than it was when he wrote, though probably surprised at how his seminal work has been used for many years to justify the neglect of inequality, under the guise that rising inequality was a price worth paying for economic development, something which he never said but is often interpreted to have meant.

With reference to contemporary patterns, Kuznets might have said that deindustrialization ought to be *equalizing* if the labour movement is from the more equal sector to the less equal sector. One question is whether the Lewisian turning point (the exhaustion of surplus rural labour) has been reached. Indonesia and Thailand are unlikely to have got to this point, given that a third of the labour force remain in agriculture. This would suggest that the upward pressure on inequality that needs counterbalancing has yet to reach the peak that comes with the transition, and thus the flow of labour remains from the more equal to the less equal sector, unequalizing without the kind of highly activist intervention noted above on the three fault lines of inequality.

However, what if—due to premature deindustrialization—there was an unequalizing effect in the urban sector and an equalizing one in the rural sector? Overall inequality may still rise—it would depend on the intra and inter-sectoral components—because the reverse flow of labour to rural areas would weaken rural wage growth. In short it would have an equalizing impact in the rural sector. Would then the departure of low- and medium-skilled workers from the urban sector strengthen wage growth for the high-skilled workers (i.e. be unequalizing)? In that case, growth with deindustrialization could potentially be inclusive (equalizing in rural sector) *and* immizering (unequalizing in the urban sector) at the same time. An additional point that needs further attention is the extent to which migration is likely to be circular (e.g. seasonal) and the related impact of the contemporary changes in the ease of transfer of urban to rural remittances, which are presumably equalizing between sectors but potentially unequalizing within sectors.

7.3.3 *How did Malaysia, Indonesia, and Thailand Achieve Such Rapid Economic and Social Transformation in a Relatively Short Space of Time? In Other Words, what does the Experience of those Countries Imply for Theories of Economic and Social Transformation?*

The thesis of this book has been that Malaysia, Indonesia, and Thailand achieved rapid economic and social transformation in a relatively short space of time through a set of varieties of developmentalism. However, each wave or variety of developmentalism sets parameters on economic and social development, and leads to the emergence of a new or different form of dependency or subordination within the global economy that will eventually lead to crisis and, in due course, regeneration in a new form of developmentalism. Thus, developmentalism is never truly emancipatory as it relates to the nature of (adverse) incorporation into the global economy of late developers. Developmentalism, though allowing considerable scope for ST-led capital accumulation under certain global conditions, also maintains peripherality, too, in the sense that the global economy frames the parameters of capital accumulation in each period, thus maintaining some countries at the periphery or quasi-periphery. There is evidently much resonance with heterodox theorists in these matters.

The thesis of this book is further that the experience of Malaysia, Indonesia, and Thailand in achieving economic and social transformation, albeit within parameters, implies the following for theories of economic and social transformation: first, what was achieved in MIT was a product of a state–elite nationalistic pact of intra-elite cohesion, or at least that conflict within elites was individual rather than structural between groups. These regimes maintained their social basis through rising living standards, and the visibility of the fruits of growth in terms of physical infrastructure, employment growth, and cheap, widely available, and affordable basic foodstuffs.

Second, what was achieved in MIT was a product of the hyperactive state in the extensive protection of domestic capital, and selective management of international capital (which unravelled in the case of managing international financial capital in the late 1990s). It was also the product of the counterbalancing of prevailing inequality currents associated with structural transformation, though not through traditional redistributive policies (e.g. transfers) but managing divergences, that is, in the fault lines of inequality that ST-led capital accumulation tends to exacerbate. Governments in MIT in each period ensured domestic capital was afforded substantial support and wide-ranging protection from international competition in numerous ways, and openness to international capital was highly selective in production. What was achieved in MIT was a product not of getting prices 'wrong' or 'right' but of the inseparability of the state and markets or a vindication of Polanyi in terms of the state as the 'handmaiden' or 'regulator' of economic development. In short, there is much resonance with heterodox theory on the essential role of the state in late economic development.

Third and finally, with an eye again to heterodox theory, what was achieved in MIT was a product of fortuitous changes in global capital accumulation and the global economy that would be difficult to replicate. This included the Cold War context and the threat domestic communist movements posed to the social structure, which induced a strong sense of elite cohesion. There was also economic fortune in terms of exchange rate movements, and geographical location, as well as interest rate differentials and the temporal fortune of industrializing whilst China was 'sleeping' and had not yet entered the global economy fully. Such good fortune can of course reverse, as happened vis-à-vis many of these circumstances.

If the scholars of heterodox theory were asked today—e.g. Prebisch, Singer, Furtado, Myrdal, Sunkel or Cardoso, Dos Santos, Frank, Baran, Warren, Sweezy Wallerstein, Arrighi, or Emmanuel, what would they say? They may well feel vindicated about many aspects of their theorizing even if none were perfect and the heterogeneity of late capitalism undermined unifying theory. They would certainly have noted the persistent importance of the state in late development and the role the global economy plays.

They would have argued that what was achieved in MIT demonstrated that much heterodox theorizing remains relevant in some way in terms of structural barriers, dependency, and subordination which persists. Developmentalism in various guises has made substantial achievements and has the ability to reincarnate, but developing countries remain subordinate despite higher levels of economic development. In this way, peripherality is reproduced because of the changing nature of industrialization from infant industry-building, which comprises vertically integrated production controlled by the reins of the state, to horizontal integration of developing countries into global value chains, the reins of which sit with international capital. Looking ahead, visible signs of the persistent nature of dependency and subordination that developing countries seek to overcome can be seen in slowing growth rates, premature deindustrialization, and weaker employment growth.

7.4 Conclusion

At the time of writing prospects for economic development under nascent, new developmentalism in South East Asia are unclear. Certainly, for Malaysia and Thailand, political turbulence still prevails. In all three countries—Malaysia, Indonesia, and Thailand—three interrelated economic issues are likely to become more pressing in the not too distant future: first, the extent to which premature deindustrialization is (i) real and (ii) a problem vis-à-vis productivity growth and employment growth, and the extent to which the service sector might provide productivity growth and employment growth or whether new developmentalism will energize manufacturing sufficiently.

Second, and related, is the issue of weakening employment growth or jobless growth, by which we mean not literally growth with no employment creation, but weak growth elasticity of employment growth and particularly non-agricultural employment growth. Third, the 'middle-income trap', by which we mean a growth slowdown or more accurately a weakening of productivity growth. Prior to the Asian financial crisis, the growth elasticities of employment in manufacturing were stronger. One thesis is that rises in real wages as trade unions have become freer—notably in Indonesia—may also mean that productivity gains are translated into increases in real wages rather than employment growth. That said, some alternative hypotheses are as follows: (i) it could simply be a lasting negative effect of the Asian financial crisis on the sector-specific investment climate, including austerity effects; (ii) the Asian financial crisis encouraged the adoption of labour-saving technologies; (iii) there could also be a 'survival effect', meaning the Asian financial crisis eliminated (less efficient) firms that were labour-absorbing to a greater extent than other firms.

What is clear is that MIT are in the process of shifting towards service-dominated economies without fuller industrialization. How much this matters depends on the view one takes of the importance of manufacturing in terms of its potency for economic growth, productivity, labour absorption, and trade. In each of MIT, the share of manufacturing in value-added and employment plateaued or turned down following the Asian financial crisis, though the precise timing differs. The decline in Indonesia was early, around 2000; in Malaysia, it was in the mid 2000s; and in Thailand, the plateauing was much more recent. However, the first, Indonesia, is at a much lower level of income per person than Malaysia or Thailand. One potential impact of premature deindustrialization is the slower growth in output and in employment growth, as experienced in the last decade. One causal factor is the commodity boom of the 2000s, which has led to larger natural resource sectors, real exchange rate appreciation, and a squeeze on other tradeable sectors. Although the commodity boom has subsided to some extent, competition from labour-intensive manufacturers, such as China and Vietnam and new South East Asian countries, is likely to intensify rather than disappear.

All of which points towards the enduring importance of studying structural transformation and the labour transition that Lewis and Kuznets and heterodox theorists considered important and further, the importance of studying government policy vis-à-vis neutralizing the forces of inequality unleashed by structural transformation.

As South East Asia looks to the future, these issues, along with how developmentalism has achieved so much and yet structural barriers and peripherality persist, despite much higher levels of economic and social development, remain pressing economic and social concerns.

References

Acemoglu, D. and Robinson, J. (2002). 'The Political Economy of the Kuznets Curve', *Review of Development Economics*, 6(2): 183–203.

Adelman, I. and Morris, C. (1973). *Economic Growth and Social Equity in Developing Countries*. Stanford, CA: Stanford University Press.

Aggarwal, V. K. and Evenett, S. J. (2010). 'Financial Crisis, "New" Industrial Policy, and the Bite of Multilateral Trade Rules', *Asian Economic Policy Review*, 5: 221–44.

Aghion, P. and Bolton, P. (1997). 'A Theory of Trickle-Down Growth and Development', *Review of Economic Studies*, 64(2): 151–72.

Aglietta, M. (1976). *A Theory of Capitalist Regulation: The US Experience*, trans. D. Fernbach. London: New Left Books.

Alavi, M. (1996). Industrialization in Malaysia: Import Substitution and Infant Industry Performance. London: Routledge.

Alavi, R. (2002). *Industrialization in Malaysia: Import Substitution and Infant Industry Performance.* (2nd edn). London: Routledge.

Ali, I. and Zhang, J. (2007). 'Inclusive Growth toward a Prosperous Asia: Policy Implications', Asian Development Bank (ADB) Economics and Research Department Working Paper. Manila: ADB.

Alkire, S., Roche, J. M., and Vaz, A. (2015). 'Changes Over Time in Multidimensional Poverty: Methodology and Results for 34 Countries', OPHI Working Paper 76, University of Oxford.

Alvaredo, F. and Gasparini, L. (2015). 'Recent Trends in Inequality and Poverty in Developing Countries', in A.B. Atkinson and F. Bourguignon (eds), *Handbook of Income Distribution*, Volume 2. Amsterdam: Elsevier.

Amsden, A. (1989). *Asia's Next Giant: South Korea and Late Industrialization*. New York and Oxford: Oxford University Press.

Amsden, A. (2001). *The Rise of 'The Rest': Challenges to the West From Late-Industrializing Economies*. Oxford: Oxford University Press.

Amsden, A., DiCaprio, A., and Robinson, J. A. (2012). *The Role of Elites in Economic Development*. Oxford: Oxford University Press.

Amsden, A. H. (1995). 'Like the Rest: South-East Asia's "Late" Industrialization', *Journal of International Development*, 7(5): 791–9.

Anand, R., Cheng, K. C., Rehman, S., and Zhang, L. (2014). 'Potential Growth in Emerging Asia', IMF Working Paper, Washington, DC: IMF.

Anand, S. and Kanbur, R. (1993a). 'The Kuznets Process and the Inequality–Development Relationship', *Journal of Development Economics*, 40(1): 25–52.

Anand, S. and Kanbur, R. (1993b). 'Inequality and Development: A Critique', *Journal of Development Economics*, 41(1): 19–43.

Arrighi, G. (1990). 'The Developmentalist Illusion: A Reconceptualization of the Semiperiphery', in W. G. Martin (ed.), *Semiperipheral States in the World Economy*. Westport, CT: Greenwood Press, pp. 11–42.

Balassa, B. (1974). 'Trade Creation and Trade Diversion in the European Common Market: An Appraisal of the Evidence', *The Manchester School*, 42: 93–135.

Ban, C. (2013). 'Brazil's Liberal Neo-developmentalism: New Paradigm or Edited Orthodoxy?', *Review of International Political Economy*, 20(2): 298–331.

Baran, P. A. (1957). *The Political Economy of Growth*. New York: Monthly Review Press.

Baran, P. A. and Sweezy, P. (1966). *Monopoly Capital: An Essay on the American Economic and Social Order*. New York: Monthly Review Press.

Bastos, P. P. Z. (2012). 'A economia política do novo-desenvolvimentismo e do social desenvolvimentismo', *Economia e Sociedade*, 21(special): 779–810.

Basu, D. and Foley, D. K. (2013). 'Dynamics of Output and Employment in the US Economy', *Cambridge Journal of Economics*, 37(5): 1077–106.

Basu, K. (1997). *Analytical Development Economics*. Cambridge, MA: MIT Press.

Bauer, P. (1981). *Equality, the Third World, and Economic Delusion*. Cambridge, MA: Harvard University Press.

Baymul, C. and Sen, K. (2017). 'What do we know about the Relationship between Structural Change, Inequality and Poverty in Developing Countries?', ESRC GPID Research Network Working Paper. London: King's College London.

Bello, W. and Rosenfield, S. (1991). *Dragons in Distress: Asia's Miracle Economies in Crisis*. London: Penguin.

Besley, T. and Cord, L. J. (eds) (2006). *Delivering on the Promise of Pro-poor Growth: Insights and Lessons from Country Experiences*. Washington, DC: World Bank.

Betcherman, G. (2012). 'Labor Market Institutions: A Review of the Literature', World Development Report background. Washington, DC: World Bank.

Bhagwati, J. (1958). 'Immiserizing Growth: A Geometrical Note', *Review of Economic Studies*, 25(June): 201–5.

Bhagwati, J. N. (1978). *Foreign Trade Regimes and Economic Development: Anatomy and Consequences of Exchange Control Regimes*. New York: National Bureau of Economic Research.

Boo Teik, K. (2010). 'Development Strategies and Poverty Reduction', in K. Boo Teik (ed.), *Policy Regimes and the Political Economy of Poverty Reduction in Malaysia*. Commissioned for the UNRISD Flagship Report on Poverty Project on Poverty Reduction and Policy Regimes. UNRISD: Geneva, pp. 25–72.

Booth, A. (1999). 'Initial Conditions and Miraculous Growth: Why is South East Asia Different From Taiwan and South Korea?', *World Development*, 27(2): 301–21.

Booth, A. (2016). *Economic Change in Modern Indonesia: Colonial and Post-colonial Comparisons*. Cambridge: Cambridge University Press.

Bourguignon, F. (2003). 'The Growth Elasticity of Poverty Reduction: Explaining Heterogeneity across Countries and Time Periods', in T. Eicher and S. Turnovsky (eds), *Inequality and Growth: Theory and Policy Implications*. Cambridge, MA: MIT Press, pp. 3–26.

Boyer, R. and Saillard, Y. (1995). *Théorie de la regulation: l'état des savoirs*. Paris: La Découverte.

Boyer, R., Uemura, H., and Isogai, A. (eds) (2012). *Diversity and Transformations of Asian Capitalisms*. London: Routledge.

Brenner, R. (1977). 'The Origins of Capitalist Development: A Critique of Neo-Smithian Marxism', *New Left Review*, I/104: 25–92.

Bresser-Pereira, L. C. (2011). 'From old to new developmentalism in Latin America', in J. O. Ocampo and J. Ross (eds), *The Oxford Handbook of Latin American Economics*. Oxford: Oxford University Press, pp. 108–29.

Bresser-Pereira, L. C. (2013). 'Developmental Capitalism', Paper presented at the Annual Conference of SASE, June 27–8.

Bruton, H. J. (1981). 'The Import-Substitution Strategy of Economic Development: A Survey', *Pakistan Development Review*, 10(2): 123–46.

Bruton, H. J. (1998). 'A Reconsideration of Import Substitution', *Journal of Economic Literature*, 36(June): 903–36.

Buehler, M. (2016). *The Politics of Shari'a Law: Islamist Activists and the State in Democratizing Indonesia*. Cambridge: Cambridge University Press.

Cardoso, F. H. and Faletto, E. (1979). *Dependency and Development in Latin America*. Berkeley and Los Angeles, CA: University of California Press.

Carneiro, R. de M. (2012). 'Velhos e novos desenvolvimentismos', *Economia e Sociedade*, 21(special): 749–78.

Carney, R. W. and Witt, M. A. (2012). The Role of the State in Asian Business Systems. In M.A. Witt & G. Redding (Eds.) Oxford Handbook of Asian Business Systems. Oxford: Oxford University Press.

Chang, H.-J. (1994). *The Political Economy of Industrial Policy*. New York: St. Martin's Press.

Chang, H.-J. (2008). Bad Samaritans: The Myth of Free Trade and the Secret History of Capitalism. London: Bloomsbury.

Chang, H.-J. (2010). *23 Things They Don'*t Tell You About Capitalism. London: Penguin Books.

Chenery, H. (1960). 'Patterns of Industrial Growth', *The American Economic Review*, 50(4): 624–54.

Chenery, H. (1975). 'The Structuralist Approach to Development Policy', *The American Economic Review*, 65(2): 310–16.

Chenery, H. (1979). *Structural Change and Development Policy*. Oxford: Oxford University Press.

Chenery, H., Ahluwalia, M., Bell, C., Duloy, J., and Jolly, R. (1974). *Redistribution with Growth*. Oxford: Oxford University Press for the World Bank.

Cimoli, M. and Porcile, G. (2014). 'Technology, Structural Change and the BOP-Constraint: Why did Latin America Fail to Converge?', *Cambridge Journal of Economics*, 38(1): 215–37.

Cimoli, M., Martins, A., Porcile, G., and Sossdorf, F. (2015). 'Productivity, Social Expenditure and Income Distribution in Latin America', Desarrollo Productivo 201, Naciones Unidas Comisión Económica para América Latina y el Caribe (CEPAL).

Clark, C. (1957). *The Conditions of Economic Progress* (3rd edn). London: Macmillan.

Cobb, C. and Douglas, P. (1928). 'A Theory of Production', *The American Economic Review*, 18(1): 139–65.

Cobham, A., Davis, W., Ibrahim, G., and Sumner, A. (2016). 'Hidden Inequality: How Much Difference Would Adjustment for Illicit Financial Flows Make to National Income Distributions?', *Journal of Globalization and Development*, 7(2): 1–18.

Copestake, J. (2003). 'The Links between Social and Economic Development: The Sigma Economy of Adolfo Figueroa', Wellbeing in Developing Countries (WeD) Working Paper 3. Bath: University of Bath.

Credit Suisse (2016). Global Wealth Report. Zurich: Credit Suisse.

Cunha Neves P. and Tavares Silva, S. (2014). 'Inequality and Growth: Uncovering the Main Conclusions from the Empirics', *The Journal of Development Studies*, 50(1): 1–12.

Deininger, K. and Squire, L. 1998. 'New Ways of Looking at Old Issues: Inequality and Growth', *Journal of Development Economics*, 57: 259–87.

Diao, X., McMillan, M., and Rodrik, D. (2017). 'The Recent Growth Boom in Developing Economies: A Structural Change Perspective', NBER Working Paper N. 23132. Cambridge, MA: NBER.

Dick, H. (2002). *The Emergence of a National Economy: An Economic History of Indonesia, 1800–2000*. Sydney: Allen and Unwin.

Dirlik, A. (2006). 'Beijing Consensus: Beijing "Gongshi". Who Recognizes Whom and to What End?' Mimeograph, University of Oregon.

Dixon, C. (1999). *The Thai Economy: Uneven Development and Internationalisation*. London and New York: Routledge.

Dollar, D. and Kraay, A. (2002). 'Growth Is Good for the Poor', *Journal of Economic Growth*, 7: 195–225.

Dollar, D., Kleineberg, T., and Kraay, A. (2013). 'Growth Still is Good for the Poor', World Bank Policy Research Working Paper. Washington, DC: World Bank.

Doner, R. (2009). *The Politics of Uneven Development: Thailand's Economic Growth in Comparative Perspective*. New York and London: Cambridge University Press.

Doner, R. F., Ritchie, B. K., and Slater, D. (2005). Systemic Vulnerability and the Origins of Developmental States: Northeast and Southeast Asia in Comparative Perspective. *International Organization*, 59(2): 327–61.

Dong, S. X. and Manning, C. (2017). 'Labour-Market Developments at a Time of Heightened Uncertainty', *Bulletin of Indonesian Economic Studies*, 53: 1–25.

Dos Santos, T. (1970). 'The Structure of Dependence', *American Economic Review*, 60(2): 231–6.

Duarte, M. and Restuccia, D. (2010). 'The Role of the Structural Transformation in Aggregate Productivity', *The Quarterly Journal of Economics*, 125(1): 129–73.

Ebenau, M., Bruff, I., and May, C. (2015). *New Directions in Comparative Capitalism Research: Critical and Global Perspectives*. Basingstoke: Palgrave Macmillan.

Edward, P. and Sumner, A. (2014). 'Estimating the Scale and Geography of Global Poverty Now and in the Future: How Much Difference do Method and Assumptions Make?', *World Development*, 58: 67–82.

Edward, P. and Sumner, A. (2015). 'New Estimates of Global Poverty and Inequality: How Much Difference do Price Data Really Make?', Centre for Global Development (CGD) Working Paper (and Data Set). Washington, DC: CGD.

Emmanuel, A. (1972). *Unequal Exchange: A Study of the Imperialism of Trade*. New York; London: Monthly Review Press.

Epstein, G. (2001). 'Financialization, Rentier Interests, and Central Bank Policy', manuscript, Department of Economics, University of Massachusetts, Amherst, MA, December.

Esping-Andersen, G. (1990). *The Three Worlds of Welfare Capitalism*. Princeton, NJ: Princeton University Press.

Esping-Andersen, G. (1999). *Social Foundations of Postindustrial Economies*. New York: Oxford University Press.

Evans, P. B. (1995). *Embedded Autonomy: States and Industrial Transformation*. Princeton, NJ: Princeton University Press.

Fainshmidt, S., Judge, W. Q., Aguilera, R. V., and Smith, A. (2016). 'Varieties of Institutional Systems: A Contextual Taxonomy of Understudied Countries', *Journal of World Business*.

Feenstra, R. C., Inklaar, R., and Timmer, M. P. (2015). 'The Next Generation of the Penn World Table', *American Economic Review*, 105(10): 3150–82.

Fei, J. C. H. and Ranis, G. (1964). *Development of the Labor Surplus Economy: Theory and Policy*. Homewood IL: Richard A. Irwin.

Fei, J. C. H., Ranis, G., and Kuo, S. W. Y. (1979). Growth with Equity: The Taiwan Case. A World Bank research publication. Washington, DC: The World Bank.

Felipe, J., Mehta, A., and Rhee, C. (2015). *Manufacturing Matters... But it's the Jobs that Count*. Manila: ADB.

Ferrari Filho, F. and Fonseca, P. C. D. (2015). 'Which Developmentalism? A Keynesian-Institutionalist Proposal', *Review of Keynesian Economics*, 3(1): 90–107.

Fields, G. S. (2001). *Distribution and Development: A New Look at the Developing World*. Cambridge, MA: MIT Press.

Fields, G. S. (2004). 'Dualism in the Labor Market: A Perspective on the Lewis Model after Half a Century', *The Manchester School*, 72: 724–35.

Fine, B. (2013). 'Beyond the Developmental State: An Introduction', in B. Fine, J. Saraswati, and D. Tavasci (eds), *Beyond the Developmental State: Industrial Policy into the Twenty-first Century*. London: Pluto Press, pp. 1–32.

Fine, B. and Van Waeyenberge, E. (2013). 'A Paradigm Shift that Never Was: Justin Lin's New Structural Economics', *Competition and Change*, 17(4): 355–71.

Fischer, A. (2011). 'Beware the Fallacy of Productivity Reductionism', *The European Journal of Development Research*, 23(4): 521–6.

Fischer, A. M. (2014). The Social Value of Employment and the Redistributive Imperative for Development. UNDP Human Development Report Office, Occasional Paper. New York: UNDP.

Fischer, A. M. (2015). 'The End of Peripheries? On the Enduring Relevance of Structuralism for Understanding Contemporary Global Development', *Development and Change*, 46(4): 700–32.

Frank, A. G. (1966). 'The Development of Underdevelopment', *Monthly Review*, 18(4): 17–31.

Frank, A. G. (1972). *Lumpenbourgeoisie and Lumpendevelopment: Dependency, Class and Politics in Latin America*. London; New York: Monthly Review Press.

Furtado, C. (1956). Uma economia dependente. RJ, Ministério da Educação e Cultura.

Furtado, C. (1961). *Development and Underdevelopment.* Los Angeles, CA: University of California Press.

Furtado, C. (1971). *The Economic Growth of Brazil: A Survey from Colonial to Modern Times.* Los Angeles, CA: University of California Press.

Galbraith, J. K. (2011). 'Inequality and Economic and Political Change: A Comparative Perspective', *Cambridge Journal of Regions, Economy and Society*, 4(1): 13–27.

Gallup, J. (2012). *Is There a Kuznets Curve?* Portland, OR: Portland State University.

Geertz, C. (1973). 'Thick Description: Toward an Interpretive Theory of Culture', in C. Geertz (ed.), *The Interpretation of Cultures: Selected Essays.* New York: Basic Books, pp. 3–30.

Gereffi, G. (1994). 'The Organization of Buyer-Driven Global Commodity Chains: How U.S. Retailers Shape Overseas Production Networks', in G. Gereffi and M. Korzeniewicz (eds), *Commodity Chains and Global Capitalism*, Westport: Praeger, pp. 95–122.

Gereffi, G. (2005). 'The Global Economy: Organization, Governance, and Development', in N. J. Smelser and R. Swedberg (eds), *The Handbook of Economic Sociology* (2nd edn). Princeton, NJ: Princeton University Press, pp. 160–82.

Gerschenkron, A. (1953). 'Social Attitudes, Entrepreneurship and Economic Development', *Explorations in Entrepreneurial History*, 6(1): 1–19.

Gerschenkron, A. (1962). *Economic Backwardness in Historical Perspective: A Book of Essays.* Cambridge, MA: Belknap Press of Harvard University Press.

Gollin, D. (2014). 'The Lewis Model: A 60-Year Retrospective', *Journal of Economic Perspectives*, 28(3): 71–88.

Gollin, D., Jedwab, R., and Vollrath, D. (2016). 'Urbanization With and Without Structural Transformation', *Journal of Economic Growth*, 21(1): 35–70.

Gollin, D. M., Parente, S., and Rogerson, R. (2004). 'Farm Work, Home Work and International Productivity Differences', *Review of Economic Dynamics*, 7(4): 827–50.

Gomez, E. and Jomo, K. S. (1997). *Malaysia's Political Economy: Politics, Patronage and Profits.* Cambridge: Cambridge University Press.

Gordon, D. (1978). 'Up and Down the Long Roller Coaster', In The Union for Radical Political Economics (eds.), *U.S. Capitalism in Crisis.* New York: The Union for Radical Political Economics.

Gordon, D., Edwards, R., and Reich, M. (1982). *Segmented Work, Divided Workers: The Historical Transformation of Labor in the United States.* Cambridge: Cambridge University Press.

Gordon, D., Weisskopf, T. E., and Bowles, S. (1996). 'Power, Accumulation and Crisis: The Rise and Demise of the Postwar Social Structure of Accumulation', in V. D. Lippit (ed.), *Radical Political Economy: Explorations in Alternative Economic Analysis.* Armonk, NY: M.E. Sharpe, pp. 226–44.

Gordon, D. M. (1980). 'Stages of Accumulation and Long Economic Cycles', in T. K. Hopkins and I. Wallerstein (eds), *Process of the World System.* Beverly Hills: Sage, pp. 9–45.

Gordon, D. M., Edwards, R., and Reich, M. (1994). 'Long Swings and Stages of Capitalism', in D. M. Kotz, T. McDonough, and M. Reich (eds), *Social Structures of*

Accumulation: The Political Economy of Growth and Crisis. Cambridge. Cambridge University Press, pp. 11–28.

Gordon, D. M., Reich, M., and Edwards, R. (1982). *Segmented Work, Divided Workers: The Historical Transformation of Labor in the United States*. New York: Cambridge University Press.

Gore, C. (2000). 'The Rise and Fall of the Washington Consensus as a Paradigm for Developing Countries', *World Development*, 28(5): 789–804.

Gough, I. (2000). 'Welfare Regimes in East Asia and Europe: Comparisons and Lessons', Mimeo. Department of Social and Policy Sciences, University of Bath.

Green, M. and Hulme, D. (2005). 'From Correlates and Characteristics to Causes: Thinking About Poverty from a Chronic Poverty Perspective', *World Development*, 33(6): 867–79.

Greenwood, J. and Seshadri, A. (2005). 'Technological Progress and Economic Transformation', in P. Aghion and S. Durlauf (eds), *Handbook of Economic Growth*, Vol. 1B. Amsterdam and New York: North Holland, chapter 19, pp. 1225–73.

Grimm, M., Klasen, S., and McKay, A. (2007). *Determinants of Pro-Poor Growth: Analytical Issues and Findings from Country Cases*. Basingstoke: Palgrave Macmillan.

Hadiz, V. (2004). *Reorganising Power in Indonesia: The Politics of Oligarchy in an Age of Markets*. Routledge/City University of Hong Kong Southeast Asia Series.

Hadiz, V. R. (2010). *Localising Power in Post-Authoritarian Indonesia: A Southeast Asia Perspective*. Stanford, CA: Stanford University Press.

Hall, P. A. and Soskice, D. W. (2001). *Varieties of Capitalism: The Institutional Foundations of Comparative Advantage*. Oxford: Oxford University Press.

Harris, J. R. and Todaro, M. P. (1970). 'Migration, Unemployment and Development: A Two- Sector Analysis', *American Economic Review*, 60: 126–42.

Harriss, J. (2007). 'Bringing Politics back into Poverty Analysis: Why Understanding Social Relations Matters More for Policy on Chronic Poverty than Measurement', Chronic Poverty Research Centre (CPRC) Working Paper. Manchester: CPRC.

Harriss-White, B. (2003). *India Working*. Cambridge: Cambridge University Press.

Hausmann, R. and Rodrik, D. (2003). 'Economic Development as Self-discovery', *Journal of Development Economics*, 72(2): 603–33.

Heintz, J. (2009). 'Employment, Economic Development and Poverty Reduction: Critical Issues and Policy Challenges', UNRISD Working Paper. Geneva: UNRISD.

Henderson, J. and Phillips, R. (2007). 'Unintended Consequences: Social Policy, State Institutions and the "Stalling" of the Malaysian Industrialization Project', *Economy and Society*, 36(1): 78–102.

Herrendorf, B., Rogerson, R., and Valentinyi, A. (2013). 'Growth and Structural Transformation', NBER Working Paper No. 18996. Cambridge, MA: NBER.

Hewison, K. (1989). *Power and Politics in Thailand*. Manila: Journal of Contemporary Asia Publishers.

Hilferding, R. (1981 [1910]). *Finance Capital: A Study of the Latest Phase of Capitalist Development*. London and Boston: Routledge & Kegan Paul.

Hill, H. (1996). *The Indonesian Economy*. Cambridge: Cambridge University Press.

Hill, H. (2002). *The Indonesian Economy* (2nd edn). Cambridge: Cambridge University Press.

Hill, H. (ed.) (2012). *Malaysia's Development Challenges*. London: Routledge.

Hirschman, A. (1958). *The Strategy of Economic Development*. New Haven, CT: Yale University.

Hirschman, A. (1968). 'The Political Economy of Import-Substituting Industrialization in Latin America', *The Quarterly Journal of Economics*, 82(1, February): 1–32.

Houston, D. (1992). 'Is there a New Social Structure of Accumulation?', *Review of Radical Political Economics*, 24(2): 60–7.

Hoy, C. and Sumner, A. (2016). 'Global Poverty and Inequality: Is There New Capacity for Redistribution in Developing Countries?', *Journal of Globalization and Development*, 7(1): 117–57.

ILO (2017). ILOSTAT. Geneva: ILO.

Inglehart, R. and Welzel, C. (2005). *Modernization, Cultural Change, and Democracy: The Human Development Sequence*. Cambridge: Cambridge University Press.

Inklaar, R. and Timmer, M. P. (2013). 'Capital and TFP in PWT8.0', mimeo. https://rug.nl/ggdc/productivity/pwt/.

Jenkins, R. (1991). 'The Political Economy of Industrialization: A Comparison of Latin American and East Asian Newly Industrialising Countries', *Development and Change*, 22: 197–231.

Jin, K. K. (2012). 'Poverty and Inequality', in K. Boo Teik (ed.), *Policy Regimes and the Political Economy of Poverty Reduction in Malaysia*. Geneva: UNRISD.

Johnston, B., Darbar, S. M., and Echeverria, C. (1997). 'Sequencing Capital Account Liberalisaton: Lessons from the Experience of Chile, Indonesia, Korea and Thailand', IMF Working Paper 97/157. Washington, DC: IMF.

Jomo, K. S. (1986). *A Question of Class: Capital, the State and Uneven Development in Malaya*. Singapore: Oxford University Press. (Paperback edition, New York: Monthly Review Press).

Jomo, K. S. (1988). *A Question of Class: Capital, the State and Uneven Development in Malaya*. New York: Monthly Review Press/Manila: Journal of Contemporary Asia.

Jomo, K. S. (1990). *Growth and Structural Change in the Malaysian Economy*. London: Macmillan; New York: St. Martin's Press.

Jomo, K. S. (ed.) (1993). *Industrialising Malaysia: Policy, Performance, Prospects*. London: Routledge.

Jomo, K. S. (1994). *U-Turn? Malaysian Economic Development Policies After 1990*. Centre for East and Southeast Asian Studies, James Cook University of North Queensland, Townsville.

Jomo, K. S. (2003). 'Growth with Equity In East Asia?', in K. S. Jomo (ed.), *Southeast Asian Paper Tigers? From Miracle to Debacle and Beyond*. London: Routledge, pp. 81–135.

Jomo, K. S. (2006). *The Great Divergence: Hegemony, Uneven Development, and Global Inequality*. Oxford: Oxford University Press.

Jomo, K. S. and Tan, K. W. (1999). *Industrial Policy in East Asia*. Kuala Lumpur: Penerbit Universiti Malaya.

Jomo, K. S. and Wee, C. H. (2014). *Malaysia@50: Economic Development, Distribution, Disparities*. Singapore: World Scientific Publishing.

Jomo, K. S. with Edwards, C. B. (1993). 'Malaysian Industrialisation in Historical Perspective', in K. S. Jomo (ed.), *Industrialising Malaysia: Policy, Performance, Prospects*. London: Routledge, pp. 14–39.

Judge, W., Fainshmidt, S., and Brown, J. (2014). 'Which Model of Capitalism Best Delivers both Wealth and Equality?', *Journal of International Business Studies*, 45: 363–86.

Kakwani, N. and Pernia, E. (2000). 'What Is Pro-Poor Growth?', *Asian Development Review: Studies of Asian and Pacific Economic Issues*, 18(1): 1–16.

Kaldor, N. (1957). A Model of Economic Growth, *The Economic Journal*, 67(268): 591–624.

Kaldor, N. (1966). *The Causes of the Slow Rate of Growth of the United Kingdom Economy*. Cambridge: Cambridge University Press.

Kaldor, N. (1967). *Strategic Factors in Economic Development*. Ithaca: New York State School of Industrial and Labor Relations, Cornell University.

Kalecki, M. (1954). *Theory of Economics Dynamics: An Essay on Cyclical and Long-run Changes in Capitalist Economy*. London: George Allen and Unwin.

Kalecki, M. (1955). 'The Problem of Financing of Economic Development', *Indian Economic Review*, 2(3, February): 1–22.

Kalecki, M. (1967). 'Observations on Social and Economic Aspects of "Intermediate Regimes"', *Coexistence*, 4(1): 1–5.

Kalecki, M. (1976). *Essays on Developing Economies*. Hassocks: Harvester Press.

Kanbur, R. (1999). 'Income Distribution Implications of Globalization and Liberalization in Africa', Working Paper, Cornell University, Department of Applied Economics and Management, Ithaca, New York.

Kanbur, R. (2012). 'Does Kuznets Still Matter?', in S. Kochhar (ed.), *Policy-Making for Indian Planning: Essays on Contemporary Issues in Honor of Montek S. Ahluwalia*. Academic Foundation Press, pp. 115–28.

Kanbur, R. (2016). 'W. Arthur Lewis and the Roots of Ghanaian Economic Policy', Working Paper. Charles H. Dyson School of Applied Economics and Management Cornell University, Ithaca, New York.

Kanbur, R. (2017). 'Structural Transformation and Income Distribution: Kuznets and Beyond', ESRC GPID Working Paper. London: KCL.

Kanbur, R. and Zhuang, J. (2013). 'Urbanization and Inequality in Asia', *Asian Development Review*, 30(1, March): 131–47.

Khan, M. (2010). *Political Settlements and the Governance of Growth-Enhancing Institutions*. London: University of London.

Khay Jin, K. (2010). 'Poverty and Inequality', in Policy Regimes and the Political Economy of Poverty Reduction in Malaysia. Commissioned for the UNRISD Flagship Report on Poverty Project on Poverty Reduction and Policy Regimes. UNRISD: Geneva, pp. 73–114.

Khoo, B. T. (1995). *Paradoxes of Mahathirism*. Kuala Lumpur: Oxford University Press.

Khoo, B. T. (2003). Beyond Mahathir: Malaysian Politics and its Discontents. London and New York: Zed Books.

Khoo, K. J. (2008). 'Poverty and Inequality', Malaysia Country Study Report No. 3, UNRISD Project on Poverty Reduction and Policy Regimes. Geneva: UNRISD.

Khoo, B. T. (2010). Country Study: Malaysia. Policy Regimes and the Political Economy of Poverty Reduction in Malaysia. UNRISD: Geneva.

Kindleberger, C. P. (1967). *Europe's Postwar Growth*. Cambridge, MA: Harvard University Press.

Kirkpatrick, C. and Barrientos, A. (2004). 'The Lewis Model after 50 Years', *The Manchester School*, 72(6): 679–90.

Kitchin, J. (1923). 'Cycles and Trends in Economic Factors', Review of Economics and Statistics, 5(1): 10–16.

Klasen, S. (2010). 'Measuring and Monitoring Inclusive Growth: Multiple Definitions, Open Questions, and Some Constructive Proposals', Asian Development Bank Working Paper Series. Manila: ADB.

Kohli, A. (2004). State-Directed Development: Political Power and Industrialization in the Global Periphery. Cambridge: Cambridge University Press.

Kondratieff, N. D. (1935). 'The Long Waves in Economic Life', *Review of Economic Statistics*, 17(6): 105–15.

Korinek, A., Mistiaen, J. A., and Ravallion, M. (2006). 'Survey Nonresponse and the Distribution of Income', *Journal of Economic Inequality*, 4: 33–55.

Kotz, D. M. (1994). 'The Regulation Theory and the Social Structure of Accumulation Approach', in D. M. Kotz, T. McDonough, and M. Reich (eds), *Social Structures of Accumulation: The Political Economy of Growth and Crisis*. Cambridge: Cambridge University Press, pp. 85–97.

Kotz, D. M. (2015). The Rise and Fall of Neoliberal Capitalism. Cambridge, MA: Harvard University Press.

Kotz, D. M. (2016). 'Roots of the Current Economic Crisis: Capitalism, Forms of Capitalism, Policies, and Contingent Events', in T. Subasat (ed.), *The Great Financial Meltdown of 2008: Systemic, Conjunctural or Policy-created?* Cheltenham, UK and Northampton, MA: Edward Elgar, pp. 18–34.

Kotz, D., McDonough, T., and Reich, M. (1994). *Social Structures of Accumulation: The Political Economy of Growth and Crisis*. Cambridge: Cambridge University Press.

Kraay, A. (2006). 'When Is Growth Pro-Poor? Evidence from a Panel of Countries', *Journal of Development Economics*, 80(1): 198–227.

Krueger, A. (1974a). *Liberalization Attempts and Consequences*. Cambridge, MA: Ballinger Publishing Company.

Krueger, A. (1974b). 'The Political Economy of the Rent-Seeking Society', *The American Economic Review*, 64(3): 291–303.

Krueger, A. O. (1983). *Trade and Employment in Developing Countries, Volume 3: Synthesis and Conclusions*. Cambridge, MA: National Bureau of Economic Research.

Kuruvilla, S. (1995). 'Industrialization Strategy and Industrial Relations Policy in Malaysia', (Electronic version), in S. Frenkel and J. Harrod (eds), *Industrial and Labor Relations: Contemporary Research in Seven Countries*. Ithaca, NY: ILR Press.

Kuznets, S. (1930). *Secular Movements in Production and Prices: Their Nature and their Bearing upon Cyclical Fluctuations*. Boston, MA: Houghton Mifflin.

Kuznets, S. (1955). 'Economic Growth and Income Inequality', *American Economic Review*, 45(1): 1–28.

Kuznets, S. (1966). *Modern Economic Growth: Rate, Structure, and Spread*. New Haven, CT: Yale University Press.

Kuznets, S. (1971). *Economic Growth of Nations. Total Output and Production Structure*. Cambridge, MA: The Belknap Press of Harvard University Press.

Kim, K., Sumner, A., and Yusuf, A. A. (2017). 'How Inclusive is Structural Change? The Case of Indonesia', ESRC GPID Working Paper 3. London: KCL.

Lal, D. (1983). *The Poverty of Development Economics*. London: Institute of Economic Affairs.

Lal, D. and Rajapathirana, S. (1987). 'Foreign Trade Regimes and Growth in Developing Countries', *World Bank Research Observer*, 2: 189–217.

Leibenstein, H. (1957). *Economic Backwardness and Economic Growth*. New York: John Wiley; London: Chapman & Hall.

Leigh, A. and van der Eng, P. (2009). 'Inequality in Indonesia: What can we Learn from Top Incomes?', *Journal of Public Economics*, 93 (1–2): 209–12.

Lenin, V. I. (1985 [1917]). *Imperialism: The Highest Stage of Capitalism*. New York: International Publishers.

Lewis, W. A. (1953). *Report on Industrialisation of the Gold Coast*. Accra: Government Printer.

Lewis, W. A. (1954). 'Economic Development with Unlimited Supplies of Labour', *The Manchester School*, 22(2): 139–91.

Lewis, W. A. (1955). *The Theory of Economic Growth*. Homewood, IL: Richard D. Irwin.

Lewis, W. A. (1958). 'Employment Policy in an Underdeveloped Area', *Social and Economic Studies*, 7(3): 42–54.

Lewis, W. A. (1969). *Aspects of Tropical Trade, 1883–1965*. Stockholm: Almqvist and Wicksell.

Lewis, W. A. (1972). 'Reflections on Unlimited Labour', in L. E. diMarco (ed.), *International Economics and Development (Essays in Honour of Raoul Prebisch)*. New York: Academic Press, pp. 75–96.

Lewis, W. A. (1976). 'Development and Distribution', in A. Cairncross and M. Puri (eds), *Employment, Income Distribution and Development Strategy: Essays in Honour of Hans Singer*. London: Macmillan, pp. 26–42.

Lewis, W. A. (1979). 'The Dual Economy Revisited', *The Manchester School*, 47(3): 211–29.

Lewis, W. A. (1984). 'Development Economics in the1950s', in G. Meier and D. Seers (eds), *Pioneers in Development*. Oxford: Oxford University Press for the World Bank, pp. 121–37.

Lewis, W. A. (1985). *Racial Conflict and Economic Development*. Cambridge, MA: Harvard University Press.

Lin, J. (2012). *New Structural Economics: A Framework for Rethinking Development and Policy*. Washington, DC: World Bank.

Lindbeck, A. (ed.) (1992). *Nobel Lectures, Economics 1969–1980*. Singapore: World Scientific Publishing Co.

Lindblad, J. T. (2015). 'Foreign Direct Investment in Indonesia: Fifty Years of Discourse', *Bulletin of Indonesian Economic Studies*, 51(2): 217–37.

Lindert, P. (1986). 'Unequal English Wealth since 1670', *Journal of Political Economy*, 94(6): 1127–62.

Lindert, P. and Williamson, J. (2001). 'Does Globalization Make the World More Unequal?', National Bureau of Economic Research (NBER) Working Paper. Cambridge, MA: NBER.

Lindert, P. H. (2000). 'Three Centuries of Inequality in Britain and America', in A. B. Atkinson and F. Bourguignon (eds), *Handbook of Income Distribution*. Amsterdam: Elsevier, 167–216.

Little, I. M. D., Scitovsky, T., and Scott, M. (1970). *Industry and Trade in Some Developing Countries*. Oxford: Oxford University Press.

López-Calva, L. F. and Ortiz-Juarez, E. (2014). 'A Vulnerability Approach to the Definition of the Middle Class', *The Journal of Economic Inequality*, 12(1): 23–47.

Mandel, E. (1964). 'After Imperialism?' *New Left Review*, 25(May–June): pp. 17–25.

Mandelbaum, K. (1954 [1945]). *The Industrialization of Backward Areas* (2nd edn). Oxford: Basil Blackwell.

Manning, C. and Purnagunawan, R. M. (2017). 'Has Indonesia Passed the Lewis Turning Point and does it Matter?', in H. Hill and J. Menon (eds), *Managing Globalization in the Asian Century: Essays in Honour of Prema-Chandra Athukorala*. Singapore: ISEAS Publishing.

Marquetti, A., and Foley, D. (2011). 'Extended Penn World Tables v. 4.0', Available at: https://sites.google.com/a/newschool.edu/duncan-foley-homepage/home/EPWT.

Martinez-Bravo, M., Mukherjee, P., and Stegmann, A. (forthcoming). 'The Non-democratic Roots of Elite Capture: Evidence from Soeharto Mayors in Indonesia', *Econometrica*.

Marx, K. (1885 [1972]). *Capital, Volume II: The Circulation Process of Capital*. London: Lawrence and Wishart.

Matsuyama, K. (2008). 'A One-Sector Neoclassical Growth Model with Endogenous Retirement', *Japanese Economic Review*, 59: 139–55.

McDonough, T. (1994). 'Social Structures of Accumulation, Contingent History, and Stages of Capitalism', in D. M. Kotz, T. McDonough, and M. Reich (eds), *Social Structures of Accumulation: The Political Economy of Growth and Crisis*. Cambridge: Cambridge University Press.

McDonough, T. (2008). 'Social Structures of Accumulation: The State of the Art', *Review of Radical Political Economics*, 40(2): 153–73.

McDonough, T. (2014). *Social Structure of Accumulation Theory*. The International Library of Critical Writings in Economics Series, T. McDonough, D. M. Kotz, and M. Reich (eds). Cheltenham: Edward Elgar.

McKinley, T. (2010). *Inclusive Growth Criteria and Indicators: An Inclusive Growth Index for Diagnosis of Country Progress*. Manila: ADB.

McMillan, M. S. and Rodrik, D. (2011). 'Globalization, Structural Change and Productivity Growth', NBER Working Paper No. 17143. Cambridge, MA: NBER.

Minami, R. (1973). *The Turning Point in Economic Development: Japan's Experience*. Tokyo: Kinokuniya.

Mishra, S. (2009). 'Economic Inequality in Indonesia: Trends, Causes, and Policy Response', New York: UNDP.

Mohd, S. (2010). 'Welfare Regime, Social Protection and Poverty Reduction', in *Policy Regimes and the Political Economy of Poverty Reduction in Malaysia*. Commissioned for the UNRISD Flagship Report on Poverty Project on Poverty Reduction and Policy Regimes. UNRISD: Geneva, pp. 115–47.

Mollo, M. de L. R. and Amado, A. (2015). 'The "Developmentalism" Debate in Brazil: Some Economic and Political Issues', *Review of Keynesian Economics*, 3(1): 77–89.

Mosley, P. (2004). 'Institutions and Politics in a Lewis-Type Growth Model', *The Manchester School*, 72(6): 751–73.

Musacchio, A. and Lazzarini, S. G. (2012). 'Leviathan in Business: Varieties of State Capitalism and their Implications for Economic Performance', Harvard Business School Working Paper, No. 12–108, June.

Musacchio, A. and Lazzarini, S. G. (2014). *Reinventing State Capitalism*. Cambridge, MA: Harvard University Press.

Myrdal, G. (1956). *An International Economy, Problems and Prospects*. New York: Harper & Brothers.

Myrdal, G. (1957a). *Rich Lands and Poor*. New York: Harper & Brothers.

Myrdal, G. (1957b). *Economic Theory and Underdeveloped Regions*. London: Gerald Duckworth & Co. Ltd.

Myrdal, G. (1968). *Asian Drama: An Inquiry into the Poverty of Nations*. New York: Pantheon Books.

Myrdal, G. (1970). *The Challenge of World Poverty*. New York: Penguin Press.

Nurkse, R. (1944). *International Currency Experience: Lessons of the Interwar Period*. Geneva: League of Nations.

Nurkse, R. (1953). *Problems of Capital Formation in Underdeveloped Countries*. Oxford: Basil Blackwell.

OECD (2017). *OECD's FDI Regulatory Restrictiveness Index*. Paris: OECD. Available at: http://www.oecd.org/investment/fdiindex.htm.

Okun, A. M. (1962). 'Potential GNP: Its Measurement and Significance', American Statistical Association, Proceedings of the Business and Economics Statistics Section, pp. 98–104.

Oyvat, C. (2016). 'Agrarian Structures, Urbanization, and Inequality', *World Development*, 83(C): 207–30.

Page, J. (1994). 'The East Asian Miracle: Four Lessons for Development Policy', in S. Fischer and J. J. Rotemberg (eds), *NBER Macroeconomics Annual*, Volume 9. Cambridge, MA: MIT Press, pp. 219–82.

Palley, T. (2007). 'Financialization: What It Is and Why It Matters', Levy Economics Institute Working Paper. Bard College.

Palma, G. (1978). 'Dependency: A Formal Theory of Underdevelopment or a Methodology for the Analysis of Concrete Situations of Underdevelopment?', *World Development*, 6(7–8): 881–924.

Palma, J. G. (2005). 'Four Sources of De-industrialisation and a New Concept of the Dutch- Disease', in J. A. Ocampo (ed.), *Beyond Reforms: Structural Dynamic and Macroeconomic Vulnerability*. Stanford, CA: Stanford University Press and the World Bank.

Pangestu, M., Rahardja, S., and Ing, L. Y. (2015). 'Fifty Years of Trade Policy in Indonesia: New World Trade, Old Treatments', *Bulletin of Indonesia Economic Studies*, 51(2): 239–61.

Pasinetti, L. L. (1983). *Structural Change and Economic Growth: A Theoretical Essay on the Dynamics of the Wealth of Nations*. Cambridge: Cambridge University Press.

Pasinetti, L. L. (1991). *Structural Economic Dynamics*. Cambridge: Cambridge University Press.

Perraton, J. (2004). 'Joseph Stiglitz's, Globalization and its Discontents', *Journal for International Development*, 16: 897–905.

Piketty, T. (2006). 'The Kuznets' Curve, Yesterday and Tomorrow', in A. Banerjee, R. Benabou, and D. Mookherjee (eds), *Understanding Poverty*. Oxford: Oxford University Press.

Piketty, T. (2014). *Capital in the Twenty-First Century*. Cambridge, MA: The Belknap Press of Harvard University Press.

Poczter, S. and Pepinsky, T. B. (2016). 'Authoritarian Legacies in Post-New Order Indonesia: Evidence from a New Dataset', *Bulletin of Indonesian Economic Studies*, 52(1): 77–100.

Polanyi, K. (1957 [1944]). *The Great Transformation: The Political and Economic Origins of Our Time*. Boston, MA: Beacon Press.

Prates, D. M. (2016). *Developmentalism at the Periphery: Can Productive Change and Income Distribution be Compatible with Global Financial Asymmetries?* Available at: http://paperroom.ipsa.org/app/webroot/papers/paper_58077.pdf.

Prebisch, R. (1949). *The Economic Development of Latin America and Its Principal Problems*. UN document no. E/CN.12/89/Rev.1. Lake Success, NY: United Nations.

Pritchett, L., Woolcock, M., and Andrews, M. (2010). 'Capability Traps? The Mechanisms of Persistent Implementation Failure', Center for Global Development Working Paper 234. Washington, DC: Center for Global Development.

Ramo, J. C. (2004). *The Beijing Consensus*. London: The Foreign Policy Centre.

Ranis, G. (2004). 'Arthur Lewis' Contribution to Development Thinking and Policy', Economic Growth Center Yale University, Discussion Paper 891.

Ranis, G. and Stewart, F. (1999). 'V-Goods and the Role of the Urban Informal Sector in Development', *Economic Development and Cultural Change*, 47(2): 259–88.

Raquiza, A. R. (2012). *State Structure, Policy Formation, and Economic Development in Southeast Asia: The Political Economy of Thailand and the Philippines*. London and New York: Routledge.

Rauniyar, G. and Kanbur, R. (2010). Inclusive growth and inclusive development: a review and synthesis of Asian Development Bank literature. Manila: ADB.

Ravallion, M. (2004). 'Measuring Pro-Poor Growth: A Primer', World Bank Working Paper 3242. Washington, DC: World Bank.

Ray, D. (2010). 'Uneven Growth: A Framework for Research in Development Economics', *Journal of Economic Perspectives*, 24(3): 45–60.

Rebol, M. (2010). 'Public Perceptions and Reactions: Gauging African Views of China in Africa', *Alternatives: Turkish Journal of International Relations*, 9(4): 149–86.

Reich, M. (1994). How Social Structures of Accumulation Decline and are Built', in D. M. Kotz, T. McDonough, and M. Reich (eds), *Social Structures of Accumulation: The Political Economy of Growth and Crisis*. Cambridge: Cambridge University Press.

Reich, M. (1997). 'Social Structure of Accumulation Theory: Retrospect and Prospect', *Review of Radical Political Economics*, 29(3): 1–10.

Reinert, E. (2007). *How Rich Countries Got Rich... and Why Poor Countries Stay Poor.* New York: Carroll & Graf Publishers.

Ricklefs, M. C., Lockhart, B., Lau, A., Reyes, P., and Aung-Thwin, M. (2010). *A New History of Southeast Asia.* Basingstoke: Palgrave MacMillan.

Rigg, J. (2012). *Unplanned Development: Tracking Change in South-East Asia.* London: Zed Books.

Rigg, J. (2015). *Challenging Southeast Asian Development: The Shadows of Success.* London: Routledge.

Robison, R. (1986). *Indonesia: The Rise of Capital.* Sydney: Allen & Unwin.

Robison, R. (1990). *Power and Economy in Suharto's Indonesia.* Manila: Journal of Contemporary Asia Publishers.

Robison, R. (2009). 'Strange Bedfellows: Political Alliances in the Making of Neo-liberal Governance', in W. Hout and R. Robison (eds), *Governance and the Depoliticisation of Development.* London: Routledge, pp. 15–28.

Robison, R. (ed.) (2012). *Routledge Handbook of Southeast Asian Politics.* Oxford and New York: Routledge.

Rock, M. (2017). *Dictators, Democrats, and Development in Southeast Asia.* Oxford: Oxford University Press.

Rodrik, D. (1999). 'Where Did All the Growth Go? External Shocks, Social Conflict, and Growth Collapses', *Journal of Economic Growth*, 4(4): 385–412.

Rodrik, D. (2002). 'Feasible Globalizations', Discussion Papers 3524. London: CEPR.

Rodrik, D. (2004). 'Industrial Policy for the Twenty-First Century', Discussion Papers 4767. London: CEPR.

Rodrik, D. (2013). 'The Past, Present, and Future of Economic Growth', Global Citizen Foundation Working Paper 1. Available at: http://www.law.nyu.edu/sites/default/files/upload_documents/GCF_Rodrik-working-paper-1_-6.17.131_0.pdf.

Rodrik, D. (2015). 'Premature Deindustrialization', NBER Working Paper No. 20935. Cambridge, MA: NBER.

Roine, J. and Waldenström, D. (2014). 'Long-run Trends in the Distribution of Income and Wealth'. IZA (Institute for the Study of Labour) Discussion Paper No. 8157. Bonn: IZA.

Rosenstein-Rodan, P. (1943). 'Problems of Industrialisation in Eastern and Southeastern Europe', *The Economic Journal*, 53: 202–11.

Rosenzweig, M. (1988). 'Labor Markets in Low Income Countries', in H. Chenery and T. N. Srinivasan (eds), *Handbook of Development Economics*, Volume 1. Amsterdam: North Holland Press.

Rostow, W. (1960). *The Stages of Economic Growth: A Non-Communist Manifesto.* Cambridge: Cambridge University Press.

Rowthorn, R. and Ramaswamy, R. (1999). 'Growth, Trade, and Deindustrialization', IMF Staff Papers, Washington, DC: IMF.

Roy, A. D. (1951). 'Some Thoughts on the Distribution of Earnings', *Oxford Economic Papers*, 3: 135–46.

Saad-Filho, A. (2005). 'The Rise and Decline of Latin American Structuralism and Dependency Theory', in K. S. Jomo and E. S. Reinert (eds), *Origins of Development Economics: How Schools of Economic Though Addressed Development*. London and New York: Zed Books.

Salleh, H. (2010). 'Welfare Regimes, Social Services and Poverty Reduction', in *Policy Regimes and the Political Economy of Poverty Reduction in Malaysia*. Commissioned for the UNRISD Report on Poverty Project on Poverty Reduction and Policy Regimes. UNRISD: Geneva, pp. 148–205.

Santos, M. E., Dabus, C., and Delbianco, F. (2016). 'Growth and Poverty Revisited from a Multidimensional Perspective', OPHI Working Paper 105, University of Oxford.

Schlogl, L. (2017). 'Middle Class Struggles: Socioeconomic and Demographic Determinants of Collective Action in Indonesian Social Media', PhD Dissertation, King's College London.

Schneider, B. (2001). 'Issues in Capital Account Convertibility in Developing Countries', *Development Policy Review*, 19(1): 31–82.

Schultz, T. W. (1964). *Transforming Traditional Agriculture*. New Haven, CT: Yale University Press.

Schumpeter, J. A. (1942). *Capitalism, Socialism and Democracy*. Floyd, VA: Impact Books.

Schumpeter, J. A. (2006 [1939]). *Business Cycles: A Theoretical, Historical, and Statistical Analysis of the Capitalist Process*. Mansfield Centre, CT: Martino Pub.

Seers, D. (1963). 'The Limitations of the Special Case', *Bulletin of the Oxford Institute of Economics and Statistics*, 25(2): 77–98; reprinted in K. Martin and J. Knapp (eds), *The Teaching of Development Economics: Its Position in the Present State of Knowledge* (1967). London: Frank Cass, pp. 1–27.

Sen, K. (2014). 'Inclusive Growth: When May We Expect It? When May We Not?', *Asian Development Review*, 31(1): 136–62.

Sen, K. and Tyce, M. (2017). 'The Politics of Structural (De)transformation: The Unravelling of Malaysia and Thailand's Dualistic Deals Strategies', in L. Pritchett, K. Sen, and E. Werker (eds), *Deals and Development: The Political Dynamics of Growth Episodes*. Oxford: Oxford University Press.

Shaffer, P. (2017). 'Immiserizing Growth', ESRC GPID Working Paper 8. London: King's College London.

Shorrocks, A. and van der Hoeven, R. (eds) (2004). *Growth, Inequality and Poverty: Prospects for Pro-poor Economic Development*. Oxford: Oxford University Press.

Singer, H. W. (1950). 'Economic Progress in Underdeveloped Countries', *Social Research: An International Quarterly of Political and Social Science*, 16(1): 1–11.

Singer, H. W. (1975 [1950]). 'The Distribution of Gains between Investing and Borrowing Countries', in A. Cairncross and M. Puri (eds), *The Strategy of International Development: Essays in the Economics of Backwardness*. London: Macmillan.

Singh, A. (1977). 'UK Industry and the World Economy: A Case of De-industrialisation?', *Cambridge Journal of Economics*, 1: 113–36.

Siriprachai, S. (1997). *Export-Oriented Industrialisation Strategy with Land-Abundance: Some of Thailand's Shortcomings*. Available at: http://econ.tu.ac.th/class/archan/Rangsun/EC%20460/EC%20460%20Readings/Thai%20Economy/Industrialization/

Export-Oriented%20Industrialization/EOI%20Strategy%20with%20Land%20Abundance.pdf.
Solow, R. M. (1956). 'A Contribution to the Theory of Economic Growth', *The Quarterly Journal of Economics*, 70(1): 65–94.
Stiglitz, J. (1998a). 'More Instruments and Broader Goals: Moving Towards the Post-Washington Consensus', UNU WIDER Annual Lecture, Helsinki, 7 January.
Stiglitz, J. (1998b). 'Towards a New Paradigm for Development: Strategies, Policies and Processes', Prebisch Lecture at UNCTAD, Geneva, 19 October.
Stiglitz, J. (2002). *Globalization and its Discontents*. London: Penguin Press.
Stiglitz, J. and Greenwald, B. (2014). *Creating a Learning Society: A New Approach to Growth, Development, and Social Progress*. New York: Columbia University Press.
Stiglitz, J. and Weiss, A. (1981). 'Credit Rationing in Markets with Imperfect Information', *The American Economic Review*, 71(3): 393–410.
Storm, S. (2015). 'Structural Change', *Development and Change*, 46: 666–99.
Storm, S. (2017). 'The Political Economy of Industrialization', *Development and Change*. Virtual issue.
Storm, S. and Naastepad, C. W. M. (2005). 'Strategic Factors in Economic Development: East Asian Industrialization 1950–2003', *Development and Change*, 36: 1059–94.
Sumner, A. (2002). 'Poverty During an Economic Crisis: Indonesia 1997–9', PhD Thesis, London: South Bank University.
Sumner, A. (2016a). *Global Poverty: Deprivation, Distribution, and Development Since the Cold War*. Oxford: Oxford University Press.
Sumner, A. (2016b). 'The World's Two New Middles', UNU WIDER Working Paper 2016/34. Helsinki: UNU-WIDER.
Sunkel, O. (1966). 'The Structural Background of Development Problems in Latin America', *Weltwirtschaftliches Archiv*, 97(1): 22 ff.
Sunkel, O. (1972). 'Big Business and "Dependencia"', *Foreign Affairs*, April. Available at: https://www.foreignaffairs.com/articles/south-america/1972-04-01/big-business-and-dependencia.
Sunkel, O. (1989). 'Structuralism, Dependency and Institutionalism: An Exploration of Common Ground and Disparities', *Journal of Economic Issues*, 23(2): 519–33.
Sunkel, O. (1993). 'Development from Within: Toward a Neostructuralist Approach for Latin America', Boulder, CO: Lynne Rienner Publishing.
Syrquin, M. (1986). *Structural Change and Economic Development: The Role of the Service Sector: Norman Gemmell*. London: Macmillan.
Syrquin, M. (2007). 'Kuznets and Pasinetti on the Study of Structural Transformation: Never the Twain Shall Meet?', International Centre for Economic Research Working Paper, 46, Torino, Italy.
Tan, J. (2014). 'Running out of Steam? Manufacturing in Malaysia', *Cambridge Journal of Economics*, 38(1): 153–80.
Taylor, L. (1983). *Structuralist Macroeconomics: Applicable Models for the Third World*. New York: Basic Books.
Taylor, L. (1991). *Income Distribution, Inflation, and Growth*. Cambridge, MA: MIT Press.
Taylor, L. (2004). *Reconstructing Macroeconomics: Structuralist Proposals and Critiques of the Mainstream*. Cambridge: Harvard University Press.

Thee, K. W. (2012). *Indonesia's Economy Since Independence.* Singapore: Institute of Southeast Asian Studies.

Thirlwall, A. P. (1979). 'The Interaction between Income and Expenditure in the Absorption Approach to the Balance of Payments', *Journal of Macroeconomics, Elsevier,* 1(2): 237–40.

Thirlwall, A. P. (2011). 'Balance of Payments Constrained Growth Models: History and Overview', *PSL Quarterly Review,* 64(259): 307–51.

Timmer, M. P., de Vries, G. J., and de Vries, K. (2015). 'Patterns of Structural Change in Developing Countries', in J. Weiss and M. Tribe (eds), *Routledge Handbook of Industry and Development.* London: Routledge, pp. 65–83.

Tinbergen, J. (1974). 'Substitution of Graduate by Other Labour', *Kyklos,* 27(2): 217–26.

Tinbergen, J. (1975). 'Substitution of Academically Trained by Other Manpower', Review of World Economics (Weltwirtschaftliches Archiv), 111(3): 466–76, 09.

Todaro, M. P. (1969). 'A Model of Labor Migration and Urban Unemployment in Less Developed Countries', *The American Economic Review,* 59: 138–48.

UNCTAD (2017). Trade and Development Report 2017. Geneva, UNCTAD.

UNIDO (2016). Industrial Development Report 2016. Geneva, UNIDO.

UN Population Division (2015). UN Population Division's World Population Prospects (2015 Revision). New York: United Nations.

UNRISD (2010). *Combatting Poverty and Inequality: Structural Change, Social Policy and Politics.* Geneva: UN Publications.

UNU-WIDER (forthcoming). The Standardized World Income Inequality Database. UNU-WIDER: Helsinki.

van Zanden, J. L. and Marks, D. (2013). *An Economic History of Indonesia 1800–2010.* Abingdon: Routledge.

Verdoorn, P. J. (1949). 'Fattori che Regolano lo Sviluppo Delia Produttivita del Lavoro', *L'Industria* (translated in Thirlwall, A. P. (1988). 'Population Growth and Economic Development', in D. Ironmonger, J. Perkins, and T. Hoa (eds), *National Income and Economic Progress: Essays in Honour of Colin Clark.* London: Macmillan).

Vu, T. (2010). Paths to Development in Asia: South Korea, Vietnam, China, and Indonesia. Cambridge: Cambridge University Press.

Wade, R. (1990). *Governing the Market: Economic Theory and the Role of Government in East Asian Industrialization.* Princeton, NJ: Princeton University Press.

Wade, R. (1996). 'Japan, The World Bank, and the Art of Paradigm Maintenance: The East Asian Miracle in Political Perspective', *New Left Review,* 217, May–June, 3–36.

Wade, R. H. (2011). Return of Industrial Policy? *International Review of Applied Economics,* 26(2): 223–39.

Wade, R. H. (2014). 'Market versus State or Market with State: How to Impart Directional Thrust', *Development and Change,* 45(4): 777–98.

Wallerstein, I. (1979). *The Capitalist World Economy: Essays.* New York: Cambridge University Press.

Walter, A. and Zhang, X. (2014). *East Asian Capitalism: Diversity, Continuity, and Change.* Oxford: Oxford University Press.

Warr, P. (1993). 'Thailand's Economic Miracle', National Thai Studies Centre, Australian National University.

Warr, P. (1994). *The Thai Economy in Transition*. Cambridge: Cambridge University Press.

Warr, P. (2004). *Thailand Beyond the Crisis (Rethinking Southeast Asia)*. London: Routledge.

Warr, P. and Nidhiprabha, B. (1996). Thailand's Macroeconomic Miracle: Stable Adjustment and Sustained Growth (World Bank Comparative Macroeconomic Studies). Washington, DC: World Bank.

Warren, B. (1973). 'Imperialism and Capitalist Industrialization', *New Left Review*, 81(September–October): 3–44.

Warren, B. (1980). *Imperialism: Pioneer of Capitalism*. London: NLB and Verso.

White, G. (1995). 'Towards a Democratic Developmental State', *IDS Bulletin*, 26(2): 27–35.

White, G. (1998). 'Building a Democratic Developmental State: Social Democracy in the Developing World', *Democratization*, 5(3): 1–32.

Whitley, R. (1991). 'The Social Construction of Business Systems in East Asia', *Organization Studies*, 12(1): 1–28.

Whitley, R. (1999). *Divergent Capitalisms: The Social Structuring and Change of Business Systems*. Oxford: Oxford University Press.

Whitley, R. (2000). The Institutional Structuring of Innovation Strategies: Business Systems, Firm Types and Patterns of Technical Change in Different Market Economies', *Organization Studies*, 21(5): 855–86.

Wie, T. K. (2012). *Indonesia's Economy Since Independence*. Singapore: ISEAS–Yusof Ishak Institute.

Williamson, J. (1990). 'What Washington Means by Policy Reform', in J. Williamson (ed.), *Latin American Adjustment: How Much Has Happened?* Washington, DC: Institute for International Economics.

Williamson, J. (2012). 'Is the "Beijing Consensus" Now Dominant?', *Asia Policy*, 13: 1–16.

Williamson, O. E. (1985). *The Economic Institutions of Capitalism*. New York: The Free Press.

Wolfson, M. H. (1994). 'The Financial System and the Social Structure of Accumulation', in D. M. Kotz, T. McDonough, and M. Reich (eds), *Social Structures of Accumulation: The Political Economy of Growth and Crisis*. Cambridge: Cambridge University Press.

Wolfson, M. H. and Kotz, D. M. (2009). *A Re-conceptualization of SSA Theory*. Amherst, MA: University of Massachusetts.

Wood, G. and Gough, I. (2006). 'A Comparative Welfare Regime Approach to Global Social Policy', *World Development*, 34: 1696–712.

World Bank (1991). *World Development Report*. Washington, DC: World Bank.

World Bank (1993). *East Asia Miracle: Economic Growth and Public Policy*. Oxford: Oxford University Press.

World Bank (2008). *The Growth Report: Strategies for Sustained Growth and Inclusive Development*. Washington, DC: World Bank.

World Bank (2010). *Indonesia Jobs Report: Towards Better Jobs and Security For All*. Jakarta: World Bank.

World Bank (2016). *World Development Indicators*. Washington, DC: World Bank.

World Bank (2017). *Trouble in the Making? The Future of Manufacturing-Led Development*. Washington, DC: World Bank.

Yusuf, A. and Sumner, A. (2015). 'Growth, Poverty and Inequality under Jokowi', *Bulletin of Indonesian Economics Studies*, 51(3): 323–48.

Index

Index